THE
FORMULA
ONE
MISCELLANY

I wish to dedicate my *Formula One Miscellany* to several very special people: firstly, to Eugen Tripon, just for being at the end of an email when I needed advice; secondly, to a very good friend of mine, and a Formula One fanatic, Philip Crummy; thirdly, to a man who is as mad about cars as I am, another very good friend of mine, John Dempsey; fourthly, to Wilson Steele, a friend always; fifthly, to Frankie Connor; and last but by no means least, to my late father, Johnny White, whose love of cars knew no bounds.

Thank you one and all.

John White

First edition published in 2007
Second Edition 2008
Third Edition 2014

Carlton Books Limited
20 Mortimer Street
London W1T 3JW

A CIP catalogue record for this book is available from the British Library

ISBN: 978-1-78097-460-6

Commissioning Editor: Martin Corteel
Assistant Editor: David Ballheimer
Project Art Editor: Darren Jordan & Paul Chattaway
Production: Maria Petalidou

Printed and bound by CPI Group (UK) Ltd,
Croydon, CR0 4YY

JOHN WHITE

THE
FORMULA
ONE
MISCELLANY

THIRD EDITION

❂ ALSO BY THE SAME AUTHOR ❂

❖ *The Boxing Miscellany* ❖
❖ *The Celtic Football Miscellany* ❖
❖ *The England Cricket Miscellany* ❖
❖ *The England Football Miscellany* ❖
❖ *The Golf Miscellany* ❖
❖ *The Horse Racing Miscellany* ❖
❖ *The Liverpool Football Miscellany* ❖
❖ *The Manchester United Miscellany* ❖
❖ *The Olympic Games Miscellany* ❖
❖ *The Premiership Football Miscellany* ❖
❖ *The Rangers Football Miscellany* ❖
❖ *The Six Nations Rugby Miscellany* ❖
❖ *The Tour de France Miscellany* ❖

❀ FOREWORD ❀

Motor racing is in my genes. My father drove in the Indianapolis 500 five years before I was born. I was a few weeks short of my tenth birthday when War was declared so things were very tough for a young man growing up in England. However, I fell in love with cars and motor racing in particular, especially the Grand Prix machines.

From the moment Luigi Villoresi won the 1948 British GP at Silverstone in his Maserati I knew that this was something I wanted to do and that year I participated in my first motor race, a hill climb, driving a Cooper 500. I will never forget watching the inaugural F1 World Championship Grand Prix, the British, in May 1950 as I watched Nino Farina race to victory in his beautiful Alfa Romeo. What a driver he was, and he went on to win that first official World Drivers' Championship. But as we all know the sport has been graced by so many other wonderful drivers including Alberto Ascari, Juan Manuel Fangio, Jim Clark, Graham Hill, Jackie Stewart, Nelson Piquet, Alain Prost, Ayrton Senna and, of course, the seven times F1 World Champion, Michael Schumacher. Only time will tell whether or not the young Spaniard, Fernando Alonso, or Britain's new star Lewis Hamilton will be good enough to have their names included alongside the legends of the sport. The same must be said for 2007 World Champion Kimi Raikkonen

I enjoyed racing cars of all shapes and sizes and when I retired in 1962, I had managed to win 212 of the 525 races I entered, including 16 Formula One world championship Grands Prix. Although the World Drivers' crown eluded me, I am very honoured to have finished runner-up in the Championship on four occasions (from 1955 to 1958). One of my proudest moments in racing is without doubt my first ever F1 Grand Prix win and what made that extra special was the fact that it was the British Grand Prix at Aintree. In the 1950s the famous Grand National course had a motor racing circuit inside it. I won driving a Mercedes, while Juan Manuel Fangio was second.

In *The Formula One Miscellany*, John White has produced a wonderful little book, bringing back memories of friends and competitors alike, as well raising subjects I had almost forgotten about. His research resources appear to be boundless and he has the knack of finding the sparkiest and most interesting stories. Quite simply, this is a true treasure trove of facts and figures about a subject very close to my heart. I hope it gives you as much reading pleasure as it gave me.

Sir Stirling Moss, OBE

❀ ACKNOWLEDGEMENTS ❀

Special thanks to the webmaster at http://en.wikipedia.org/wiki/ Formula One for providing such an informative database on Formula One grand prix circuits, drivers and teams that has helped me verify data and which also helped me obtain information on a number of related subjects.

Eugen Tripon was a fantastic help to me in compiling my book and his website, www.4mula1.ro, was of invaluable assistance as it just contains so much information on F1.

Steven De Groote's excellent website, www.f1technical.net, also provides a lot of interesting material on F1.

❁ INTRODUCTION ❁

Formula One has witnessed so many special moments and had so many wonderfully gifted drivers since the inaugural grand prix in 1950 was raced. Indeed, the sport has been graced by many exceptional drivers from the first World Champion, Giuseppe Farina, to Alberto Ascari, Juan Manuel Fangio, Jim Clark, Jackie Stewart, Graham Hill, Nelson Piquet, Alain Prost, Ayrton Senna and Michael Schumacher. The 2014 Formula 1 season promises to be one of the most exciting, with Kimi Raikkonen returning to Ferrari with whom he won the World Championship in 2007. He joins the 2005 and 2006 World Champion, Fernando Alonso, to create a Ferrari "Dream Team", but waiting in the slipstream to reclaim their crowns are other former world champions, Lewis Hamilton (2008), Jenson Button (2009), and the man they all have to beat, Sebastian Vettel, winner of the last four titles (2010–13).

I got hooked on Formula One from an early age and will never forget the BBC's coverage of grand prix racing during the 1970s and early 1980s when Murray Walker captivated my imagination with his colourful, and sometimes very emotional, race commentaries. And how appropriate was Fleetwood Mac's "The Chain", the song the BBC adopted as the theme tune to their highlights show? Even today, when I hear this refrain it brings back memories of James Hunt's 1976 World Championship success and visions of Ayrton Senna streaking across the television screen in the famous John Player Special Lotus Renault 98T. In addition to the JPS Lotus, Formula One has also had so many other superb cars gifted to us by creative constructors such as Alfa-Romeo, Brabham, Cooper, Ferrari, Jordan, McLaren, Maserati, Mercedes, Matra, Renault, Tyrrell and Williams.

In compiling my book I owe a huge thanks to Eugen Tripon and his absolutely superb website – http://www.4mula1.ro. Eugen was an invaluable help with information on the circuits, the constructors, the drivers, the rules, the sponsors and so much more. His website is a one-stop location to find out all you ever wanted to know about the sport's thrilling history on the web, and I thoroughly recommend a visit to it.

So in closing, I hope all motor racing fans enjoy my book and it helps you to recall your own special memories down the years from the sport's illustrious history. And who knows you might just find the odd surprise or two inside where you discover something you had forgotten about or an entry in the book that leaves you totally surprised.

Yours in sport,

John White
Spring 2014

❂ 1950 DRIVERS' WORLD CHAMPIONSHIP ❂

Pos Driver	Nationality	Team	Pts
1. Giuseppe Farina	Italian	Alfa Romeo	30
2. Juan Manuel Fangio	Argentinian	Alfa Romeo	27
3. Luigi Fagioli	Italian	Alfa Romeo	24
4. Louis Rosier	French	Talbot-Lago-Talbot	13
5. Alberto Ascari	Italian	Ferrari & Ferrari-Jaguar	11
6. Johnnie Parsons	American	Kurtis Kraft-Cummins & Kurtis Kraft-Offenhauser	9
7. Bill Holland	American	Deidt-Offenhauser	6
8. Prince Bira	Thai	Maserati & Maserati-Milano & Maserati-Offenhauser	5
9. Peter Whitehead	British	Ferrari & Ferrari-Jaguar	4
10. Louis Chiron	Monegasque	Maserati & Maserati-Milano & Maserati-Offenhauser	4

❂ POLE RACES FOR POLE ❂

On 6 August 2006, Robert Kubica (Sauber-BMW) became the first Polish driver to compete in an F1 GP when he started from ninth place on the grid in the Hungarian GP. It was a dream debut for the flying Pole as he took seventh place and two World Championship points at the Hungaroring. However, later that evening Kubica received bad news in that he had been disqualified from the race because F1.06 was 2 kg underweight caused by tyre wear. However, the weather was to blame and not any of the team because during the GP it rained heavily for the first time in the history of the race and all of the team's data were amassed from dry-road tyre wear. Neither the World Championship leader, Fernando Alonso (Renault), nor the second-placed driver in the table, Ferrari's Michael Schumacher, managed to finish the GP, although Schumacher received an unexpected point as a result of Kubica's disqualification. Schumacher now trailed Alonso by 10 points with only five Grands Prix left.

❂ 1982 SWISS GP IN FRANCE ❂

The 1982 Swiss Grand Prix took place in Dijon, France, on 29 August 1982. Two laps from the end of the race, Keke Rosberg (Williams-Ford) overtook a slow-moving Alain Prost (Renault), who finished in second place. With this win Rosberg moved into the lead in the Drivers' Championship on 42 points just ahead of Ferrari's Didier Pironi (39) and McLaren-Ford's John Watson (30).

❋ A HISTORY OF THE BRITISH GP ❋

Grand Prix motor racing was introduced in Britain by Harry Seagrave at the Brooklands course in Surrey when he organised the 1926 British Grand Prix. Seagrave, a racing driver himself, won the 1923 French GP and the 1924 Spanish GP. The first ever British Grand Prix was won by the French pair, Robert Senechal and Louis Wagner, driving a Delage 155B. The first official F1 Grand Prix was the 1950 British Grand Prix, which took place at Silverstone on 13 May 1950 and was won by Giuseppe Farina in an Alfa Romeo.

Since 1950 Silverstone has hosted the British Grand Prix on a regular basis and in 1987 it was made the official home of the event. The race was shared with Aintree between 1955 and 1962 and with Brands Hatch between 1964 and 1986. In 2003 a dispute arose between Silverstone's owners, the British Racing Drivers' Club (BRDC), and the Formula One authorities over the funding for necessary improvements to the circuit's facilities. The dispute led to doubts over the future of the race and in October 2004 the British Grand Prix was left off the preliminary F1 race schedule for 2005 because the BRDC refused to pay the race fee demanded by Bernie Ecclestone. However, after months of hard-fought negotiations, a deal was agreed whereby Silverstone would host the British GP until 2009. On 4 July 2008, it was announced that Donington Park would host the British Grand Prix for 10 years from 2010, but the owners could not secure the necessary funding to host the race, so the contract was terminated in November 2009. Shortly thereafter, Silverstone signed a 17-year contract to host the British Grand Prix from 2010 onwards.

Did You Know That?
The Silverstone circuit was originally an airstrip, and during World War II it was used as a bomber training centre. The BRDC purchased the lease of the circuit from the RAC in 1952 and ownership of it from the Ministry of Defence in 1971. On a day-to-day basis, the Silverstone circuit is operated by Silverstone Motorsport Limited.

❋ HAMILTON MAKES IT NINETEEN ❋

When Lewis Hamilton (McLaren-Mercedes) claimed his first Formula One victory in the 2007 Canadian GP at Montreal, he became the 19th British driver to win an F1 World Drivers' Championship race. The last British driver to win an F1 Grand Prix prior to Hamilton was Jenson Button (Honda), who won the Hungarian GP in 2006.

❀ ALBERTO ASCARI ❀

Alberto Ascari was born on 13 July 1918 in Milan, Italy. His father, Antonio, had raced Alfa Romeos in Grands Prix during the 1920s. When Alberto was just seven years old, his father was killed while leading the 1925 French GP at the Monthlery circuit near Paris.

In his youth Alberto rode motor cycles, but by the time he was 22 he had turned his attention to four wheels. In 1940 he participated in the famous Mille Miglia road race for Enzo Ferrari, a former team-mate of his father's. World War II interrupted Ascari's career, but after the war he raced in Grands Prix for Maserati. In 1948 he won his first Grand Prix at San Remo, Italy, and won a second GP in 1949. In 1950 the inaugural F1 Drivers' World Championship commenced, but Ferrari did not compete in the first official Grand Prix, instead making their debut in the next race, the Monaco GP. Ascari finished second in the race and went on to claim fifth place in the Championship with 11 points for Ferrari. In 1951 he won two Grands Prix, his first success coming in the German GP, on 29 July 1951. At the end of the 1951 season, Ascari finished runner-up to the new World Champion, Juan Manuel Fangio.

In 1952 Ascari was unstoppable, winning six of the eight Grands Prix for Ferrari to claim his first World Championship. Alberto missed the opening GP of the 1952 season, the Swiss, taking time out to prepare to compete for Ferrari in the gruelling Indianapolis 500 race in the USA. It was the only Grand Prix he entered that year that he failed to win, and during his 11 years of Formula One competition he was the only European driver to race in the Indy 500.

In 1953 Ascari retained the Formula One Drivers' World Championship, the first driver to do so, claiming victory in five of the nine Grands Prix raced. Ascari moved to Lancia in 1954 but had a disappointing season, although he did win the 1954 Mille Miglia in a Lancia sports car. The 1955 season arrived and the new Lancia D50 was finally up to speed with its competitors. However, in only the second Grand Prix of the year, Ascari crashed into the harbour at Monaco on 22 May and nearly drowned. Four days later, testing a new Ferrari sports car at Monza, he crashed while taking one of the track's tight corners and was killed. The corner where Alberto Ascari died on 26 May 1955 is now called the "Variante Ascari". He took part in 31 Grands Prix and won 13.

Did You Know That?
Alberto Ascari is one of only two Italians to be crowned the F1 Drivers' Champion.

⚙ 1951 DRIVERS' WORLD CHAMPIONSHIP ⚙

Pos	Driver	Nationality	Team	Pts
1.	Juan Manuel Fangio	Argentinian	Alfa Romeo	31
2.	Alberto Ascari	Italian	Ferrari	25
3.	Jose Froilan Gonzalez	Argentinian	Ferrari	24
4.	Giuseppe Farina	Italian	Alfa Romeo	19
5.	Luigi Villoresi	Italian	Ferrari	15
6.	Piero Taruffi	Italian	Ferrari	10
7.	Lee Wallard	American	Kurtis Kraft-Novi & Kurtis Kraft-Offenhauser	9
8.	Felice Bonetto	Italian	Alfa Romeo	7
9.	Mike Nazaruk	American	Kurtis Kraft-Novi & Kurtis Kraft-Offenhauser	6
10.	Reg Parnell	British	BRM & Ferrari	5

⚙ THE GUNNAR NILSSON CANCER FOUNDATION ⚙

Following the death of the Swedish racing driver, Gunnar Nilsson, from testicular cancer on 20 October 1978, his mother Elisabeth established "The Gunnar Nilsson Cancer Foundation" in memory of her son. Nilsson entered 32 Grands Prix, qualifying for all but one of them, and in 1977 he won the Belgian GP, his solitary F1 victory.

Did You Know That?
Gunnar Nilsson won the Formula Three World Championship driving for March-Toyota in 1975.

⚙ FERRARI GO BACKWARDS ⚙

In 1980 Jody Scheckter (Ferrari), the reigning World Champion, failed to secure a single podium position. His best finish was his fifth place in the US West GP. Just as Colin Chapman had failed to follow up his 1978 World Championship success, so did Enzo Ferrari, the new Ferrari 312T5 turning out to be nothing short of a failure.

⚙ THE THREE "FS" ⚙

The top three places in the Drivers' World Championship table in 1950, Formula One's inaugural season, were occupied by drivers whose surnames all began with the letter "F" and who all drove Alfa Romeo 158s. The final places were as follows: Giuseppe (Nino) Farina – first, Juan Manuel Fangio – second, and Luigi Fagioli – third.

❂ 1952 DRIVERS' WORLD CHAMPIONSHIP ❂

Pos	Driver	Nationality	Team	Pts
1.	Alberto Ascari	Italian	Ferrari	36
2.	Nino Farina	Italian	Ferrari	24
3.	Piero Taruffi	Italian	Ferrari	22
4.	Rudi Fischer	Swiss	Ferrari	10
5.	Mike Hawthorn	British	Cooper-Bristol	10
6.	Robert Manzon	French	Gordini	9
7.	Troy Ruttman	American	Kuzma-Offenhauser	8
8.	Luigi Villoresi	Italian	Ferrari	8
9.	Jose Froilan Gonzalez	Argentinian	Maserati-Plate & Maserati	6.5
10.	Jim Rathmann	American	Kurtis Kraft-Novi & Kurtis Kraft-Offenhauser	6

❂ THE F1 POINTS SYSTEM ❂

Since the inception of the Drivers' World Championship in 1950, the points system used by the sport's governing body, FIA, has evolved down the years.

❂ PIAN SUFFERS TOO MUCH PAIN TO GO ON ❂

Alfredo Pian from Argentina entered the 1950 Monaco Grand Prix in a Maserati owned by the Scuderia Achille Varzi racing team. During practice sessions on the Saturday, Pian hit an oil patch on the circuit and spun off, crashing against the guard-rail. He was thrown from the cockpit of his car and sustained injuries to his leg. Pian never started the 1950 Monaco GP and never raced an F1 car again.

❂ BACK-TO-BACK FOR MIKA ❂

Mika Hakkinen (McLaren-Mercedes) knew he had to win the final race of the 1999 season, the Japanese Grand Prix at Suzuka, to stand any chance of winning back-to-back World Championships. He trailed Ferrari's Eddie Irvine by four points, but starting the race from P2 on the grid behind Michael Schumacher (Ferrari), the Finn led all the way to victory. Schumacher finished second and Irvine was third. If Schumacher had allowed his team-mate to pass him, Irvine and Hakkinen would have finished level on 76 points, but Hakkinen would still have been crowned champion as he had won five GPs to Irvine's four.

◉ FAST TALK (1) ◉

"Aerodynamics is for those who cannot manufacture good engines."
Enzo Ferrari

◉ SPOILER FAILS TO SPOIL VICTORY ◉

In the German Grand Prix on 2 August 1981, Nelson Piquet suffered left front spoiler damage to his Brabham-Ford at the very first corner. However, despite having under-steer for the 45-lap race he somehow managed to adjust his driving to claim the win. After the race he said: "Well, I had a big under-steer after a touch and I tried some way to adjust my driving. When I achieved it, I really was very fast and so I could catch everyone in front and win."

◉ HILL GRABS VICTORY IN FINAL GP ◉

In the final Grand Prix of the 1962 season, the South African GP at East London, Jim Clark (Lotus-BRM & Lotus-Climax) went into the race in second place in the Drivers' Championship table, three points behind Graham Hill (BRM). However, while he was leading the GP, Clark's car suffered an oil leak after 62 laps which forced him to abandon the race while Hill drove to victory and took the championship crown by 12 points.

Did You Know That?
If Clark had won the 1962 South African GP and Hill had finished second, the two drivers would have been level on 39 points. However, as only the best five results from nine GPs counted, Clark would have been crowned World Champion as he would have had one victory more than Hill.

◉ FERRARI STAY AWAY FROM THE USA ◉

Following the death of Wolfgang von Trips (Ferrari) in the penultimate GP of the 1961 season, Ferrari decided not to race in the final Grand Prix in the USA. The Ferrari team were heavily criticised for electing not to retire Phil Hill's car after the death of von Trips at Monza. Hill took the chequered flag at Monza, a victory that guaranteed him the 1961 Drivers' World Championship as he had 34 points to von Trips' 33. However, Hill, the first North American to win the F1 Drivers' Championship, was not able to celebrate his victory in front of his home crowd.

❀ FANTASY BRITISH STARTING GRID ❀

(to the end of the 2007 season)

1
Nigel Mansell
*(31 GP wins,
187 GPs, World
Champion 1992)*

2
Jackie Stewart
*(27 GP wins, 99 GPs,
World Champion
1969, 1971, 1973)*

3
Jim Clark
*(25 GP wins, 72,
GPs, World
Champion 1963,
1967)*

4
Lewis Hamilton
Lewis Hamilton
*(22 GP wins, 120
GPs, World Champion
2008)*

5
Damon Hill
*(22 GP wins, 115
GPs, World
Champion 1996)*

6
Stirling Moss 1
*(16 GP wins, 66 GPs,
World Champion best
2nd, 4 times)*

7
Jenson Button
*(15 GP wins, 238
GPs, World
Champion 2009)*

8
Graham Hill
*(14 GP wins, 176,
GPs, World Champion
1962, 1968)*

9
David Coulthard
*(13 GP wins, 229
GPs, World
Champion best 2nd
2001)*

10
James Hunt
*(10 GP wins, 92 GPs,
World Champion
1976)*

◉ 1953 DRIVERS' WORLD CHAMPIONSHIP ◉

Pos Driver	Nationality	Team	Pts
1. Alberto Ascari	Italian	Ferrari	34.5
2. Juan Manuel Fangio	Argentinian	Maserati	28
3. Nino Farina	Italian	Ferrari	26
4. Mike Hawthorn	British	Ferrari	19
5. Luigi Villoresi	Italian	Ferrari	17
6. Jose Froilan Gonzalez	Argentinian	Maserati	13.5
7. Bill Vukovich	American	Kurtis Kraft-Novi & Kurtis Kraft-Offenhauser	9
8. Toulo de Graffenried	Swiss	Maserati	7
9. Felice Bonetto	Italian	Maserati	6.5
=9. Art Cross	American	Kurtis Kraft-Novi & Kurtis Kraft-Offenhauser	6

◉ NO SAMBA FOR RAIKKONEN ◉

On lap 52 of the 2003 Brazilian Grand Prix, David Coulthard (McLaren-Mercedes) pitted while Giancarlo Fisichella (Jordan-Ford) closed in and overtook Kimi Raikkonen (McLaren-Mercedes) in lap 53, to the absolute delight of team boss Eddie Jordan. However, Mark Webber made a mistake at the main straight, shunting his Jaguar-Cosworth car, which disintegrated on the track. Immediately the race marshals produced the yellow flags as the cars attempted to avoid the green pieces of metal strewn across the track. Fernando Alonso (Renault) then hit a tyre, spun and crashed, which blocked the track and caused the race to be abandoned. Although Fisichella just managed to pass the finish line at the same time the race was officially ended, Raikkonen was declared the winner, Fisichella second and Alonso third. Five days later, FIA awarded the victory to Fisichella when the video tape of the race showed that he had crossed the finish line seven seconds before the red flag was shown.

◉ LAUDA BACK WHERE HE BELONGS ◉

In only his third comeback race after retirement, Niki Lauda won the US West Grand Prix in his McLaren-Ford.

Did You Know That?
Lauda and all the drivers in the points were in non-turbo cars, while Gilles Villeneuve was disqualified from his third-place finish because of an irregular wing.

❀ 1954 DRIVERS' WORLD CHAMPIONSHIP ❀

Pos Driver	Nationality	Team	Pts
1. Juan Manuel Fangio	Argentinian	Maserati & Mercedes	42
2. Jose Froilan Gonzalez	Argentinian	Ferrari	25.14
3. Mike Hawthorn	British	Ferrari	24.64
4. Maurice Trintignant	French	Ferrari	17
5. Karl Kling	German	Mercedes	12
6. Bill Vukovich	American	Kurtis Kraft-Offenhauser	8
7. Hans Herrmann	German	Mercedes	8
8. Nino Farina	Italian	Ferrari	6
9. Luigi Musso	Italian	Maserati	6
10. Jimmy Bryan	American	Kuzma-Offenhauser	6

❀ SWEDISH-FINNISH-GERMAN CONNECTION ❀

Nico Rosberg, the son of the 1982 F1 World Champion Keke Rosberg (born in Sweden but with adopted Finnish nationality), was born in Wiesbaden, Germany on 27 June 1985 and drives under the German flag. In 2002 Nico, aged just 17, became the youngest man ever to drive a Grand Prix car when he tested for Williams-BMW. In 2005, Nico won the newly created GP2 series with the ART Grand Prix Racing Team.

Did You Know That?
In November 2005, Nico Rosberg was officially confirmed as a Williams F1 driver for the 2006 GP season. When Nico's father claimed his world championship in 1982, he too was driving for Frank Williams' team.

❀ WING-CARS ABANDONED ❀

At the start of the 1983 F1 season, FISA introduced a new regulation stating that the teams had to abandon their traditional wing-cars and replace them with a flat under-body car which would provide down-force with a perfectly shaped aerodynamic body. In 1983, many of the constructors also adopted the turbo-charged engine, but the costs of running an F1 team were getting increasingly higher.

❀ NEW FACES IN '69 ❀

In 1969 Francois Cevert made his Grand Prix debut while the Williams team entered the world of F1 racing.

❀ ANDRETTI MARK II ❀

In 1993 Michael Andretti, son of Mario, the 1978 F1 Drivers' Champion, made his Formula One debut driving for the McLaren racing team. He drove alongside the legendary Ayrton Senna, but in the 13 GPs he entered in 1993, he only managed to secure one podium finish. Ironically he finished in third place in his last ever F1 race, the Italian Grand Prix at Monza on 12 September 1993. Andretti then returned to America and the Champ Car Series, in which he enjoyed a successful career, finishing runner-up in 1996. In 2003, Michael started his own Indy Racing League team, "Andretti Green Racing", after buying into Barry and Kim Green's "Team Green" and moving it to Indy from the Champ Car Series. Dan Wheldon won the Indianapolis 500 for Andretti Green Racing in 2003.

Did You Know That?
After a number of collisions, Michael Andretti had only managed to finish three laps in his first three GPs.

❀ EDDIE'S EASTERN DELIGHT ❀

On 17 October 1999, Eddie Irvine (Ferrari) won the inaugural Malaysian Grand Prix held in Sepang. The victory put the Ulsterman four points ahead of his nearest challenger, Mika Hakkinen (McLaren-Mercedes) going into the final race of the season, the Japanese Grand Prix at Suzuka.

❀ AWESOME SENNA ❀

Ayrton Senna (Lotus-Renault) claimed two firsts in the second Grand Prix of the 1985 season, the Portuguese. He took his first ever pole position after practice and when the race started he shot away from the field despite the extremely poor weather conditions and awful visibility. Senna quite simply annihilated his opponents, finishing the race 1'02.978 ahead of the second-placed driver, Michele Alboreto (Ferrari), and one lap ahead of Patrick Tambay (Renault) in third place.

Did You Know That?
Senna almost caused an accident just after taking the chequered flag. He got out of his car to celebrate when Nigel Mansell (Williams-Honda) was just behind him. Thankfully, Mansell managed to swerve and miss the Brazilian.

⚙ 1955 DRIVERS' WORLD CHAMPIONSHIP ⚙

Pos Driver	Nationality	Team	Pts
1. Juan Manuel Fangio	Argentinian	Mercedes	40
2. Stirling Moss	British	Mercedes	23
3. Eugenio Castellotti	Italian	Ferrari & Lancia	12
4. Maurice Trintignant	French	Ferrari	11.33
5. Nino Farina	Italian	Ferrari	10.33
6. Piero Taruffi	Italian	Mercedes	9
7. Bob Sweikert	American	Kurtis Kraft-Offenhauser	8
8. Roberto Mieres	Argentinian	Maserati	7
9. Luigi Musso	Italian	Maserati	6
10. Jean Behra	French	Maserati	6

⚙ FAST TALK (2) ⚙

"If someone said to me that you can have three wishes, my first would have been to get into racing, my second to be in Formula One, my third to drive for Ferrari."
Gilles Villeneuve

⚙ FIRST GP WIN FOR A SIX-WHEELED CAR ⚙

Ken Tyrrell's revolutionary six-wheeled Tyrrell-Ford P34 created history on 13 June 1976 when Jody Scheckter drove it to victory in the Swedish Grand Prix. It was the first win by a six-wheeled vehicle in F1 racing.

⚙ THE FIRST US GRAND PRIX ⚙

The first US Grand Prix took place at Sebring on 12 December 1959 and was won by Bruce McLaren in a Cooper-Climax. In 1960, the US race moved to Riverside, California, before switching to Watkins Glen, New York. Eight times between 1966 and 1983 a race called the Grand Prix USA-West was held at Long Beach, California. During the 1980s, Dallas and Las Vegas both staged one Grand Prix, while seven were held in Detroit. From 1989 to 1991, Phoenix also staged GPs.

Did You Know That?
Up to the end of the 2013 season, only four drivers have won the US Grand Prix and the Indy 500: Mario Andretti, Jim Clark, Emerson Fittipaldi and Graham Hill.

❀ SELECTED F1 DRIVERS IN TV ADS ❀

Jenson Button............Head & Shoulders Shampoo & Santander Bank
Damon Hill & Murray Walker...Pizza Hut
Nigel Mansell..London Buses
Kimi Raikkonen & Giancarlo Fisichella.......................Mercedes
Michael Schumacher & Nico Rosberg.........................Mercedes
Jackie Stewart.....................Highways Agency & Ford Pinto
Sebastian Vettel................Head & Shoulders Shampoo
Mark Webber......................................Canberra Milk

❀ BUTTON CLEARS MONKEY OFF HIS BACK ❀

On 6 August 2006, Jenson Button (Honda) claimed his first F1
GP victory in 114 races when he took victory in the Hungarian
GP at the Hungaroring. Amazingly Button claimed victory from
14th position on the grid and was the first British winner of a
GP in 63 attempts dating back to David Coulthard's win in the
2003 Australian GP in Melbourne. Meanwhile Pedro de la Rosa's
(McLaren-Mercedes) second-place finish was his first podium and
Nick Heidfeld claimed third place to give newcomers Sauber-BMW
their first Championship points. Button's removal of the monkey
from his back bettered team-mate, Rubens Barrichello's 124-race
wait for his maiden F1 GP victory.

Did You Know That?
Damon Hill (Williams-Renault) and Fernando Alonso (Renault)
both claimed their first Grand Prix victories at the Hungaroring.

❀ ANDERSON DIES AT SILVERSTONE ❀

In 1961, Bob Anderson, a motor-cycle racer from Hendon, North
London, switched to racing cars. At the start of 1963 he purchased
an ex-Bowmaker-Lola and began racing in F1 as a privateer with his
own team comprising himself and his French wife. Then in 1964,
he switched to a Brabham and enjoyed a brief moment of glory in
the Austrian Grand Prix that year, finishing in third place behind
Lorenzo Bandini (Ferrari) and Richie Ginther (BRM). In 1967, he
was thinking of retiring from F1 but continued racing until he had
an accident while testing at Silverstone. He slid off the track in very
wet conditions and crashed into a marshal's post. Anderson suffered
serious chest and neck injuries and died later in Northampton
General Hospital.

❀ SIR JACK BRABHAM, OBE ❀

John Arthur "Jack" Brabham was born on 2 April 1926 in Hurstville, Australia. During World War II Jack served in the Royal Australian Air Force. In his first season of racing he won the New South Wales Championship and forged an alliance with Ron Tauranac, with whom he would later form Brabham Racing. When the Australian authorities would not permit him to advertise on his Cooper, he went overseas and shone in the 1954 non-Championship New Zealand Grand Prix.

On 16 July 1955 he made his F1 debut when he drove a Cooper-Bristol in the British Grand Prix at Aintree. In 1959 he won the opening GP of the season in Monaco and then won the British Grand Prix at Aintree on his way to clinching the 1959 F1 Drivers' World Championship. In 1960 Brabham (Cooper-Climax) won five of the ten Grands Prix raced to claim back-to-back Drivers' Championships. John Cooper provided Brabham with a new car for the 1961 F1 season and it impressed when raced at the Indianapolis 500, finishing a respectable eighth in a race traditionally dominated by front-engine cars. However, 1961 belonged to Phil Hill, who became the first American to be crowned World Champion in his shark-nosed Ferrari, which won five of the eight GPs raced.

In 1962, along with Tauranac, Brabham founded the Brabham Racing Organisation. On 28 June 1964 the Brabham-Climax claimed its first ever GP victory when Dan Gurney took the chequered flag in the French Grand Prix. Jim Clark dominated F1 in 1965, and Gurney outdid Brabham in the Drivers' Championship, finishing in fourth place – Brabham was eighth. F1 history was made in 1966 when Jack Brabham became the first and only man to win the F1 Drivers' Championship in a car bearing his own name (Brabham-Repco). Perhaps his proudest moment came on 3 July 1966 when he finally won an F1 race, the French GP at Reims, in his own car. A year later the world title went to his team-mate, Denny Hulme. After sustaining injuries in a 1969 race, Brabham decided to retire after the final Grand Prix of the 1970 season. In total, Brabham took part in 126 Grands Prix, winning 14 of them, and securing 31 podium finishes, 13 pole positions and 12 fastest laps.

In 1979 Jack Brabham was knighted, and in 1990 he was inducted into the International Motorsports Hall of Fame.

Did You Know That?
Jack Brabham was awarded the OBE in 1966 for winning his third Drivers' World Championship.

❀ 1956 DRIVERS' WORLD CHAMPIONSHIP ❀

Pos	Driver	Nationality	Team	Pts
1.	Juan Manuel Fangio	Argentinian	Ferrari	30
2.	Stirling Moss	British	Maserati	27
3.	Peter Collins	British	Ferrari	25
4.	Jean Behra	French	Maserati	22
5.	Pat Flaherty	American	Watson-Offenhauser	8
6.	Eugenio Castellotti	Italian	Ferrari	7.5
7.	Paul Frere	Belgian	Ferrari	6
8.	Sam Hanks	American	Kurtis Kraft-Novi & Kurtis Kraft-Offenhauser	6
9.	Paco Godia	Spanish	Maserati	6
10.	Jack Fairman	British	Connaught-Alta	5

❀ THE MASTER OF MONACO ❀

Ayrton Senna, nicknamed "Magic" by his adoring fans, won the Monaco Grand Prix six times, a record which earned him the title "Master of Monaco".

❀ AN ALL-FORD PODIUM ❀

Michele Alboreto, driving a Tyrrell-Ford, won the 1983 US East Grand Prix in Detroit, the home of the Ford motor car company. It was an excellent day for Ford as they supplied the engines for every place on the podium.

1983 US East Grand Prix

Pos	Driver	Team	Laps	Time/Retired	Grid	Pts
1.	Michele Alboreto	Tyrrell-Ford	60	1:50'53.669	6	9
2.	Keke Rosberg	Williams-Ford	60	+ 7.702	12	6
3.	John Watson	McLaren-Ford	60	+ 9.283	21	4

Did You Know That?

Of the 12 cars that finished the 1983 US East GP, eight were equipped with a Ford engine.

❀ WILLIAMS SHOW OFF FW09 ❀

At the 1983 South African Grand Prix, Williams-Ford paraded their new Honda turbo-engine and were rewarded with a respectable fifth position by the reigning World Champion, Keke Rosberg.

☗ ALFA 1-2-3 ☗

The top three places in the first official Formula One GP, the British Grand Prix at Silverstone on 13 May 1950, were all occupied by Alfa Romeos, with Giuseppe Farina first, Luigi Fagioli second and Reg Parnell third.

Did You Know That?
Leslie Johnson became the first driver to abandon an official F1 race when his ERA had to leave the 1950 British GP after lap two with a failed compressor.

☗ MAIDEN GP ENDS IN TRAGEDY ☗

On 7 July 1968, Jo Schlesser (Honda) participated in his maiden Grand Prix, the French GP at Rouen. The Honda team had manufactured an experimental air-cooled F1 car, known as the RA302, which was tested for the team by the 1964 F1 World Champion, John Surtees. Following testing, Surtees said that the car was not ready for racing and that it was a potential death-trap. However, Honda went ahead and entered the car for the French Grand Prix and hired local driver Jo Schlesser to drive it. On lap 2 of the race, the car slid wide going into the Six Freres corner and crashed sideways into a nearby bank. The car, with a full tank of petrol, ignited, leaving Schlesser with no chance of survival. Honda withdrew from F1 racing at the end of the 1968 season.

☗ HUNT'S ARRIVAL ☗

James Hunt made his Formula One debut at the Monaco Grand Prix on 3 June 1973 driving a March owned by Lord Hesketh. Hunt managed ninth place in the March-Ford after his race ended five laps from the end with engine trouble. Jackie Stewart (Tyrrell-Ford) won his third GP of the season in the Principality.

☗ DUREX ENTERS F1 ☗

Throughout its history G1 GP racing had attracted a somewhat very wide, yet very diverse, range of sponsors including:

7-Up • Brooke Bond • Durex • Embassy • Fruit of the Loom
LEC Refrigeration • Lockheed • Martini • Matchbox
Oxo • Penthouse

❀ 1957 DRIVERS' WORLD CHAMPIONSHIP ❀

Pos Driver	Nationality	Team	Pts
1. Juan Manuel Fangio	Argentinian	Maserati	40
2. Stirling Moss	British	Vanwall & Maserati	25
3. Luigi Musso	Italian	Ferrari	16
4. Mike Hawthorn	British	Ferrari	13
5. Tony Brooks	British	Vanwall	11
6. Masten Gregory	American	Maserati	10
7. Harry Schell	American	Maserati	10
8. Sam Hanks	American	Epperly-Offenhauser	8
9. Peter Collins	British	Ferrari	8
10. Jim Rathmann	American	Epperly-Offenhauser	7

❀ F1 MANAGEMENT GAMES ❀

F1 Manager • Grand Prix Manager 2 • Grand Prix World

❀ PESCARA DELIGHT FOR MOSS ❀

When the Belgian and Dutch Grands Prix of 1957 were cancelled, an additional Italian GP was held, this time at Pescara. Stirling Moss drove his Vanwall to victory on the tortuous circuit. Ferrari did not enter the race.

❀ SUPER SLICK CANADIAN ❀

Jacques Villeneuve (Williams-Renault) won seven of the 17 GPs raced in 1997 to claim the F1 Drivers' Championship. Michael Schumacher (Ferrari) led by a single point from the young Canadian going into the last race of the season, the European Grand Prix at Jarama, Spain. However, Schumacher's attempt to put both himself and Villeneuve out of the GP on lap 47 going into the Dry Sack hairpin backfired on him as he succeeded only in eliminating himself. If both drivers had left the race, Schumacher would have won his third championship, but as it turned out, Villeneuve finished third in the race to claim the four points which gave him the title.

❀ IRELAND WIN ❀

Innes Ireland won his first and only F1 race, the US Grand Prix at Watkins Glen, on 8 October 1961. It was the first GP won by the works Lotus team.

❂ 1958 DRIVERS' WORLD CHAMPIONSHIP ❂

Pos Driver	Nationality	Team	Pts
1. Mike Hawthorn	British	Ferrari F2 & Ferrari	42
2. Stirling Moss	British	Cooper-Climax F2 & Cooper-Climax & Vanwall	41
3. Tony Brooks	British	Vanwall	24
4. Roy Salvadori	British	Cooper-Climax F2 & Cooper-Climax	15
5. Peter Collins	British	Ferrari F2 & Ferrari	14
6. Harry Schell	American	BRM	14
7. Maurice Trintignant	French	Cooper-Climax F2 & Cooper-Climax	12
8. Luigi Musso	Italian	Ferrari F2 & Ferrari	12
9. Stuart Lewis-Evans	British	Vanwall	11
10. Phil Hill	American	Ferrari F2 & Ferrari	9

❂ 1958 CONSTRUCTORS' CUP ❂

Pos Constructor	Pts
1. Vanwall	48
2. Ferrari	40
3. Cooper-Climax	31
4. BRM	18
5. Maserati	6
6. Lotus-Climax	3

❂ SIMPLY TWO GOOD ❂

In 1992, the Williams FW14B, designed by Patrick Head and Adrian Newey, took the F1 world by storm. Mod cons in the car included a semi-automatic gearbox, active suspension, traction control and a host of other gadgets. Of the 16 GPs raced in 1992, the Williams FW14B won 10 of them, took 15 pole positions and had 11 fastest laps. Nigel Mansell won nine of the ten for Williams with their powerful and superbly reliable Renault V10 engine and his teammate Ricardo Patrese won one. At the end of 1992, active suspension and traction control were both banned, and thus F1 fans only saw the FW14B race for a single all-conquering season.

Did You Know That?
In 1992 Williams won the Constructors' Cup by a massive margin of 65 points from McLaren (164 points to 99).

✪ BACK TO THE DRAWING BOARD ✪

The 1969 season was a transitional one for Formula One. Several teams were plagued with wing failures in their cars, with Graham Hill and Jochen Rindt both being involved in accidents caused by ruptured wings. Discussion among the teams resulted in new limits being introduced to the permitted size of a car's wing, its structure and its distance from the ground. Many of the constructors went back to the drawing board with their research, while the Lotus, Matra and McLaren teams tested their four-wheel-drive cars without ever being able to develop a car that was both competitive and financially viable.

✪ FIRST NON-EUROPEAN GP ✪

On 18 January 1953, Argentina hosted the opening GP of the 1953 season in Buenos Aires. It was the first Formula One race (excluding the Indianapolis 500) to be held outside Europe and was won by the reigning World Champion, Alberto Ascari (Ferrari). However, the race was full of unsavoury incidents because of an unruly crowd and Giuseppe (Nino) Farina (Ferrari) hit and killed a young boy who was running across the circuit. Nine more people were killed in the trouble that followed. The deaths were the first fatalities in F1 racing.

✪ WORLD TITLE ELUDES MANSELL ✪

Going into the last Grand Prix of the 1986 season, Nigel Mansell was seven points ahead of his nearest challengers for the world crown, his Williams-Honda team-mate Nelson Piquet and McLaren-TAG's Alain Prost. On lap 62 of the 82-lap race Piquet was in first place, with Mansell second and Prost third. All Mansell had to do now was finish the race in the position he was in and he would be crowned the new World Champion. However, his dreams were shattered along with his left rear tyre on lap 63 as he hit the barriers. Mansell's loss was Piquet's gain as he was still in the lead by five seconds from Prost with 19 laps to go, knowing that victory in the GP would net him his fourth Drivers' World Championship. With 18 laps to go, Williams called Piquet into the pit to change his tyres and when he re-entered the race, he was 22 seconds behind Prost. He then proceeded to make an amazing recovery, setting a new track record fastest lap of 1'20.787 in the last lap, finishing the race a mere four seconds behind Prost. Prost claimed his first World Drivers' Championship and was now only one GP win behind Jackie Stewart's world record of 27 GP victories.

❂ 1959 DRIVERS' WORLD CHAMPIONSHIP ❂

Pos Driver	Nationality	Team	Pts
1. Jack Brabham	Australian	Cooper-Osca, Cooper-Borgward, Cooper-Climax & Cooper-Maserati	31
2. Tony Brooks	British	Ferrari	27
3. Stirling Moss	British	BRM, Cooper-Osca, Cooper-Borgward, Cooper-Climax & Cooper-Maserati	25.5
4. Phil Hill	American	Ferrari	20
5. Maurice Trintignant	French	Cooper-Osca, Cooper-Borgward, Cooper-Climax & Cooper-Maserati	19
6. Bruce McLaren	NZ	Cooper-Osca, Cooper-Borgward, Cooper-Climax & Cooper-Maserati	16.5
7. Dan Gurney	American	Ferrari	13
8. Jo Bonnier	Swedish	BRM	10
9. Masten Gregory	American	Cooper-Osca, Cooper-Borgward, Cooper-Climax & Cooper-Maserati	10
10. Rodger Ward	American	Watson-Offenhauser	8

❂ 1959 CONSTRUCTORS' CUP ❂

Pos Constructor	Pts
1. Cooper-Climax	40
2. Ferrari	32
3. BRM	18
4. Lotus-Climax	5

❂ TESTING AND QUALIFYING RULE CHANGES ❂

Over the years, the FIA has made many changes to the rules regarding testing, practice and qualifying. The 2013 regulations did not allow testing other than at specific times of the year, a rule instituted to stop the wealthiest teams gaining even more of an advantage. With only one tyre manufacturer, there was a strict limit on this testing and Mercedes were punished for breaking the rules. At each Grand Prix weekend, there were two Friday practice sessions, Saturday morning practice, Saturday's three-part qualifying session and the race on Sunday.

❀ HILL ACHIEVES GRAND SLAM ❀

Graham Hill is the only driver to achieve the Motor Racing Grand Slam of Formula One World Champion (1962 & 1968), Le Mans 24 Hours Champion (1972) and Indianapolis 500 Champion (1966).

❀ FAST TALK (3) ❀

"If I have a serious crash, I'd rather lose my life in it than be stuck in a wheelchair … I have such an intense life …"
Ayrton Senna

❀ BRABHAM PUSHES HIS CAR HOME ❀

At the Monaco Grand Prix on 19 May 1957, Jack Brabham pushed his car across the line after a fuel pump failure to claim sixth place in the race.

❀ AN UNWANTED NO. 2 RECORD ❀

In 1972, the Australian driver, David Walker, was the second driver to Emerson Fittipaldi in the Lotus F2 Formula One racing team. During the 1972 season, Lotus dropped Walker from the team for the Italian and Canadian GPs after they discovered he had tested a Two car for another team. His place at Lotus was taken by Reine Wisell. Walker returned for the US Grand Prix but then retired. Fittipaldi went on to win five times in 1972, scoring 61 points, which gave him the Drivers' Championship title, while Walker never finished better than ninth place (in Spain). When the 1973 season arrived, Walker was replaced by Ronnie Peterson.

Did You Know That?
David Walker remains the only driver in the history of F1 not to score a single championship point in the same season his team-mate won the F1 Drivers' World Championship title.

❀ CASTELLOTTI GIVEN LANCIA'S LAST DRIVE ❀

After announcing their withdrawal from F1 racing following the death of Alberto Ascari on 26 May 1955, Lancia allowed Eugenio Castellotti one final drive in a Lancia car as a privateer. In the Belgian Grand Prix at Spa on 5 June 1955, he had to withdraw after lap 16 with gearbox trouble.

◉ THE NEARLY MAN ◉

Between 1955 and 1958, Britain's Stirling Moss finished runner-up in the Formula One Drivers' Championship four consecutive times. He lost out in 1955 to his Mercedes team-mate Juan Manuel Fangio; in 1956 his Maserati was second to Fangio's Ferrari; in 1957 he drove for Vanwall and Maserati but for the third year in a row he lost out to Fangio (Maserati); and in 1958 it was fellow Brit Mike Hawthorn (Ferrari F2 & Ferrari) who was crowned World Champion ahead of Moss driving a Cooper-Climax F2, a Cooper-Climax and a Vanwall.

◉ THE DEATH OF A GENIUS ◉

On 1 May 1994, the world of Formula One was rocked to its core following the death of two drivers at Imola in the San Marino Grand Prix. First, Roland Ratzenberger died when he crashed his Simtek-Ford into a wall at 190mph during qualifying. Then, JJ Lehto (Benetton-Ford), who was nursing a broken neck, stalled on the grid and was hit from behind by Pedro Lamy's Lotus-Mugen-Honda resulting in wreckage from the cars flying into the grandstand opposite, injuring eight spectators. On lap five of the GP, Senna's Williams-Renault hit a bump as he turned into the left-hand Tamburello curve, causing his car to spear into the retaining wall. The three times former World Champion died instantly.

◉ FIRST ACTIVE SUSPENSION WIN ◉

Ayrton Senna (Lotus-Honda) won the 1987 Monaco Grand Prix to record the first ever F1 victory for an active suspension car. He finished the race 33.212 seconds ahead of Nelson Piquet (Williams-Honda) and 1'12.839 ahead of the third-placed driver Michele Alboreto (Ferrari).

◉ 100% WINNING RECORD ◉

After Niki Lauda won the Swedish Grand Prix at Anderstorp on 17 June 1978, his new Brabham-Alfa Romeo "Fan-car" was banned by the FIA. The Brabham B46B was designed by Gordon Murray for team owner Bernie Ecclestone and generated a tremendous amount of down-force by means of a revolutionary fan which extracted air from beneath the car and aided the cooling of the engine. Therefore, as it only raced once before it was declared illegal, the BT46B is the only car in F1 history with a 100% winning record.

✪ 1960 DRIVERS' WORLD CHAMPIONSHIP ✪

Pos Driver	Nationality	Team	Pts
1. Jack Brabham	Australian	Cooper-Climax, Cooper-Castellotti & Cooper-Maserati	43
2. Bruce McLaren	NZ	Cooper-Climax, Cooper-Castellotti & Cooper-Maserati	34
3. Stirling Moss	British	Lotus-Climax	19
4. Innes Ireland	British	Lotus-Climax	18
5. Phil Hill	American	Cooper-Climax, Cooper-Castellotti, Cooper-Maserati & Ferrari	16
6. Olivier Gendebien	Belgian	Cooper-Climax, Cooper-Castellotti & Cooper-Maserati	10
7. Wolfgang von Trips	German	Ferrari	10
8. Jim Rathmann	American	Watson-Offenhauser	8
9. Richie Ginther	American	Ferrari	8
10. Jim Clark	British	Lotus-Climax	8

✪ 1960 CONSTRUCTORS' CUP ✪

Pos Constructor	Pts
1. Cooper-Climax	48
2. Lotus-Climax	34
3. Ferrari	26
4. BRM	8
5. Cooper-Maserati	3
6. Cooper-Castellotti	3
7. Porsche	1

✪ MASERATI CLAIM FIRST WIN ✪

In the final Grand Prix of the 1953 season, the Italian GP held on 13 September 1953, Maserati claimed their first ever F1 victory when Juan Manuel Fangio took the chequered flag at Monza. Amazingly, Fangio was in third place going into the final lap but somehow Alberto Ascari (Ferrari) spun off, taking Giuseppe (Nino) Farina (Ferrari) with him, leaving Fangio to emerge from the dust cloud and take his first victory since his win in the last Grand Prix of the 1951 season, the Spanish.

❀ JIM CLARK, OBE ❀

James Clark was born on 4 March 1936 in Kilmany, Fifeshire, Scotland. Aged 17, a local garage owner, Jock McBain, persuaded him to enter an auto test, which he won. Following this first win his appetite for racing was all-consuming and in 1957 Ian Scott-Watson purchased Clark a Porsche, and the following year Jock McBain reformed the Border Reivers racing team. Jim won 12 times in 20 starts driving a Jaguar D-type for the team.

In 1959 he made his single-seater debut in Formula Junior, and a year on he was a member of Lotus's Formula Junior team before being sensationally moved up to Formula One. On 6 June 1960, Clark made his F1 debut in the Dutch Grand Prix in a Lotus-Climax and managed to score his first Drivers' Championship points in his very next Grand Prix, the Belgian. In 1961 Clark was involved in the accident that killed Wolfgang von Trips at Monza in the Italian Grand Prix, and the racing authorities placed the blame for the accident on Clark's shoulders. His first GP victory came on 17 June 1962 when he took the chequered flag in the Belgian Grand Prix at Spa-Francorchamps. Two more wins followed in 1962 in the British and US Grands Prix, enabling him to finish runner-up to Graham Hill (BRM) in the Drivers' Championship.

Jim's first World Championship arrived in 1963, when his Lotus-Climax raced to victory in seven of the season's ten Grands Prix. The Lotus team also won their first ever Constructors' Championship. Despite winning three GPs in the 1964 F1 season, Clark was prevented from retaining his world title as a result of poor reliability from his Climax engine. He finished third in the 1964 Drivers' World Championship table. However, in 1965 Clark, Lotus and Climax bounced back in style with Clark winning six of the ten GPs raced to claim his second drivers' crown. A disappointing 1966 followed with just one GP win (the US) and sixth place in the World Championship. Four GP victories in 1968 was only good enough for third place in the Drivers' Championship, and after winning the opening Grand Prix of the 1968 season in South Africa, Jim crashed and died in a Formula Two race at Hockenheim on 7 April 1968. In 1990 he was inducted into the International Motorsports Hall of Fame. Clark participated in 72 Grands Prix, winning 25, with 32 podium finishes, 33 pole positions and 28 fastest laps.

Did You Know That?
Jim Clark (Lotus-Climax) is the only driver to win the Indianapolis 500 and the F1 Drivers' World Championship in the same year (1965).

⚙ 1961 DRIVERS' WORLD CHAMPIONSHIP ⚙

Pos	Driver	Nationality	Team	Pts
1.	Phil Hill	American	Ferrari	34
2.	Wolfgang von Trips	German	Ferrari	33
3.	Stirling Moss	British	Lotus-Climax & Lotus-Maserati	21
4.	Dan Gurney	American	Porsche	21
5.	Richie Ginther	American	Ferrari	16
6.	Innes Ireland	British	Lotus-Climax & Lotus-Maserati	12
7.	Jim Clark	British	Lotus-Climax & Lotus-Maserati	11
8.	Bruce McLaren	NZ	Cooper-Climax & Cooper-Maserati	11
9.	Giancarlo Baghetti	Italian	Ferrari	9
10.	Tony Brooks	British	BRM-Climax	6

⚙ 1961 CONSTRUCTORS' CUP ⚙

Pos	Constructor	Pts
1.	Ferrari	45
2.	Lotus-Climax	35
3.	Porsche	22
4.	Cooper-Climax	14
5.	BRM-Climax	7

⚙ F1 WORLD CHAMPIONS & LE MANS MASTERS ⚙

Graham Hill (1962 & 1968 F1, 1972 Le Mans)
Phil Hill (1961 F1, 1958, 1961 & 1962 Le Mans)
Jochen Rindt (1970 F1, 1965 Le Mans)

⚙ FURTHER FUEL REDUCTION ⚙

Following on from the 1984 rule obligating constructors to limit their fuel capacity in a car to 220 litres, in 1985 FISA reduced the maximum capacity of fuel tanks to 195 litres. FISA's overall aim was to reduce the speed of the cars and thereby improve the overall safety of the drivers. In direct response, teams positioned buttons in the cockpit for controlling the fuel in the car. This became redundant from 2012, when the FIA changed the rules again and outlawed refuelling altogether.

❀ 1962 DRIVERS' WORLD CHAMPIONSHIP ❀

Pos Driver	Nationality	Team	Pts
1. Graham Hill	British	BRM	42
2. Jim Clark	British	Lotus-BRM & Lotus Climax	30
3. Bruce McLaren	NZ	Cooper-Alfa Romeo & Cooper-Climax	27
4. John Surtees	British	Lola-Climax	19
5. Dan Gurney	American	Porsche	15
6. Phil Hill	American	Ferrari	14
7. Tony Maggs	S African	Cooper-Alfa Romeo & Cooper-Climax	13
8. Richie Ginther	American	BRM	10
9. Jack Brabham	Australian	Lotus-BRM, Brabham-Climax & Lotus-Climax	9
10. Trevor Taylor	British	Lotus-BRM & Lotus-Climax	6

❀ 1962 CONSTRUCTORS' CUP ❀

Pos	Constructor	Pts
1.	BRM	42
2.	Lotus-Climax	36
3.	Cooper-Climax	29
4.	Lola-Climax	19
5.	Porsche	18
6.	Ferrari	18
7.	Brabham-Climax	6
8.	Lotus-BRM	1

❀ WILLIAMS IN THE USA ❀

Up to the end of the 2013 season (there was no US GP 2008–11), Williams has won five US Grands Prix: Alan Jones at Watkins Glen in 1980, Jones again at Las Vegas and Long Beach in 1981, Keke Rosberg at Dallas in 1984 and Rosberg again at Detroit in 1985.

❀ RAISING THE BAR ❀

In 1999 BAR failed to score a single championship point in their F1 debut season, but in the first race of the 2000 season, the Australian Grand Prix, Jacques Villeneuve claimed three points for the team when he took fourth place in his BAR-Honda. His team-mate, Ricardo Zonta, claimed another point, finishing in sixth position.

❀ BRIDGESTONE TAKE OVER ❀

Bridgestone Tyres signed a three-year deal in 2008 to become the exclusive Formula One tyre manufacturer. Michelin pulled out of F1 after 2007. Bridgestone, a Japanese rubber conglomerate, based in Fukuoka, took their name from the founder Shojiro Ishibashi. *Ishibashi* literally means Stone Bridge. From 2012, Pirelli became the tyre manufacturers, but some teams struggled with their rubber.

❀ ECCLESTONE FAILS TO QUALIFY ❀

In 1957 Bernie Ecclestone was the manager of Formula One driver Stuart-Lewis Evans who finished in 12th place in the F1 Drivers' Championship driving a Connaught-Alta and a Vanwall. In 1958 Ecclestone purchased the Connaught-Alta racing team and attempted to qualify for the 1958 Monaco Grand Prix in one of his own cars. He failed to qualify for the GP and returned to concentrating on management.

❀ FISA VERSUS FOCA ❀

During the early 1980s, a power struggle developed between the Federation Internationale du Sport Automobile (FISA, the sporting arm of FIA) and the Formula One Constructors' Association (FOCA). The manufacturer-entered teams, Alfa Romeo, Ferrari and Renault, sided with FISA, while the British "garagistes" sided with FOCA. FOCA had grown very strong during the 1970s with Brabham's owner, Bernie Ecclestone, guiding the organisation. Indeed, such was Ecclestone's influence back then that race organisers used to give him the GP's prize money to distribute. This resulted in the FISA-backed teams withdrawing from the 1980 Spanish Grand Prix after the race organiser supported the FOCA-backed teams in an argument. In the end the Spanish GP went ahead with 22 cars but was subsequently declared null and void in the Drivers' and Constructors' Championship race.

❀ POSTHUMOUS F1 WORLD CHAMPION ❀

In 1970 Jochen Rindt (Lotus-Ford) was killed during practice for the Italian Grand Prix at Monza. It was the tenth of 13 GP races that year and although Jacky Ickx (Ferrari) won two of the remaining races, Rindt still won the title by five points from Ickx to become the first, and to date only, posthumous F1 Drivers' World Champion.

❀ 1963 DRIVERS' WORLD CHAMPIONSHIP ❀

Pos Driver	Nationality	Team	Pts
1. Jim Clark	British	Lotus-Borgward, Lotus-Ford, Lotus-BRM & Lotus-Climax	63
2. Graham Hill	British	BRM	29
3. Richie Ginther	American	BRM	29
4. John Surtees	British	Ferrari	22
5. Dan Gurney	American	Brabham-Climax	19
6. Bruce McLaren	NZ	Cooper-Maserati & Cooper-Climax	17
7. Jack Brabham	Australian	Brabham-Climax	14
8. Tony Maggs	S African	Cooper-Maserati & Cooper-Climax	9
9. Innes Ireland	British	BRP-BRM	6
10. Lorenzo Bandini	Italian	BRM & Ferrari	6

❀ 1963 CONSTRUCTORS' CUP ❀

Pos	Constructor	Pts
1.	Lotus-Climax	54
2.	BRM	36
3.	Brabham-Climax	28
4.	Ferrari	26
5.	Cooper-Climax	25
6.	BRP-BRM	6
7.	Porsche	5
8.	Lotus-BRM	4

❀ PIT BABES AND GRID GIRLS ❀

Prior to every F1 Grand Prix, especially in the early 2000s, "Pit Babes", usually glamorous models of the like of Jordan, Jodie Marsh and Melinda Messenger, were found on the grid holding an umbrella over the driver's head. They were dressed in the team's colours and held the driver's board which displayed his name and grid position. The most renowned troupes were the Marlboro Grid Girls, the Jordan F1 ladies, *Las Chicas de la F1* and the RaceQueens of Japan.

❀ EUROPEAN MASTER ❀

On 7 May 2006, Michael Schumacher (Ferrari) won the European GP at the Nurburgring, his 86th career victory in F1.

⚙ FANTASY ITALIAN STARTING GRID ⚙

(to the end of the 2013 season)

1
Alberto Ascari
*(13 GP wins, 31
GPs, World
champion 1952,
1953)*

2
Riccardo Patrese
*(6 GP wins, 256
GPs, World champion
best 2nd 1992)*

3
Giueseppe Farina
*(5 GP wins, 33
GPs, World
champion 1950)*

4
Michele Alboreto
*(5 GP wins, 194 GPs,
World champion, best
2nd 1985)*

5
Giancarlo
Fisichella *(3 GP
wins, 231 GPs,
World champion
best 5th 2005)*

6
Elio de Angelis
*(2 GP wins, 108
GPs, World champion
best 3rd 1984*

7
Alessandro
Nannini *(1 GP
win, 77 GPs,
World champion
best 6th 1989)*

8
Giancarlo Baghetti
*(1 GP win, 21 GPs,
World champion best
9th 1961*

9
Jarno Trulli
*(1 GP win, 256
GPs, World
champion best 6th
2004)*

10
Lorenzo Bandini
*(1 GP win, 42 GPs,
World champion best
4th 1964)*

❂ 1964 DRIVERS' WORLD CHAMPIONSHIP ❂

Pos	Driver	Nationality	Team	Pts
1.	John Surtees	British	Ferrari	40
2.	Graham Hill	British	BRM	39
3.	Jim Clark	British	Lotus-BRM & Lotus-Climax	32
4.	Lorenzo Bandini	Italian	Ferrari	23
5.	Richie Ginther	American	BRM	23
6.	Dan Gurney	American	Brabham-Ford, Brabham-BRM & Brabham-Climax	19
7.	Bruce McLaren	NZ	Cooper-Climax	13
8.	Jack Brabham	Australian	Brabham-Ford, Brabham-BRM & Brabham-Climax	11
9.	Peter Arundell	British	Lotus-BRM & Lotus-Climax	11
10.	Jo Siffert	Swiss	Brabham-Ford, Brabham-BRM & Brabham-Climax	7

❂ 1964 CONSTRUCTORS' CUP ❂

Pos	Constructor	Pts
1.	Ferrari	45
2.	BRM	42
3.	Lotus-Climax	37
4.	Brabham-Climax	30
5.	Cooper-Climax	16
6.	Brabham-BRM	7
7.	BRP-BRM	5
8.	Lotus-BRM	3

❂ 1950–1957 ❂

8-6-4-3-2 points awarded to the first five placed drivers. One extra point was awarded to the driver who recorded the fastest lap in the race. Drivers were also permitted to share drives, with points divided accordingly.

❂ NEW RULES AND SOME CHANGES IN 1965 ❂

In 1965 BRM unveiled their new four-wheel-drive racing car that never raced while Honda transversely mounted their 12-cylinder engine. Additionally, the tyres used became wider and much lower than before, and were made with nylon as opposed to cotton fibres. The 1965 season also marked the end of the 1.5-litre engine capacity rule.

❁ A VERY POPULAR CAR ❁

So popular was the Cooper T51 racing car, designed by Owen Maddock, and driven to World Championship glory by Jack Brabham in 1959 and 1960, that nine T51s appeared on the grid for the 1960 British GP. They had been entered by no fewer than six different teams, but the race was inevitably won by the reigning World Champion, Jack Brabham – in his T51.

❁ SCHUMI IN A CLASS OF HIS OWN ❁

Going into the final GP of the 2003 season, Kimi Raikkonen (McLaren-Mercedes) needed to win the Japanese Grand Prix, and hope Michael Schumacher (Ferrari) did not finish in the top eight positions, to claim his first Drivers' Championship. Raikkonen finished second to Rubens Barrichello (Ferrari) in the GP, while Schumacher finished eighth to win his fourth consecutive F1 World Championship. Schumacher's sixth title took him one past the legendary Juan Manuel Fangio's five World Championship victories. After the race a modest Schumacher said: "Fangio is above me..."

❁ ALL-CONQUERING McLAREN ❁

In 1984 Team McLaren-TAG established a new record for points won in a season with their total of 143.5 (drivers and constructors) and also set a new record for the most GP wins in a season when Niki Lauda (5) and Alain Prost (7) won 12 of the 16 races between them.

❁ HILL DEATH ❁

On 29 November 1975, the former two-times F1 World Champion Graham Hill died when his light Piper Aztec aeroplane crashed while returning from a test session at the Paul Ricard circuit in France. Five of Hill's Embassy-Hill racing team, including the promising young driver Tony Brise, also lost their lives in the crash. Hill was piloting the plane when it encountered foggy conditions over Arkley Golf Course in north London.

❁ BRM'S FIRST WIN ❁

Joakim Bonnier secured the BRM racing team their first ever Grand Prix win after nine years of trying when he took the chequered flag at Zandvoort in the Dutch GP on 31 May 1959.

❀ FAST TALK (4) ❀

"The crashes people remember, but drivers remember the near misses."
Mario Andretti

❀ OUT OF AFRICA ❀

There were 18 Grands Prix on the 2006 F1 calendar but Africa was the only continent not visited.

❀ JOHNNY DELIGHTS STEWART ❀

Johnny Herbert gave Stewart-Ford their first ever Formula One victory when he took the chequered flag in the 1999 European Grand Prix at the Nurburgring. Team owner Jackie Stewart was ecstatic with delight. Herbert finished in eighth place in the World Championship table of 1999, one place below his team-mate, Rubens Barrichello.

❀ ALMOST A CLIMAX ❀

Cliff Allison narrowly missed out on giving Lotus-Climax its first ever Formula One victory in the 1958 Belgian Grand Prix, and had the race lasted 25 laps instead of 24, he would surely have done so. Tony Brooks won in his Vanwall, but his car crossed the line with its gearbox practically seized. Mike Hawthorn finished second in his Ferrari, which broke its engine as it approached the chequered flag, and Stuart Lewis-Evans's Vanwall broke a steering arm just yards from the finishing line. Allison finished in fourth place.

❀ 10 AND OUT ❀

At the first S bend during the 2006 US GP at the Indianapolis Motor Speedway circuit, 10 of the 22 cars in the race were forced to retire after a huge pile-up.

❀ MR MONACO MAKES IT FIVE ❀

Graham Hill (Lotus-Ford) won the Monaco Grand Prix for the fifth time in 1969, and this remained a record until the magical Ayrton Senna surpassed Hill's achievement in 1993. During his driving career, Hill was known as "Mr Monaco", such was his dominance on the Principality's narrow and tricky street circuit.

❀ 1965 DRIVERS' WORLD CHAMPIONSHIP ❀

Pos	Driver	Nationality	Team	Pts
1.	Jim Clark	British	Lotus-BRM, Lotus-Ford & Lotus-Climax	54
2.	Graham Hill	British	BRM	40
3.	Jackie Stewart	British	BRM	33
4.	Dan Gurney	American	Brabham-Ford, Brabham-BRM & Brabham-Climax	25
5.	John Surtees	British	Ferrari	17
6.	Lorenzo Bandini	Italian	Ferrari	13
7.	Richie Ginther	American	Honda	11
8.	Mike Spence	British	Lotus-BRM, Lotus-Ford & Lotus-Climax	10
9.	Bruce McLaren	NZ	Cooper-Ford & Cooper-Climax	10
10.	Jack Brabham	Australian	Brabham-Ford, Brabham-BRM & Brabham-Climax	9

❀ 1965 CONSTRUCTORS' CUP ❀

Pos	Constructor	Pts
1.	Lotus-Climax	54
2.	BRM	45
3.	Ferrari	26
4.	Brabham-Climax	21
5.	Cooper-Climax	14
6.	Honda	11
7.	Brabham-BRM	5
8.	Lotus-BRM	2

❀ A MAN OF MANY TALENTS ❀

In 1992 Phillipe Alliot and Mauro Baldi won two races and helped Peugeot to the World Sports Car Championship. Peugeot then named Alliot as a McLaren-Peugeot F1 driver in 1994, although he only took part in one Grand Prix for the team, the Hungarian GP. In August 1994, Alliot rejoined Larrousse for one race, the Belgian Grand Prix, but at the beginning of 1995 he announced his retirement from racing, having opted for a career in politics. He also did some television commentary work for a while and competed in ice racing and in the Paris–Dakar Rally, but then moved on to run his own team in GP racing.

❀ JUAN MANUEL FANGIO ❀

Many motor racing writers consider Juan Manuel Fangio, who was born on 24 June 1911 in Balcarce, Argentina, to be the greatest racing driver ever.

Fangio began motor racing in Argentina in 1934 after military service and won the Argentine National Championship in 1940 and 1941. However, World War II put the brakes on his racing career. Fangio raced at a time when legends sat alongside him on the grid including Alberto Ascari (twice World Champion in 1952 and 1953), Giuseppe Farina (inaugural World Champion in 1950) and Britain's Stirling Moss. In 1950, driving an Alfa Romeo, he finished runner-up in the inaugural F1 World Championship to Farina and the following year he won his first world title with Alfa Romeo. During the 1952 season he suffered a neck injury at Monza which ended his Championship hopes and when he returned to F1 racing in 1954 he was a Maserati driver, although Mercedes took over mid-season. In 1954, Fangio won six of the Championship's eight races (8 wins from 12 in total) to claim his second World crown.

Fangio won his second successive, and third overall, F1 World Drivers' Championship in 1955, but following the death of 77 spectators at Le Mans in 1955, Mercedes, who won all of the motor racing Championships that year, took the decision to withdraw from motor racing. In 1956, Fangio was a Ferrari driver, hired by Enzo Ferrari to replace Ascari, who had been killed in an accident. The Argentinian maestro won his third consecutive World Championship and a fourth title overall. In 1957, Fangio made a return to Maserati and won his fifth title and the following year he decided to call it quits and retire after finishing fourth in the French GP.

On 23 February 1958, he was kidnapped by Cuban rebels and then freed some time later. After his F1 career ended, Fangio was employed as a representative of Mercedes-Benz and quite often drove his former race cars in demonstration laps prior to an F1 GP. In 1990, the maestro was inducted into the International Motorsports Hall of Fame. Juan Manuel Fangio died in Buenos Aires on 17 January 1995, aged 84 and was buried at Cludad de Balcarce Cemetery. He participated in 51 Grands Prix, winning 24 of them (the best winning percentage in F1 history) and also secured 31 podium finishes, 39 pole positions and 23 fastest laps. His nephew, Juan Manuel II, was also a successful motor racing driver.

Did You Know That?

In 2005, the Zonda 2005 C12F was named in Fangio's honour for the engineering work he did for Italian car-maker Pagani Automobili SpA.

❀ 1966 DRIVERS' WORLD CHAMPIONSHIP ❀

Pos	Driver	Nationality	Team	Pts
1.	Jack Brabham	Australian	Brabham-BRM, Brabham-Repco & Brabham-Climax	42
2.	John Surtees	British	Cooper-Ferrari, Cooper-Maserati & Ferrari	28
3.	Jochen Rindt	Austrian	Cooper-Ferrari & Cooper-Maserati	22
4.	Denny Hulme	N.Z.	Brabham-BRM, Brabham-Repco & Brabham-Climax	18
5.	Graham Hill	British	BRM	17
6.	Jim Clark	British	Lotus-BRM & Lotus-Climax	16
7.	Jackie Stewart	British	BRM	14
8.	Mike Parkes	British	Ferrari	12
9.	Lorenzo Bandini	Italian	Ferrari	12
10.	Ludovico Scarfiotti	Italian	Ferrari	9

❀ 1966 CONSTRUCTORS' CUP ❀

Pos	Constructor	Pts
1.	Brabham-Repco	42
2.	Ferrari	31
3.	Cooper-Maserati	30
4.	BRM	22
5.	Lotus-BRM	13
6.	Lotus-Climax	8
7.	Eagle-Climax	4
8.	Honda	3
9.	McLaren-Ford	2
10.	Brabham-Climax	1

❀ WILLIAMS' FIRST ❀

Clay Regazzoni gave Williams their first GP win when he took the chequered flag in the 1979 British Grand Prix at Silverstone. His team-mate, Alan Jones, went on to win four more F1 races that year for the marque: in Germany, Austria, Holland and Canada.

Did You Know That?
Regazzoni's victory at Silverstone was the fifth and final one of his career. He was seriously injured in a crash at Long Beach in 1980.

❂ LE MANS TRAGEDY ROCKS F1 ❂

At the Le Mans 24 Hours race on 11 June 1955, Pierre Levegh's Mercedes-Benz flew into the crowd, killing 77 spectators. As a result the Swiss government banned all motor sports events within their borders, and Mercedes-Benz took the decision to withdraw from F1 at the end of the 1955 season. The race was won by the future F1 World Champion, Mike Hawthorn, and Ivor Bueb in a Jaguar D-Type.

Did You Know That?
In addition to the Swiss GP, the French, German and Spanish GPs were all cancelled in 1955 following the tragedy at Le Mans.

❂ ALONSO DEDICATES WIN TO MICHELIN ❂

On 28 May 2006, Fernando Alonso (Renault) won the Monaco GP, his fourth GP win of the season from seven races, and dedicated his victory to Edward Michelin who died the previous Friday in a boating accident. All three podium places were occupied by drivers who used Michelin tyres. When the three podium placed drivers (Fernando Alonso, Pablo Montoya, McLaren-Mercedes and David Coulthard, Red Bull Racing-Ferrari) were presented with the customary bottles of champagne after the victory ceremony they did not spray it over their mechanics in memory of Edward Michelin.

❂ FERRARI'S REVOLUTIONARY MODEL 639 ❂

During the 1988 season, the Brazilian driver, Roberto Moreno, was Ferrari's test driver. He helped develop the new and revolutionary Ferrari 639 model designed by John Barnard. The car had shift gears installed in the steering wheel and had a seven-speed gearbox.

❂ BRITISH WORLD CHAMPION DIES ❂

On 7 March 1968, Jim Clark, the F1 Drivers' World Champion in 1963 and 1965, crashed and tragically died in a Formula Two race at Hockenheim. Following Clark's death, Chris Amon said: "If it could happen to him, what chance do the rest of us have?"

❂ ARGENTINIAN HILL ❂

In 1995, Argentina held its first F1 Grand Prix in 14 years and the race was dominated by Damon Hill (Williams-Renault).

❀ 1967 DRIVERS' WORLD CHAMPIONSHIP ❀

Pos Driver	Nationality	Team	Pts
1. Denny Hulme	NZ	Brabham-Climax & Brabham-Repco	51
2. Jack Brabham	Australian	Brabham-Climax & Brabham-Repco	46
3. Jim Clark	British	Lotus-Climax, Lotus-BRM & Lotus-Ford	41
4. John Surtees	British	Honda	20
5. Chris Amon	NZ	Ferrari	20
6. Pedro Rodriguez	Mexican	Cooper-ATS, Cooper-Maserati & Cooper-Climax	15
7. Graham Hill	British	Lotus-Climax, Lotus-BRM & Lotus-Ford	15
8. Dan Gurney	American	Eagle-Climax & Eagle-Weslake	13
9. Jackie Stewart	British	BRM	10
10. Mike Spence	British	BRM	9

❀ 1967 CONSTRUCTORS' CUP ❀

Pos Constructor	Pts
1. Brabham-Repco	63
2. Lotus-Ford	44
3. Cooper-Maserati	28
4. Honda	20
5. Ferrari	20
6. BRM	17
7. Eagle-Weslake	13
8. Lotus-BRM	6
9. Cooper-Climax	6
10. McLaren-BRM	3

❀ SKIRTS BANNED ❀

In 1981 the FISA took the decision to ban side-skirts, and introduced a new rule which stated: "All cars should have a minimum of 60 mm ground distance." However, the Brabham team invented a hydro pneumatic suspension that allowed the car to "graze" the ground at top speed but not when the car was driving slowly or sitting in parc fermé. The other teams immediately followed Brabham's lead and FISA accepted its legality four races later.

✺ BRITISH DRIVERS EXCEL AT HOME GP ✺

The British Grand Prix has witnessed seven British winners since 1991: Nigel Mansell (1991, 1992), Damon Hill (1994), Johnny Herbert (1995), David Coulthard (1999, 2000) and Lewis Hamilton (2008). Hamilton also claimed pole position in 2007 and 2013, but didn't win.

✺ PROUD DAD WATCHES SON'S DEBUT ✺

At the opening GP of the 2006 season, Keke Rosberg, the 1982 World Drivers' Champion, watched his son, Nico the reigning GP2 Champion, make his maiden Formula One Grand Prix start for Williams-Cosworth in Bahrain. Nico finished the race in seventh position to claim two World Championship points.

✺ SENNA TRIES OUT INDY CARS ✺

In 1993 Ayrton Senna tested for the Marlboro Team Penske in Indy Car racing, but despite setting extremely quick times he returned to Formula One with McLaren-Ford.

✺ ENZO'S LAST PICK ✺

Nigel Mansell was the last driver to be personally selected by the late Enzo Ferrari to race for Ferrari when he signed to drive for the team in 1989. Sadly Enzo died before Mansell drove for the team.

✺ THE PELE OF MOTOR RACING ✺

Before the start of the 2006 Brazilian GP, Michael Schumacher's 249th and final appearance in the cockpit of a Formula One car, the legendary Brazilian footballer, Pele, presented him with a commemorative trophy and described him as the "Pele of Motor Racing".

✺ MONZA DEATHS ✺

On 10 September 1961, Wolfgang von Trips' Ferrari collided with Jim Clark's Lotus-Climax at the end of Parabolica on the second lap of the Italian GP at Monza. The car became airborne and crashed into a side barrier, killing the German driver and 14 spectators. Wolfgang Graf Alexander Berghe von Trips won two Grands Prix (the Dutch & the British in 1961), achieved one pole position, took six podium places and scored a total of 56 championship points.

◉ 1968 DRIVERS' WORLD CHAMPIONSHIP ◉

Pos Driver	Nationality	Team	Pts
1. Graham Hill	British	Lotus-Ford	48
2. Jackie Stewart	British	Matra & Matra-Ford	36
3. Denny Hulme	NZ	McLaren-BRM & McLaren-Ford	33
4. Jacky Ickx	Belgian	Ferrari	27
5. Bruce McLaren	NZ	McLaren-BRM & McLaren-Ford	22
6. Pedro Rodriguez	Mexican	BRM	18
7. Jo Siffert	Swiss	Lotus-Ford	12
8. John Surtees	British	Honda	12
9. Jean Pierre Beltoise	French	Matra & Matra-Ford	11
10. Chris Amon	NZ	Ferrari	10

◉ 1968 CONSTRUCTORS' CUP ◉

Pos	Constructor	Pts
1.	Lotus-Ford	62
2.	McLaren-Ford	49
3.	Matra-Ford	45
4.	Ferrari	32
5.	BRM	28
6.	Honda	14
7.	Cooper-BRM	14
8.	Brabham-Repco	10
9.	Matra	8
10.	McLaren-BRM	3

◉ FAST TALK (5) ◉

"When I started racing my father told me, 'Cristiano, nobody has three balls but some people have two very good ones.'"
Cristiano Da Matta

◉ THE NEXT AYRTON SENNA ◉

In the 1997 and 1998 F1 seasons, Jan Magnussen drove for the Stewart-Ford F1 racing team. Team founder Jackie Stewart once described the young Dane as the best prospect since Ayrton Senna. Magnussen never lived up to the claim and only managed to score a single championship point in the 25 GPs he started.

❀ 1969 DRIVERS' WORLD CHAMPIONSHIP ❀

Pos	Driver	Nationality	Team	Pts
1.	Jackie Stewart	British	Matra-Ford	63
2.	Jacky Ickx	Belgian	Brabham-Climax, Brabham-Repco & Brabham-Ford	37
3.	Bruce McLaren	NZ	McLaren-Ford	26
4.	Jochen Rindt	Austrian	Lotus-Ford	22
5.	Jean Pierre Beltoise	French	Matra-Ford	21
6.	Denny Hulme	NZ	McLaren-Ford	20
7.	Graham Hill	British	Lotus-Ford	19
8.	Piers Courage	British	Brabham-Climax, Brabham-Repco & Brabham-Ford	16
9.	Jo Siffert	Swiss	Lotus-Ford	15
10.	Jack Brabham	Australian	Brabham-Climax, Brabham-Repco & Brabham-Ford	14

❀ 1969 CONSTRUCTORS' CUP ❀

Pos	Constructor	Pts
1.	Matra-Ford	66
2.	Brabham-Ford	49
3.	Lotus-Ford	47
4.	McLaren-Ford	38
5.	BRM	7
6.	Ferrari	7

❀ REAL NAMES ❀

Two drivers have won the F1 Drivers' World Championship without using their real surname:

Nelson Piquet was born *Nelson Souto Maior*
Ayrton Senna was born *Ayrton Senna Da Silva*

❀ SCHUMI KNOCKED OFF ❀

After five successive years in which he was crowned World Champion, Michael Schumacher (Ferrari), was knocked off his perch in 2005 by Fernando Alonso (Renault). Alonso became the first Spaniard to be crowned World Champion and the sport's youngest ever World Champion at the time (though he lost that record to Lewis Hamilton in 2008).

❀ NON-QUALIFYING DRIVER RACES IN GP ❀

German racing driver Hans Heyer had one attempt in his career to race in Formula One. On 31 July 1977, he entered the German Grand Prix, driving the second car of the new German team, ATS. However, Heyer failed to qualify for the race subsequently won by Niki Lauda (Ferrari). To the dismay of everyone in attendance at the Hockenheimring, when the race started Heyer left the pits and joined the race. The race stewards had not noticed Heyer's shrewd manoeuvre until his car broke down after nine laps with transmission failure. The stewards then disqualified him from the race, but a smiling Heyer was not worried about that because he had earned his 10 minutes of fame and had a story to tell everyone for years to come. In 1989 Heyer retired after participating in 999 races over a 30-year career, most of his races being in sports car racing.

Did You Know That?
In 2000 Kris Nissen, the director of Volkswagen, discovered that Heyer had ended his career just one race short of 1,000. Nissen then invited Heyer to race in the 2004 ADC Volkswagen Polo Cup at the Noisring, thereby achieving 1,000 career races.

❀ F1'S FIRST PUNCH-UP ❀

When a piston failure forced Jean Behra (Ferrari) to retire on lap 31 of the 1959 French Grand Prix, he became involved in a heated discussion with his team manager, Romolo Tavoni, and after punching him Behra was immediately dismissed from Ferrari. Less than a month later Behra crashed his Porsche RSK in the sports car race that preceded the German GP at Avus, Berlin, on 1 August 1959. Behra was thrown from his car and died from the injuries he sustained when he hit a flagpole.

❀ SIXTH IN TITLE RACE WITH ONLY ONE GP ❀

In the inaugural 1950 F1 season the American driver Johnnie Parsons finished in sixth place in the Drivers' World Championship after competing in just one of the seven Grands Prix raced. On 30 May 1950 Parsons won the Indianapolis 500, which was part of the F1 calendar at the time, but chose thereafter to concentrate on his Indy career rather than race Formula One. However, the nine points he was awarded for winning the race was still good enough to place him sixth overall in 1950.

❂ MOON SQUADRON LANDINGS ❂

George Abecassis began racing in 1935 in a modified Austin Seven and made two Grand Prix starts in a HW-Alta. During World War II Abecassis was a member of the Royal Air Force's secret Moon Squadrons, ferrying secret agents in and out of France in Lysander aeroplanes. After the war he went back to racing, initially with pre-war machinery, but then he became a partner with John Heath in HW Motors and they built the "HW-Alta", which later became known as the "HWM". Abecassis raced in two GPs in a HWM.

❂ TOTAL DOMINANCE ❂

The 2004 F1 season was the first time in the history of the sport that two drivers finished with 100 or more points in the Drivers' Championship table: Michael Schumacher (Ferrari) had 148 points and his team-mate, Rubens Barrichello, had 114 points. Not surprisingly, Ferrari won the Constructors' Cup with a record-busting 262 points, more than twice the score of their nearest challenger, BAR-Honda, with 119 points.

❂ ONCE, TWICE, THREE TIMES IN AUSTRIA ❂

The 1987 Austrian Grand Prix had to be started three times. The first time Martin Brundle (Zakspeed) broke his suspension just after the lights, which caused him to hit the barriers and cause havoc on the track. In the second start it was the turn of Riccardo Patrese (Brabham-BMW) to halt the race when his car collided with Derek Warwick's Arrows-Megatron. When the race was started a third time, Nigel Mansell drove to victory in his Williams-Honda.

Did You Know That?
After the Austrian Grand Prix Nigel Mansell (Williams-Honda), Nelson Piquet (Williams-Honda) and Teo Fabi (Benetton-Ford) all travelled to the podium on board Mansell's car. Mansell stood up just as they approached a little bridge, and got a bang on his head. Mansell was still dazed when he got on to the podium and Piquet could barely control his laughter.

❂ RENAULT'S FIRST ❂

In 1979, Jean-Pierre Jabouille gave Renault their first win in Formula One when he raced to victory in the French Grand Prix.

⊛ ALL-TIME F1 WORLD CHAMPIONS ⊛

A total of 33 different drivers from 14 countries have claimed the 64 F1 World Drivers' Championship since 1950. This is the full list:

Year	Driver	Year	Driver
1950	Giuseppe Farina	1982	Keke Rosberg
1951	Juan Manuel Fangio	1983	Nelson Piquet
1952	Alberto Ascari	1984	Niki Lauda
1953	Alberto Ascari	1985	Alain Prost
1954	Juan Manuel Fangio	1986	Alain Prost
1955	Juan Manuel Fangio	1987	Nelson Piquet
1956	Juan Manuel Fangio	1988	Ayrton Senna
1957	Juan Manuel Fangio	1989	Alain Prost
1958	Mike Hawthorn	1990	Ayrton Senna
1959	Jack Brabham	1991	Ayrton Senna
1960	Jack Brabham	1992	Nigel Mansell
1961	Phil Hill	1993	Alain Prost
1962	Graham Hill	1994	Michael Schumacher
1963	Jim Clark	1995	Michael Schumacher
1964	John Surtees	1996	Damon Hill
1965	Jim Clark	1997	Jacques Villeneuve
1966	Jack Brabham	1998	Mika Hakkinen
1967	Denny Hulme	1999	Mika Hakkinen
1968	Graham Hill	2000	Michael Schumacher
1969	Jackie Stewart	2001	Michael Schumacher
1970	Jochen Rindt	2002	Michael Schumacher
1971	Jackie Stewart	2003	Michael Schumacher
1972	Emerson Fittipaldi	2004	Michael Schumacher
1973	Jackie Stewart	2005	Fernando Alonso
1974	Emerson Fittipaldi	2006	Fernando Alonso
1975	Niki Lauda	2007	Kimi Raikkonen
1976	James Hunt	2008	Louis Hamilton
1977	Niki Lauda	2009	Jenson Button
1978	Mario Andretti	2010	Sebastian Vettel
1979	Jody Scheckter	2011	Sebastian Vettel
1980	Alan Jones	2012	Sebastian Vettel
1981	Nelson Piquet	2013	Sebastian Vettel

⊛ LOTUS AND HONDA TEAM UP ⊛

At the 1986 German Grand Prix, Lotus announced that they had signed a deal with Honda to supply their engines in 1987.

❁ GIUSEPPE FARINA ❁

Emilio Giuseppe "Nino" Farina was born on 30 October 1906 in Turin, Italy. In the 1930s he participated in hill climb racing, crashing first time out, before graduating to Grand Prix racing with Maserati. During the late 1930s Nino moved to Alfa Romeo as the second driver to the legendary Tazio Nuvolari and from 1937 to 1939 he won the Italian Drivers' Championship. In 1940 Nino secured his first major race win, the Tripoli Grand Prix in Libya, but the outbreak of World War II put the brakes on his racing career. He won the 1946 Grand Prix des Nations in Geneva for Alfa Romeo and, in 1950, the Federation Internationale de l'Automobile (FIA) announced that the inaugural Formula One Drivers' World Championship would be held the same year. Nino signed up for the Alfa Romeo team.

Nino won the first official Formula One Grand Prix, the British, at Silverstone on 13 May 1950 in the almost invincible Alfetta 158. He went on to win two more Grands Prix in 1950 and with it the inaugural Drivers' World Championship. He was 44 years old when he took the crown and it proved to be the pinnacle of his racing career. In 1951 Nino struggled, unable to match the speed of his team-mate, and new World Champion, Juan Manuel Fangio, and won only the Belgian Grand Prix during the season. He finished fourth overall in the 1951 drivers' table with 19 points, 12 behind Fangio.

In 1952 Nino moved to Ferrari but failed to win a single Grand Prix. His team-mate, Alberto Ascari, went on to win the first of his two World Championships. In 1952 Nino was runner-up to Ascari, and the following year, again driving for Ferrari, he finished third in the drivers' table behind the World Champion, Ascari, and Juan Manuel Fangio. Nino's first win for Ferrari was also the last of his five Grand Prix victories and came in the 1953 German Grand Prix at the Nurburgring. Along with co-driver Mike Hawthorn, he won the Spa 24 Hours endurance race in 1953; and in 1954 he was badly burnt when his sports car was engulfed in flames during a crash at Monza. He returned to Formula One racing in 1955 but had to inject himself with morphine to cope with the pain he suffered when driving. After securing a few points finishes he finally took the decision to retire from Formula One at the end of the 1955 season. Nino participated in 33 Grands Prix and won five of them. He died in a car crash at Chambery, France, on 30 June 1966 while driving as a spectator at the French Grand Prix.

Did You Know That?
Nino was famous for his "straight-arm" driving style.

❀ 1970 DRIVERS' WORLD CHAMPIONSHIP ❀

Pos	Driver	Nationality	Team	Pts
1.	Jochen Rindt	Austrian	Lotus-Ford	45
2.	Jacky Ickx	Belgian	Ferrari	40
3.	Clay Regazzoni	Swiss	Ferrari	33
4.	Denny Hulme	NZ	McLaren-Ford & McLaren-Alfa Romeo	27
5.	Jack Brabham	Australian	Brabham-Ford	25
6.	Jackie Stewart	British	March-Ford	25
7.	Pedro Rodriguez	Mexican	BRM	23
8.	Chris Amon	NZ	March-Ford	23
9.	Jean Pierre Beltoise	French	Matra	16
10.	Emerson Fittipaldi	Brazilian	Lotus-Ford	12

❀ 1970 CONSTRUCTORS' CUP ❀

Pos	Constructor	Pts
1.	Lotus-Ford	59
2.	Ferrari	52
3.	March-Ford	48
4.	Brabham-Ford	35
5.	McLaren-Ford	35
6.	BRM	23
7.	Matra	23
8.	Surtees-Ford	3

❀ BRITISH TOP BOTH LISTS ❀

At the end of the 1960 season, British constructors topped the Constructors' Cup table, Cooper and Lotus coming first and second respectively. Cooper drivers occupied four of the first six places in the Drivers' Championship, which was headed by Jack Brabham and Bruce McLaren, while Lotus drivers Stirling Moss and Innes Ireland came third and fourth respectively.

❀ LAUDA'S WORLD TITLE BY HALF A POINT ❀

Niki Lauda won the 1984 Drivers' World Championship by half a point over his McLaren-TAG team-mate, Alain Prost. Lauda finished the season on 72 points to Prost's 71½ points. Although Prost won five GPs during the season and the Austrian won just one, the Dutch GP, it was Lauda's consistent podium finishes that clinched the title.

❀ CRASHGATE ❀

Former Renault F1 driver Nelson Piquet Jr created a scandal when he alleged he had taken part in a race-fixing during the 2008 Singapore Grand Prix. Piquet was sacked in August 2009, after which he revealed that he had been ordered to crash in Singapore to help his team-mate Fernando Alonso, who went on to win the race. Dubbed "Crashgate", the FIA carried out a lengthy investigation and Renault were handed a 2-year suspended ban from F1, team Managing Director, Flavio Briatore was banned for life and Executive Director of Engineering, Pat Symonds, suspended for five years. The two men appealed and had their suspensions overturned in 2010.

❀ F1'S YOUNGEST EVER GP WINNER ❀

At the 2008 Italian GP, Sebastian Vettel (Toro Rosso), aged 21 years and 74 days, became the youngest driver to win a Formula One Grand Prix. He broke the previous record by 317 days, set by Fernando Alonso at the 2003 Hungarian GP. The Monza race was Vettel's first win, the first for Toro Rosso. and the team's first podium finish.

❀ BIG FALL-OUT ❀

Prior to the start of the 1991 Formula One season, Ligier and AGS protested to FISA that the Lola Larrousse team should, like them, have to participate in pre-qualifying as they did not built their own chassis in their own factory. FISA and FOCA discussed the issue and ruled that the Lola Larrousse team did not need to pre-qualify.

❀ FAMOUS F1 CORNERS AND LANDMARKS ❀

Adelaide Hairpin	Magny-Cours
Brooklands Corner	Silverstone
La Chicane	Monaco
Degner Curve	Suzuka
Eau-Rouge	Spa-Francorchamps
Expo Dome	Montreal
La Fouine	Dijon-Prenois
Hanger Straight	Silverstone
Hotel de Paris	Monaco
Ostkurve	Hockenheim
Parabolica	Monza
Stowe Corner	Silverstone
Tamburello	Monza
Texaco Chicane	Osterreichring, Zeltweg
Tunnel Oost	Zandvoort
Virage de l'ecole	Paul Ricard
Wurth Corner	Catalunya Circuit

Did You Know That?
Monaco is the only Grand Prix circuit with a tunnel.

⚙ 1971 DRIVERS' WORLD CHAMPIONSHIP ⚙

Pos	Driver	Nationality	Team	Pts
1.	Jackie Stewart	British	Tyrrell-Ford	62
2.	Ronnie Peterson	Swedish	March-Ford & March-Alfa Romeo	33
3.	Francois Cevert	French	Tyrrell-Ford	26
4.	Jacky Ickx	Belgian	Ferrari	19
5.	Jo Siffert	Swiss	BRM	19
6.	Emerson Fittipaldi	Brazilian	Lotus-Pratt, Whitney & Lotus-Ford	16
7.	Clay Regazzoni	Swiss	Ferrari	13
8.	Mario Andretti	American	Ferrari	12
9.	Peter Gethin	British	BRM	9
10.	Pedro Rodriguez	Mexican	BRM	9

⚙ 1971 CONSTRUCTORS' CUP ⚙

Pos	Constructor	Pts
1.	Tyrrell-Ford	73
2.	BRM	36
3.	Ferrari	33
4.	March-Ford	33
5.	Lotus-Ford	21
6.	McLaren-Ford	10
7.	Matra	9
8.	Surtees-Ford	8
9.	Brabham-Ford	5

⚙ FAST TALK (6) ⚙

"I make jokes about the fact that as a neuro-surgeon I shouldn't be required at a motor race because the drivers don't have any brains … otherwise they wouldn't race."
Syd Watkins, Formula One Chief Medical Officer

⚙ TAKE MY RIDE ⚙

At the 1961 Italian Grand Prix, Innes Ireland gave his Lotus-Climax car to Stirling Moss, and upset the team's owner, Colin Chapman. Both drivers failed to finish the GP in their Lotus-Climax cars, with Ireland retiring after lap 5 (chassis trouble) and Moss after lap 35 (wheel bearing). At the end of the 1961 season, Ireland was sacked.

❀ FANTASY FRENCH STARTING GRID ❀

(up to the end of the 2013 season)

1
Alain Prost
*(51 GP wins, 200
GPs, World
champion 1985,
1986, 1989, 1993)*

2
Rene Arnoux
*(7 GP wins, 149 GPs,
World champion best
3rd 1983)*

3
Jacques Laffite
*(6 GP wins, 176
GPs, World
champion best 4th
1979, 1980, 1981)*

4
Didier Pironi
*(3 GP wins, 70 GPs,
World champion best
2nd 1982)*

5
Jean-Pierre
Jabouille *(2 GP
wins, 49 GPs,
World champion
best 8th 1980)*

6
Maurice Trintignant
*(2 GP wins, 82 GPs,
World champion best
4th 1954, 1955)*

7
Patrick Depailler
*(2 GP wins, 95
GPs, World
champion best 4th
1976)*

8
Patrick Tambay
*(2 GP wins, 114 GPs,
World champion best
4th 1983)*

9
Francois Cevert
*(1 GP win, 47
GPs, World
champion best 3rd
1971)*

10
Jean Alesi
*(1 GP win, 201 GPs,
World champion best
4th 1996)*

❁ A MAN OF MANY TEAMS ❁

In 1954, Juan Manuel Fangio was the first to win the Formula One Drivers' Championship after driving for two constructors during the season. He began the 1954 season with Maserati, winning in Argentina and Belgium, before switching to Mercedes and winning the French, Swiss, German and Italian GPs.

Did You Know That?
Fangio won his five F1 championships driving for four different constructors. They were:

1951	Alfa Romeo
1954	Maserati/Mercedes
1955	Mercedes
1956	Ferrari
1957	Maserati

❁ *TIFOSI* HONOUR ENZO FERRARI ❁

The legendary Enzo Ferrari died on 14 August 1988, just one month before the Italian Grand Prix was raced on 11 September. The previous 11 GPs of 1988 had all been won by the all-conquering McLaren-Honda partnership of Ayrton Senna (seven) and Alain Prost (four). However, somehow Ferrari claimed a remarkable one-two in the race with Gerhard Berger taking the chequered flag followed across the line by Michele Alboreto. The *Tifosi* went wild with delight, as no doubt a smiling Enzo looked happily down on them.

Did You Know That?
Ayrton Senna (McLaren-Honda) claimed his tenth pole position of the 1988 season in Italy, a new F1 record. He finished in third place behind the two Ferraris.

❁ SIX PACK ❁

Alberto Ascari only competed in six Grands Prix during the 1952 season, winning them all for Ferrari. Not surprisingly, Ascari won the 1952 Drivers' World Championship with 36 points from Farina's 24 points. He missed the opening Grand Prix, the Swiss, which was won by Piero Taruffi, also for Ferrari, and the second GP, the Indianapolis 500, won by Troy Ruttman for Kuzma-Offenhauser. Thus, of the eight GPs raced in the 1952 season, Ferrari won seven.

❂ 1972 DRIVERS' WORLD CHAMPIONSHIP ❂

Pos	Driver	Nationality	Team	Pts
1.	Emerson Fittipaldi	Brazilian	Lotus-Ford	61
2.	Jackie Stewart	British	Tyrrell-Ford	45
3.	Denny Hulme	NZ	McLaren-Ford	39
4.	Jacky Ickx	Belgian	Ferrari	27
5.	Peter Revson	American	McLaren-Ford	23
6.	Francois Cevert	French	Tyrrell-Ford	15
7.	Clay Regazzoni	Swiss	Ferrari	15
8.	Mike Hailwood	British	Surtees-Ford	13
9.	Ronnie Peterson	Swedish	March-Ford	12
10.	Chris Amon	NZ	Matra	12

❂ 1972 CONSTRUCTORS' CUP ❂

Pos	Constructor	Pts
1.	Lotus-Ford	61
2.	Tyrrell-Ford	51
3.	McLaren-Ford	47
4.	Ferrari	33
5.	Surtees-Ford	18
6.	March-Ford	15
7.	BRM	14
8.	Matra	12
9.	Brabham-Ford	7

❂ LAUDA CRASHES ❂

On 1 August 1976, Niki Lauda crashed in his Ferrari in the German Grand Prix and suffered horrific burns. However, the brave Austrian, then reigning World Champion, was amazingly back behind the wheel of his car just two Grands Prix later at Monza. He went on to win two further F1 Drivers' Championships in 1977 (Ferrari) and 1984 (McLaren-Porsche).

❂ ALONSO HUNGARY TO GET OFF THE MARK ❂

On 24 August 2003, Renault's Fernando Alonso became the first Spaniard to win an official Formula One GP when he took the chequered flag in Hungary. At 22 years and 26 days, he was (by 78 days) the youngest ever F1 winner, breaking the record set by Bruce McLaren's US Grand Prix victory on 12 December 1959

❃ MUDDLY TALKER ❃

For more than 20 years, British television audiences were regaled by the commentary of Murray Walker. A former advertising executive, he became the voice of Formula One on the BBC and then he transferred to ITV when the coverage was bought by the independent broadcaster. However, Walker is equally famous for his comments, which didn't always come out quite as he hoped. Here is a selection:

> "And Edson Arantes di Nascimento, commonly known to us as Pele, hands the award to Damon Hill, commonly known to us as Damon Hill."
> *After the British driver won the Brazilian Grand Prix*

> "Michael Schumacher is 37 seconds ahead, so he can refuel the car, change all four wheels, take off his helmet, have a smoke and a cup of tea, and rejoin in first."
> *This could be during any number of races between 1994 and 2006*

> "Are they on a one-stopper? Are they on a two? And when I say they, who do I mean? Well, I don't know. It could be anybody."
> *Trousers well and truly on fire*

> "I don't know what happened, but there was a major malmisorganisation problem there."
> *Murray's impression of George W. Bush*

> "... and here comes Damon Hill in the Williams! This car is absolutely unique ... except for the one behind it ... which is exactly the same ..."
> *Murray carves up Damon again*

❃ SURTEES ADDS TWO WHEELS ❃

On 29 May 1960, John Surtees, the multiple motor-bike World Champion, made his F1 debut in a Lotus-Climax at the Monaco Grand Prix. The future F1 World Champion had to retire after 17 laps with transmission failure.

❃ ARROWS DELIGHTED ❃

Damon Hill finished second to Jacques Villeneuve (Williams-Renault) in an Arrows-Yamaha in the 1997 Hungarian Grand Prix.

❁ 1958–1959 ❁

8-6-4-3-2 points awarded to the first five placed drivers. One extra point was awarded to the driver who recorded the fastest lap in the race. Points were no longer awarded for shared drives.

❁ SIX-CAR RACE ❁

At the 2005 US Grand Prix held at the Indianapolis Motor Speedway circuit, only six cars competed as the other 14 cars, all with Michelin tyres, retired after the parade lap. The Michelin runners had a safety issue with their tyres which meant that only the Bridgestone runners competed: Ferrari, Jordan and Minardi. Michelin informed their seven teams that they could not guarantee that the tyres they brought to the US with them were safe to race on. Michael Schumacher (Ferrari) won the Grand Prix.

1983 Brazilian Grand Prix

Pos	Driver	Team	Laps	Time/Retired	Grid	Pts
1.	M. Schumacher	Ferrari	73	1:29'43.181	5	10
2.	R. Barrichello	Ferrari	73	+1.5 secs	7	8
3.	T. Monteiro	Jordan-Toyota	72	+1 Lap	17	6
4.	N. Karthikeyan	Jordan-Toyota	72	+1 Lap	19	5
5.	C. Albers	Minardi-Cosworth	71	+2 Lap	18	4
6.	P. Friesacher	Minardi-Cosworth	71	+2 Lap	20	3

❁ KING OF SIX WHEELS ❁

Going into the last race of the 1964 season, the Mexican Grand Prix, Graham Hill (BRM) led the Drivers' World Championship on 39 points (two GP wins), from John Surtees (Ferrari) on 34 points (two GP wins) and Jim Clark (Lotus-BRM and Lotus-Climax) on 30 points (three GP wins). Clark began in pole position but the turning-point of the race came on lap 63 when Lorezo Bandini's Ferrari touched wheels with Hill, forcing Hill out of the race. Jim Clark was now on course to win his second successive world crown only to see his engine blow up with two laps to go. Dan Gurney (Brabham-Climax) won the race, followed home by John Surtees. Surtees' second place was enough to win him the World Championship with a total of 40 points, one point more than Graham Hill. Surtees thus completed a unique double, having won both the 350cc and 500cc Motorbike World Championships from 1958 to 1960, all this after also winning the 500cc version in 1956.

❀ 1973 DRIVERS' WORLD CHAMPIONSHIP ❀

Pos	Driver	Nationality	Team	Pts
1.	Jackie Stewart	British	Tyrrell-Ford	71
2.	Emerson Fittipaldi	Brazilian	Lotus-Ford	55
3.	Ronnie Peterson	Swedish	Lotus-Ford	52
4.	Francois Cevert	French	Tyrrell-Ford	47
5.	Peter Revson	American	McLaren-Ford	38
6.	Denny Hulme	NZ	McLaren-Ford	26
7.	Carlos Reutemann	Argentinian	Brabham-Ford	16
8.	James Hunt	British	March-Ford	14
9.	Jacky Ickx	Belgian	Ferrari & McLaren-Ford	12
10.	Jean Pierre Beltoise	French	BRM	9

❀ 1973 CONSTRUCTORS' CUP ❀

Pos	Constructor	Pts
1.	Lotus-Ford	92
2.	Tyrrell-Ford	82
3.	McLaren-Ford	58
4.	Brabham-Ford	22
5.	March-Ford	14
6.	Ferrari	12
7.	BRM	12
8.	Shadow-Ford	9
9.	Surtees-Ford	7
10.	Iso Marlboro-Ford	2

❀ FAST TALK (7) ❀

"I consider myself one of a very small handful of drivers in the world that are top drivers. The best one? I don't think anybody can say they're the best one because, from one week to the next, you can be on form or off form a little bit."
Nigel Mansell

❀ WELL LUBRICATED ❀

In total some 31 oil companies have supplied lubricant products to F1 including:

Agip • BP • Castrol • Duckhams • Elf • Esso • Havoline • Mobil Repsol • Shell • Silkolene • STP • Texaco • Unipart • Valvoline

⚙ EMERSON FITTIPALDI ⚙

Emerson Fittipaldi was born on 12 December 1946 in Sao Paulo, Brazil. He started out as a mechanic, but began racing 50cc motor cycles before following his older brother, Wilson, into kart racing and then cars. In 1967 Emmo won the Brazilian Formula Vee Championship. Two years later he moved to Britain and was hired by Jim Russell to race his Formula Three Lotus. When he won the 1969 Lombank Formula Three title, Lotus signed him up for Formula Two in 1970.

After finishing third in the 1970 European Formula Two Championship for Lotus, team owner Colin Chapman gave Fittipaldi his F1 debut on 18 July 1970 in the British Grand Prix. He finished eighth in the Lotus-Ford. In his fifth race, the US Grand Prix at Watkins Glen on 4 October 1970, Emmo (Lotus-Ford) won his first F1 GP and ended the year 10th in the Drivers' Championship.

In 1971 Emmo (Lotus-Ford and Lotus-Pratt/Whitney) finished sixth in the World Championship. Colin Chapman produced his revolutionary Lotus 72D for the 1972 F1 season and in it Emmo won five of the 11 GPs raced to win the first of his two World Championships by 16 points from Jackie Stewart (Tyrrell-Ford). Aged 25, he was, at the time, the youngest ever F1 World Champion. After winning three of the first four GPs in 1973, Emmo looked set to win back-to-back titles. However, Chapman introduced his Lotus 72E midway through 1973 and it was not as good a car as the 72D. This enabled Stewart (Tyrrell-Ford) to win his third drivers' crown, ironically by 16 points from Emmo. Fittipaldi joined McLaren in 1974 recording three wins and four other podium places in the McLaren M23, to claim his second Drivers' World Championship by three points from Clay Regazzoni (Ferrari). A year later, Emmo (McLaren-Ford) was runner-up to Niki Lauda (Ferrari).

After four very successful years in which he claimed two World Championships and was runner-up on the other two occasions, Emmo joined his brother Wilson's Copersucar F1 team for the 1976 season. In five unsuccessful years with his brother, Emmo claimed just two top-three finishes. He retired at the end of 1980 but, after four years away, Emmo was lured into Indy Car Racing with Patrick Racing. In 1989 he won the Indy 500 and the Indy Car Championship driving for Penske-Chrevolet. He also won the 1993 Indy 500 for the same team. Emmo participated in 144 Grands Prix, winning 14 of them, and also secured 35 podium finishes, six pole positions and six fastest laps.

Did You Know That?
Emerson was named after the American author and philosopher, Ralph Waldo Emerson.

❖ F1 TOLD TO KICK THE HABIT ❖

In April 2002, a bill to abolish tobacco advertising was passed in the UK. There was a huge outcry from F1 teams and the Government agreed to give F1 until 2006 to comply. On 31 July 2005, a European Union (EU) directive banned all print advertising, radio advertising and event sponsorship in sport by tobacco companies. The sport's governing body, FIA, had originally agreed to a voluntary global ban at the end of the 2006 season. It was estimated that tobacco companies poured US$350million into motor sport in 2002, with F1 taking a huge slice of the cake. However, in a dramatic twist, F1 was excluded from the tobacco advertising ban. Many accused the government of sleaze and back-tracking when it emerged that the F1 supremo, Bernie Ecclestone, had given £1 million to the Labour Party.

The following tobacco manufacturers have all been involved in sponsorship deals with F1 teams:

British American Tobacco (Lucky Strike)
Gallaher (Benson & Hedges)
Imperial Tobacco (John Player Special, West)
Philip Morris (Marlboro)
RJ Reynolds (Camel)
Selta (Gauloises and Gitanes)

Did You Know That?
From 1972 to 1993, Camel was the title sponsor of the International Motor Sports Association series of races.

❖ ASCARI LEGACY ❖

Alberto Ascari is interred next to his father, Antonio, in the Cimitero Monumentale, Milan, Italy. Both men lost their lives driving racing cars. In 1992 Alberto Ascari, twice F1 World Champion, was inducted into the International Motorsports Hall of Fame.

❖ BRAKE DUCTS PROVE COSTLY FOR SENNA ❖

Ayrton Senna (Lotus-Honda) finished second in the last race of the 1987 season in Australia and secured second place in the Drivers' Championship. However, he was disqualified from the race, and the points, because his car was found to have irregular brake ducts. Instead, he finished in third place behind the Champion, Nelson Piquet (Williams-Honda), and Nigel Mansell (Williams-Honda).

❦ FROM THE TRACK TO THE CLOUDS ❦

After his Formula One career ended, former Williams driver Ian Ashley made a career for himself flying executive jets in the USA.

Did You Know That?
Prior to his F1 career, Ian Ashley, who was born in Wuppertal, Germany, took a driving course at the Jim Russell Racing School in 1966. Ashley was fast but somewhat erratic behind the wheel and soon earned the nickname "Crashley" from his fellow drivers.

❦ INAUSPICIOUS DEBUT FOR SCHUMACHER ❦

Michael Schumacher made his F1 debut driving for Jordan-Ford in the 1991 Belgian Grand Prix from seventh place on the grid. Eddie Jordan, the team's owner, gave him his chance when Bertrand Gachot was arrested in England following a traffic accident. However, the future seven-times World Champion had an inauspicious start to his F1 career, retiring on the first lap with clutch failure. Ayrton Senna (McLaren-Honda) won his sixth Grand Prix of the season from pole position.

❦ HAWTHORN DEBUT ❦

Mike Hawthorn made his F1 debut in the Belgian GP at Spa on 22 June 1952 in a Cooper-Bristol. By finishing fourth, he secured the highest ever final race position to date for a British car in Formula One. It was the beginning of a wonderful time for John Cooper's small company.

❦ 1983 MONACO GP MINUS McLAREN ❦

The 1983 Monaco Grand Prix is one the McLaren-Ford team will wish to forget as both their drivers, Alain Prost and John Watson, failed to qualify for the race. The GP was won by the Flying Finn, Keke Rosberg, in his Williams-Ford. Danny Sullivan (Tyrrell-Ford) finished fifth and Mauro Baldi (Alfa Romeo) finished sixth to win their first ever points in Formula One.

Did You Know That?
In 1985, Danny Sullivan joined Roger Penske's team and claimed a famous victory in the Indianapolis 500 that year. He went on to win the Indy Car title in 1988.

❀ 1974 DRIVERS' WORLD CHAMPIONSHIP ❀

Pos	Driver	Nationality	Team	Pts
1.	Emerson Fittipaldi	Brazilian	McLaren-Ford	55
2.	Clay Regazzoni	Swiss	Ferrari	52
3.	Jody Scheckter	S African	Tyrrell-Ford	45
4.	Niki Lauda	Austrian	Ferrari	38
5.	Ronnie Peterson	Swedish	Lotus-Ford	35
6.	Carlos Reutemann	Argentinian	Brabham-Ford	32
7.	Denny Hulme	NZ	McLaren-Ford	20
8.	James Hunt	British	Hesketh-Ford	15
9.	Patrick Depailler	French	Tyrrell-Ford	14
10.	Jacky Ickx	Belgian	Lotus-Ford	12

❀ 1974 CONSTRUCTORS' CUP ❀

Pos	Constructor	Pts
1.	McLaren-Ford	73
2.	Ferrari	65
3.	Tyrrell-Ford	52
4.	Lotus-Ford	42
5.	Brabham-Ford	35
6.	Hesketh-Ford	15
7.	BRM	10
8.	Shadow-Ford	7
9.	March-Ford	6
10.	Iso Marlboro-Ford	4

❀ A CAKE WALK ❀

In 2002 the Prancing Horse danced all over the opposition with Ferrari winning 15 of the 17 GPs raced. Michael Schumacher took the chequered flag 11 times and his team-mate, Rubens Barrichello, four times. Only Ralf Schumacher (Williams-BMW) and David Coulthard (McLaren-Mercedes) prevented the Scuderia from claiming a clean sweep. Indeed, such was the dominance of the Ferrari F2002 chassis that in addition to its 15 GP victories it also took 11 pole positions and secured 15 fastest laps.

❀ PIQUET MARK II ❀

Nelson Piquet's son, Nelson Jnr., raced in the British Formula Three Championship in 2006 and for Renault's F1 team in 2008 and 2009.

❂ 1975 DRIVERS' WORLD CHAMPIONSHIP ❂

Pos	Driver	Nationality	Team	Pts
1.	Niki Lauda	Austrian	Ferrari	64.5
2.	Emerson Fittipaldi	Brazilian	McLaren-Ford	45
3.	Carlos Reutemann	Argentinian	Brabham-Ford	37
4.	James Hunt	British	Hesketh-Ford	33
5.	Clay Regazzoni	Swiss	Ferrari	25
6.	Carlos Pace	Brazilian	Brabham-Ford	24
7.	Jody Scheckter	S African	Tyrrell-Ford	20
8.	Jochen Mass	German	McLaren-Ford	20
9.	Patrick Depailler	French	Tyrrell-Ford	12
10.	Tom Pryce	British	Shadow-Ford & Shadow-Matra	8

❂ 1975 CONSTRUCTORS' CUP ❂

Pos	Constructor	Pts
1.	Ferrari	72.5
2.	Brabham-Ford	54
3.	McLaren-Ford	53
4.	Hesketh-Ford	33
5.	Tyrrell-Ford	25
6.	Shadow-Ford	9.5
7.	Lotus-Ford	9
8.	March-Ford	7.5
9.	Williams-Ford	6
10.	Parnelli-Ford	5

❂ FAST TALK (8) ❂

"I have had some problems because the French don't like people to have success, they don't like the number one."
Alain Prost

❂ FERRARI NOT IN TOP 4 ❂

When the Monaco GP got under way on 1 June 2003, it was the first time in 66 Grands Prix that a Ferrari did not occupy a place in the front two rows of the grid. Ralf Schumacher (Williams-BMW) took pole position, followed by Kimi Raikkonen (McLaren-Mercedes), Juan-Pablo Montoya (Williams-BMW) and Jarno Trulli (Renault). Montoya won the Grand Prix.

❂ A COSTLY COLLISION ❂

In the final Grand Prix of the 1994 season, the Australian GP at Adelaide, Michael Schumacher (Benetton-Ford) drove into Damon Hill (Williams-Renault), forcing both drivers out of the race. Nigel Mansell (Williams-Renault) won, but Schumacher took the first of his seven Drivers' Championships by a single point from Hill.

❂ TROUBLE AT WILLIAMS ❂

For the second consecutive year, Williams started a Formula One season without their World Champion of the previous season. In 1993 the reigning World Champion, Nigel Mansell, moved to Indy Cars, and in 1994 Alain Prost retired from F1 racing when Frank Williams replaced him with his bitter rival, Ayrton Senna.

❂ DRIVER PLEDGES CASH TO TEAM ❂

In 1992 Phillipe Adams won the British Formula Three Championship and the following year he won the national British F2 series, after which he pledged a reputed $500,000 to drive for the cash-strapped Lotus Formula One team in 1994. He made his F1 debut in the 1994 Belgian Grand Prix but was forced to retire his Lotus-Mugen-Honda after spinning off the track on lap 15. He made one more GP start, the 1994 Portuguese Grand Prix, finishing in 16th and last place before deciding to return to national saloon car racing.

❂ THE BRABHAM BT19 ❂

In 1966, Jack Brabham took advantage of the new rule allowing cars to have a 3-litre engine by marrying his own car, the Brabham BT19, with a Repco V8 engine. Originally Brabham had planned to use a flat-16 Coventry Climax engine but opted for the Australian engine which proved reliable and, although not as powerful as some of the other engines, was light and compact. Brabham won four of the season's nine GPs on his way to claiming his third F1 drivers' title. The BT19 was designed by Ron Tauranac.

❂ PROST BECOMES KING IN PORTUGAL ❂

In winning the 1987 Portuguese Grand Prix, Alain Prost (McLaren-TAG) achieved the 28th GP victory of his career, to move into sole first position at the top of the GP wins table.

❈ CONSTRUCTORS' CUP WINNERS ❈

Year	Team	Year	Team
1958	Vanwall	1986	Williams-Honda
1959	Cooper-Climax	1987	Williams-Honda
1960	Cooper-Climax	1988	McLaren-Honda
1961	Ferrari	1989	McLaren-Honda
1962	BRM	1990	McLaren-Honda
1963	Lotus-Climax	1991	McLaren-Honda
1964	Ferrari	1992	Williams-Renault
1965	Lotus-Climax	1993	Williams-Renault
1966	Brabham-Repco	1994	Williams-Renault
1967	Brabham-Repco	1995	Benetton-Renault
1968	Lotus-Ford DFV	1996	Williams-Renault
1969	Matra-Ford DFV	1997	Williams-Renault
1970	Lotus-Ford DFV	1998	McLaren-Mercedes
1971	Tyrrell-Ford DFV	1999	Ferrari
1972	Lotus-Ford DFV	2000	Ferrari
1973	Lotus-Ford DFV	2001	Ferrari
1974	McLaren-Ford DFV	2002	Ferrari
1975	Ferrari	2003	Ferrari
1976	Ferrari	2004	Ferrari
1977	Ferrari	2005	Renault
1978	Lotus-Ford DFV	2006	Renault
1979	Ferrari	2007	Ferrari
1980	Williams-Ford DFV	2008	Brawn GP
1981	Williams-Ford DFV	2009	Red Bull Racing
1982	Ferrari	2010	Red Bull Racing
1983	Ferrari	2011	Red Bull Racing
1984	McLaren-TAG	2012	Red Bull Racing
1985	McLaren-TAG	2013	Red Bull Racing

❈ THE MASTER DRIVER ❈

Ayrton Senna is perhaps most renowned for his qualifying skill. He took a record 65 pole positions from 161 races, a mark that stood for 12 years, until it was passed by Michael Schumacher during qualifying for the 2006 San Marino Grand Prix – his 237th GP.

❈ PROST CLAIMS FIRST GP VICTORY ❈

On 5 July 1981, Alain Prost (Renault) achieved his first success in Formula One and he did so on home soil in the French Grand Prix.

❂ MOSS THE PERFECT GENTLEMAN ❂

At the Portuguese Grand Prix on 24 August 1958, Stirling Moss won in his Vanwall. Mike Hawthorn (Ferrari) finished second but was disqualified for pushing his car, a direct infringement of F1 rules. However, Moss interceded on behalf of Hawthorn, who was permitted to keep his second place and the six points that came with it. Moss's gentlemanly gesture backfired on him when he finished runner-up to Hawthorn in the 1958 Drivers' Championship by a single point.

Did You Know That?
At the end of the 1958 season, in which they won the inaugural Constructors' Cup, Vanwall announced their retirement from F1.

❂ RAIN STOPS PLAY IN ADELAIDE ❂

The final Grand Prix of the 1991 season, the Australian, lasted only 14 laps. The driving conditions were extremely hazardous with poor visibility as a result of the heavy rain that was falling on the circuit. At the beginning of lap 15 the race was interrupted with Ayrton Senna (McLaren-Honda) lying first, Nelson Piquet (Benetton-Ford) second, Riccardo Patrese (Williams-Renault) third, Gianni Morbidelli (Ferrari) fourth, Emanuele Pirro (Dallara-Judd) fifth and Andre de Cesaris (Jordan-Ford) sixth. Following discussions between the race officials the GP was halted and according to the rules, the final positions would be those one lap prior to the interruption of the race, lap 14. Luckily for Nigel Mansell (Williams-Renault) and Gerhard Berger (McLaren-Honda), they found themselves on the podium despite having been involved in accidents on the last completed lap. The final race positions were as follows: Senna first, Mansell second, Berger third, Piquet fourth, Patrese fifth and Morbidelli sixth.

Did You Know That?
Despite winning the 1991 Australian GP, Ayrton Senna (McLaren-Honda) was only awarded five points for the victory as a result of the race being stopped after just 14 laps. Under the rules, only half the normal points could be awarded.

❂ STEWART SECURES MAIDEN VICTORY ❂

Jackie Stewart won the first of his 27 GPs when he took the chequered flag driving for BRM in the Italian Grand Prix at Monza on 12 September 1965.

❄ SENNA MAKES IT 11 ❄

Ayrton Senna (McLaren-Honda) claimed his 11th pole position of the 1988 season at the Spanish Grand Prix but could only manage fourth place in the race as his team-mate, Alain Prost, won for the sixth time and moved 11 points ahead of him in the Drivers' World Championship. Only two GPs remained, but Senna, who had seven wins and two second places, was still in the running as only the best 11 results were counted. A win in the penultimate race, in Japan, and second in Australia, proved enough to give Senna his first title.

❄ A RACE OF NUMBERS ❄

On 23 April 2006, Michael Schumacher won the San Marino GP at Imola, his 85th career victory, an all-time record, He also set a new record with his 66th pole position. Ferrari team boss, Jean Todt, celebrated his 81st GP success in his 214th F1 GP.

❄ ONE F1 WIN WONDERS ❄

Luigi Fagioli *(French GP 1951)*
Piero Taruffi *(Swiss GP 1952)*
Luigi Musso *(Argentinian GP 1956)*
Joakim Bonnier *(Dutch GP 1959)*
Giancarlo Baghetti *(French GP 1961)*
Innes Ireland *(United States GP 1961)*
Lorenzo Bandini *(Austrian GP 1964)*
Richie Ginther *(Mexican GP 1965)*
Ludovico Scarfiotti *(Italian GP 1966)*
Peter Gethin *(Italian GP 1971)*
Francois Cevert *(United States GP 1971)*
Jean-Pierre Beltoise *(Monaco GP 1972)*
Carlos Pace *(Brazilian GP 1975)*
Jochen Mass *(Spanish GP 1975)*
Vittorio Brambilla *(Austrian GP 1975)*
Gunnar Nilsson *(Belgian GP 1977)*
Alessandro Nannini *(Japanese GP 1989)*
Jean Alesi *(Canadian GP 1995)*
Olivier Panis *(Monaco GP 1996)*
Jarno Trulli *(Monaco GP 2004)*
Robert Kubica *(Canadian GP 2008)*
Heikki Kovalainen *(Hungarian GP 2008)*
Pastor Maldonado *(Spanish GP 2012)*

❀ 1976 DRIVERS' WORLD CHAMPIONSHIP ❀

Pos	Driver	Nationality	Team	Pts
1.	James Hunt	British	McLaren-Ford	69
2.	Niki Lauda	Austrian	Ferrari	68
3.	Jody Scheckter	S African	Tyrrell-Ford	49
4.	Patrick Depailler	French	Tyrrell-Ford	39
5.	Clay Regazzoni	Swiss	Ferrari	31
6.	Mario Andretti	American	Parnelli-Ford & Lotus-Ford	22
7.	John Watson	British	Penske-Ford	20
8.	Jacques Laffite	French	Ligier-Matra	20
9.	Jochen Mass	German	McLaren-Ford	19
10.	Gunnar Nilsson	Swedish	Lotus-Ford	11

❀ 1976 CONSTRUCTORS' CUP ❀

Pos	Constructor	Pts
1.	Ferrari	83
2.	McLaren-Ford	74
3.	Tyrrell-Ford	71
4.	Lotus-Ford	29
5.	Penske-Ford	20
6.	Ligier-Matra	20
7.	March-Ford	19
8.	Shadow-Ford	10
9.	Brabham-Alfa Romeo	9
10.	Surtees-Ford	7

❀ F1'S OLDEST DRIVER ❀

On 22 May 1955, Louis Chiron became the oldest driver to compete in a Formula One race when, to the delight of Prince Rainier and his adoring fans, he guided his Lancia D50 to a sixth-place finish in Monaco, the city of his birth, to secure his first and only podium finish in the 15 GPs he raced. He was just 73 days short of his 56th birthday. After an incredible 35 years in motor racing, Chiron remained active in motor racing, organising the Monaco Grand Prix, and was honoured by having a statue erected along the Monaco GP race track and having one of its curves named after him.

Did You Know That?
Louis Chiron recorded the most podium finishes driving a Bugatti car, and the grateful manufacturer named a concept car in his honour.

❀ MIKE HAWTHORN ❀

John Michael Hawthorn was born on 10 April 1929 in Mexborough, Yorkshire, England. As a boy he watched races on the banked circuit at Brooklands and in 1950, with his father's support, entered the Brighton speed trials. In 1952 Mike was driving single-seaters and won his first race in a Formula Two Cooper-Bristol at Goodwood. On 22 June 1952, Mike made his F1 debut in the Belgian Grand Prix at Spa-Francorchamps, finishing fourth in a Cooper-Bristol. Mike achieved fourth place overall in the 1952 Drivers' Championship.

Following glowing reports from Luigi Villoresi, whom Mike had impressed with the handling of his Cooper-Bristol in wet conditions at Boreham, Enzo Ferrari offered Hawthorn a works drive for 1953. Mike accepted, and in his fourth race for the Scuderia, the French Grand Prix at Reims on 5 July 1953, Mike won for the first time in Formula One. Two more podium finishes were achieved during the year, helping him to fourth place in the 1953 Drivers' World Championship. In addition to his F1 drives in 1953, Mike also won the International Trophy, the Ulster Trophy and the Spa 24 Hours sports car race alongside his Ferrari team-mate, Giuseppe Farina. In 1954 Mike suffered burns in a race at Syracuse but he rounded the season off with victory in the final Grand Prix of the year, the Spanish GP at Pedrables, to rank third overall in the World Championship.

When his father died Mike left Ferrari so that he could stay close to home and help run the family's garage business. In 1955 he raced in the Monaco and Belgian GPs for Vanwall but was unimpressed with both the car and the team, which resulted in him returning to Ferrari. However, Ferrari's dominance of F1 had been overtaken by Mercedes in 1955, and the year will always be remembered for his involvement in an accident at the Le Mans 24 Hours race. Mike's car collided with Pierre Levegh's Mercedes, which was forced up into the air and into the crowd, killing 77 people.

In 1956 Mike moved to BRM, but managed only 12th place in the Drivers' Championship. He rejoined to Ferrari a year later and claimed fourth place in the Drivers' World Championship. In the 1958 season, Mike won only the French Grand Prix, and although it was his only victory – against four by Stirling Moss (Cooper-Climax & Vanwall) and three by Tony Brooks (Vanwall) – he won the 1958 F1 Drivers' Championship. His consistency during the year, with five second-place finishes, was enough to make him Britain's first F1 World Champion. He immediately retired, after a career spanning 45 Grands Prix, which included three wins, 17 podium finishes, four pole positions and six fastest laps. Mike died in a car crash on 22 January 1959.

❁ 1977 DRIVERS' WORLD CHAMPIONSHIP ❁

Pos	Driver	Nationality	Team	Pts
1.	Niki Lauda	Austrian	Ferrari	72
2.	Jody Scheckter	S African	Wolf-Ford	55
3.	Mario Andretti	American	Lotus-Ford	47
4.	Carlos Reutemann	Argentinian	Ferrari	42
5.	James Hunt	British	McLaren-Ford	40
6.	Jochen Mass	German	McLaren-Ford	25
7.	Alan Jones	Australian	Shadow-Ford	22
8.	Gunnar Nilsson	Swedish	Lotus-Ford	20
=8.	Patrick Depailler	French	Tyrrell-Ford	20
10.	Jacques Laffite	French	Ligier-Matra	18

❁ 1977 CONSTRUCTORS' CUP ❁

Pos	Constructor	Pts
1.	Ferrari	95
2.	Lotus-Ford	62
3.	McLaren-Ford	60
4.	Wolf-Ford	55
5.	Brabham-Alfa Romeo	27
=5.	Tyrrell-Ford	27
7.	Shadow-Ford	23
8.	Ligier-Matra	18
9.	Fittipaldi-Ford	11
10.	Ensign-Ford	10

❁ CENTURY UP FOR THE COSWORTH DFV ❁

When Jody Scheckter won the Monaco Grand Prix on 22 May 1977 in his Wolf-Ford, it was the 100th GP victory for the Cosworth DFV engine. The engine designed by Keith Duckworth made its Formula One debut in 1967 and went on to record a further 55 F1 wins.

❁ WARWICK DELAYS START OF ITALIAN GP ❁

During the 1990 Italian Grand Prix, Derek Warwick (Lotus-Lamborghini) crashed into the barriers at Parabolica and when he bounced back on to the track the race had to be stopped. Ironically, FISA was experimenting with new barriers at the circuit comprising rubber and water. Warwick was unhurt and managed to take part in the restart as Ayrton Senna (McLaren-Honda) raced to victory.

❀ F1 GP CIRCUITS* ❀

Circuit	No of GPs	Circuit	No of GPs
A1-Ring (Österreichring)	25	Melbourne	18
Adelaide	11	Mexico City	15
Aida	2	Monsanto Park	1
Ain-Diab	1	Mont-Tremblant	2
Aintree	5	Monaco	60
Anderstorp	6	Montjuich Park	4
Avus	1	Montreal	34
Brands Hatch	15	Monza	63
Bremgarten	5	Mosport Park	8
Buddh	3	Nivelles-Baulers	2
Buenos Aires	20	Nurburgring	40
Caesars Palace	2	Paul Ricard	14
Circuit de Catalunya	23	Pedralbes	2
Circuit of the Americas	2	Pescara	1
Clermont-Ferrand	4	Phoenix	3
Dallas	1	Porto	2
Detroit	7	Reims-Gueux	11
Dijon-Prenois	6	Rio de Janeiro	10
Donington Park	1	Riverside	1
East London	3	Rouen-les-Essarts	5
Estoril	13	Sakhir	9
Fuji Speedway	4	Sebring	1
Hockenheim	33	Sepang	15
Hungaroring	28	Shanghai	10
Imola	27	Silverstone	47
Indianapolis	19	Spa-Francorchamps	46
Interlagos	31	Suzuka	25
Istanbul Park	7	Valencia	5
Jarama	9	Watkins Glen	20
Jerez de la Frontera	7	Yas Marina	5
Kyalami	20	Yeongam	4
Le Mans	1	Zandvoort	30
Long Beach	8	Zeltweg	1
Magny-Cours	18	Zolder	10
Marina Bay	6		

up to the end of the 2013 F1 season

❀ SUPER CLIMAX ❀

The 1963 Italian Grand Prix saw 21 lead changes before Jim Clark (Lotus-Climax) won the race and the F1 Drivers' World Championship.

❀ FAST TALK (9) ❀

"From the five years, 1968 to '73, if you were an F1 driver at that time, there was a very likely chance that you would have died."
Jackie Stewart

❀ F1 WORLD CHAMPIONS & INDY 500 WINNERS ❀

Mario Andretti (1978 F1, 1969 Indy)
Jim Clark (1963 & 1965 F1, 1965 Indy)
Emerson Fittipaldi (1972 & 1974 F1, 1989 & 1993 Indy)
Graham Hill (1962 & 1968 F1, 1966 Indy)
Jacques Villeneuve (1995 F1, 1997 Indy)

Did You Know That?
Anthony Joseph (A.J.) Foyt won the Indianapolis 500 4 times (1961, 1964, 1967 and 1977) and the Le Mans 24 Hours race in 1967, but he never raced in Formula One.

❀ DOWN TO THE WIRE IN '81 ❀

In the last race of the 1981 GP season, only three drivers could win the Championship, Jacques Laffite (Ligier-Matra), Nelson Piquet (Brabham-Ford) and Carlos Reutemann (Williams-Ford). However, only Reutemann could be more cautious than the others as he could finish fourth if Laffite won the US East Grand Prix in Las Vegas, but then had to make sure he finished in front of Piquet. Reutemann secured pole position, with Piquet fourth on the grid and Lafitte in 12th. When the race started Alan Jones (Williams-Ford) took the lead and gradually pulled away from the field. Reutemann seemed to be controlling the race, running in fourth place, but suddenly lost his position to Nigel Mansell. Then Piquet, who narrowly avoided hitting Reutemann's car at the first corner, overtook him, as Laffite subsequently also did. Reutemann finished in seventh place in a struggling car, and although Jones took the chequered flag, Piquet became the second Brazilian F1 World Champion.

❀ 8 FROM 16 ❀

No fewer than eight different drivers won a Grand Prix during the 2003 season: Fernando Alonso, Rubens Barrichello, David Coulthard, Giancarlo Fisichella, Juan Pablo Montoya, Kimi Raikkonen, Michael Schumacher and Ralf Schumacher.

❀ FANTASY GERMAN STARTING GRID ❀

(up to the end of the 2013 season)

1
Michael Schumacher *(91 GP wins, 249 GPs, World champion 1994–95, 2000–04)*

2
Sebastian Vettel *(39 GP wins, 120 GPs, World champion 2010, 2011, 2012, 2013)*

3
Ralf Schumacher *(6 GP wins, 182 GPs, World champion best 4th, 2001, 2002)*

4
Heinz- Harald Frentzen *(3 GP wins, 160 GPs ,World champion best 2nd, 1997)*

5
Nico Rosberg *(3 GP wins, 147 GPs, World champion best 6th 2013)*

6
Wolfgang Von Trips) *(2 GP wins, 29 GPs, World champion best 2nd, 1961)*

7
Jochen Mass *(1 GP win, 114 GPs, World champion best 6th, 1977)*

8
Nick Heidfeld *(best finish 2nd {8 times}, 185 GPs, world champion best, 5th 2007)*

9
Timo Glock *(best finish 2nd {twice}, 95 GPs, World champion best 10th, 2008, 2009)*

10
Nico Hülkenberg *(best finish 4th {twice}, 58 GPs, World champion best 10th 2013)*

❂ 1978 DRIVERS' WORLD CHAMPIONSHIP ❂

Pos	Driver	Nationality	Team	Pts
1.	Mario Andretti	American	Lotus-Ford	64
2.	Ronnie Peterson	Swedish	Lotus-Ford	51
3.	Carlos Reutemann	Argentinian	Ferrari	48
4.	Niki Lauda	Austrian	Brabham-Alfa Romeo	44
5.	Patrick Depailler	French	Tyrrell-Ford	34
6.	John Watson	British	Brabham-Alfa Romeo	25
7.	Jody Scheckter	S African	Wolf-Ford	24
8.	Jacques Laffite	French	Ligier-Matra	19
9.	Gilles Villeneuve	Canadian	Ferrari	17
10.	Emerson Fittipaldi	Brazilian	Fittipaldi-Ford	17

❂ 1978 CONSTRUCTORS' CUP ❂

Pos	Constructor	Pts
1.	Lotus-Ford	86
2.	Ferrari	58
3.	Brabham-Alfa Romeo	53
4.	Tyrrell-Ford	38
5.	Wolf-Ford	24
6.	Ligier-Matra	19
7.	Fittipaldi-Ford	17
8.	McLaren-Ford	15
9.	Williams-Ford	11
10.	Arrows-Ford	11

❂ CARS GIVEN WINGS ❂

Aerofoils were introduced in 1968, offering Formula One cars improved handling and road-holding. The new wings began life as small tabs situated either side of the nose cone, and then Lotus supremo Colin Chapman mounted wings on pillars on to the car's suspension, producing down-force of approximately 160kg. However, after breakages and accidents in the 1969 Spanish Grand Prix, these were banned and had to be replaced by lower and sturdier wings.

❂ THREE LIONS ❂

Nigel Mansell's, the F1 World Champion in 1992, two sons, Greg and Leo, both raced in the British Formula BMW Championship during the 2006 season.

⊛ TWO UNFORTUNATE RACING BROTHERS ⊛

Pedro Rodriguez was born on 18 January 1940 in Mexico City and two years later his brother Ricardo was born. Both brothers raced motor-bikes during their teens, with Pedro winning the Mexican National Championship in 1953 and 1954. On 1 November 1962, Ricardo died following a horrific accident in their Ferrari 250 Testa Rossa during practice for the Le Mans 24 Hours race. Despite his young age Pedro considered retiring from motor racing, but changed his mind. In 1963 he won at the Daytona International Speedway and on 6 October that year he made his F1 debut in the US Grand Prix in a Lotus-Climax. His maiden Grand Prix was over after 36 laps owing to engine failure. Pedro died on 11 July 1971 following an accident in a minor sports car race in Nuremberg, Germany.

Did You Know That?
The first hairpin at the Daytona International Speedway circuit is called the "Pedro Rodriguez curve".

⊛ NEW RULES FOR '82 ⊛

FISA introduced a number of new rules for the 1982 F1 season, including: carbon-fibre mixed with kevlar or aluminium for chassis, brakes and wings; refuelling and tyre changes during the race and a new minimum weight for a car of 580kg.

⊛ STEWART OFF THE MARCH ⊛

At the 1970 Dutch Grand Prix, Piers Courage crashed his Frank Williams-run De Tomasso-Ford car on lap 23 of the race. After hitting one of the banks surrounding the Zandvoort track the car rolled over and burst into flames, killing Courage.

⊛ A BRITISH 1-2-3 ⊛

In 1958, British drivers occupied the first three places in the Formula One Drivers' World Championship:

Pos Driver	Nationality	Team	Pts
1. Mike Hawthorn	British	Ferrari F2 & Ferrari	42
2. Stirling Moss	British	Cooper-Climax F2, Cooper-Climax & Vanwall	41
3. Tony Brooks	British	Vanwall	24

🎖 1979 DRIVERS' WORLD CHAMPIONSHIP 🎖

Pos	Driver	Nationality	Team	Pts
1.	Jody Scheckter	S African	Ferrari	51
2.	Gilles Villeneuve	Canadian	Ferrari	47
3.	Alan Jones	Australian	Williams-Ford	40
4.	Jacques Laffite	French	Ligier-Ford	36
5.	Clay Regazzoni	Swiss	Williams-Ford	29
6.	Patrick Depailler	French	Ligier-Ford	20
7.	Carlos Reutemann	Argentinian	Lotus-Ford	20
8.	Rene Arnoux	French	Renault	17
9.	John Watson	British	McLaren-Ford	15
10.	Didier Pironi	French	Tyrrell-Ford	14

🎖 1979 CONSTRUCTORS' CUP 🎖

Pos	Constructor	Pts
1.	Ferrari	113
2.	Williams-Ford	75
3.	Ligier-Ford	61
4.	Lotus-Ford	39
5.	Tyrrell-Ford	28
6.	Renault	26
7.	McLaren-Ford	15
8.	Brabham-Alfa Romeo	7
9.	Arrows-Ford	5
10.	Shadow-Ford	3

🎖 SCORCHING SCHUMI 🎖

On 14 September 2003, Michael Schumacher (Ferrari) delighted the home crowd at Monza by setting two records as took the chequered flag. First of all he set the all-time official quickest lap in F1 history with 254.8 kmph and the quickest ever race average at a blistering 247.5 kmph. The reigning World Champion also set the fastest lap in the race with a scorching 1'21.832 as he reached 362.5 kmph.

🎖 MOSS IN CASABLANCA 🎖

On 19 October 1958, Stirling Moss (Vanwall) won the Moroccan Grand Prix in Casablanca. Sadly Stuart Lewis-Evans crashed his Vanwall and, despite being flown to the famous burns unit at East Grinstead, England, he died of his injuries six days later.

❀ UNLUCKY DRIVER ❀

In a career spanning 13 years, New Zealander Chris Amon drove in almost 100 Grands Prix, led races for over 180 laps, and yet never won a single GP.

❀ SENNA ROBBED OF VICTORY ❀

Ayrton Senna (McLaren-Honda) went into the penultimate Grand Prix of the 1989 season, the Japanese, knowing that victory in the race, followed by victory in the Australian Grand Prix, would make him the World Champion for the second successive year. Senna started from pole position with his team-mate and closest challenger for the title, Alain Prost, alongside him on the grid. On lap 47, Senna took Prost completely by surprise as he dived into the chicane at the braking point, and when Prost moved across to block his team-mate, their cars touched. This resulted in both cars spinning off the track, and Prost jumped out of his car, but Senna asked for help from a nearby marshal and re-entered the race despite losing his front wing. Amazingly, Senna made a pit stop and drove majestically to win the Grand Prix. However, joy turned to sadness for Senna when he was disqualified for "reckless driving", which meant that Alain Prost was the World Champion for the third time.

❀ JOHNNY RULES BRITAIN ❀

On 16 July 1995, Johnny Herbert (Benetton-Renault) won his first ever F1 race when he took the chequered flag at Silverstone in the British Grand Prix.

❀ PENALTY FINES ❀

During the 1987 Spanish Grand Prix, Nigel Mansell (Williams-Honda) jumped out of his car when the technicians were checking the equipment. FISA fined him US$3,000. Shortly afterwards, at the Mexican Grand Prix, Ayrton Senna (Lotus-Honda) spun off the track with a broken clutch and, when the race marshals decided to push him to a safe place, he became furious with one of them, resulting in FISA handing him a US$15,000 fine.

❀ DRIVER TURNED OWNER ❀

Graham Hill quit Brabham in 1973 to set up his own racing team.

⚙ 1980 DRIVERS' WORLD CHAMPIONSHIP ⚙

Pos	Driver	Nationality	Team	Pts
1.	Alan Jones	Australian	Williams-Ford	67
2.	Nelson Piquet	Brazilian	Brabham-Ford	54
3.	Carlos Reutemann	Argentinian	Williams-Ford	42
4.	Jacques Laffite	French	Ligier-Ford	34
5.	Didier Pironi	French	Ligier-Ford	32
6.	Rene Arnoux	French	Renault	29
7.	Elio de Angelis	Italian	Lotus-Ford	13
8.	Jean Pierre Jabouille	French	Renault	9
9.	Riccardo Patrese	Italian	Arrows-Ford	7
10.	Keke Rosberg	Finnish	Fittipaldi-Ford	6

⚙ 1980 CONSTRUCTORS' CUP ⚙

Pos	Constructor	Pts
1.	Williams-Ford	120
2.	Ligier-Ford	66
3.	Brabham-Ford	55
4.	Renault	38
5.	Lotus-Ford	14
6.	Tyrrell-Ford	12
7.	Arrows-Ford	11
8.	Fittipaldi-Ford	11
9.	McLaren-Ford	11
10.	Ferrari	8

⚙ FAST TALK (10) ⚙

"The years I raced in were fantastic. There was so much change in the cars. We went from treaded tyres and no wings right through to slicks and enormous wings."
Jackie Stewart

⚙ MARIMON DIES IN PRACTICE ⚙

Onofre Agustin Marimon of Argentina participated in 11 Grands Prix, making his debut on 1 July 1951, in the Swiss Grand Prix. He achieved two podium finishes and scored a total of 8.14 Championship points. Marimon was killed on 31 July 1954, during practice at the Nurburgring for the German GP and became the first driver to die at a Formula One World Championship event.

❀ 1981 DRIVERS' WORLD CHAMPIONSHIP ❀

Pos	Driver	Nationality	Team	Pts
1.	Nelson Piquet	Brazilian	Brabham-Ford	50
2.	Carlos Reutemann	Argentinian	Williams-Ford	49
3.	Alan Jones	Australian	Williams-Ford	46
4.	Jacques Laffite	French	Ligier-Matra	44
5.	Alain Prost	French	Renault	43
6.	John Watson	British	McLaren-Ford	27
7.	Gilles Villeneuve	Canadian	Ferrari	25
8.	Elio de Angelis	Italian	Lotus-Ford	14
9.	Rene Arnoux	French	Renault	11
9=.	Hector Rebaque	Mexican	Brabham-Ford1	11

❀ 1981 CONSTRUCTORS' CUP ❀

Pos	Constructor	Pts
1.	Williams-Ford	95
2.	Brabham-Ford	61
3.	Renault	54
4.	Ligier-Matra	44
5.	Ferrari	34
6.	McLaren-Ford	28
7.	Lotus-Ford	22
8.	Arrows-Ford	10
9.	Alfa Romeo	10
10.	Tyrrell-Ford	10

❀ COME IN CAR NUMBER 208 ❀

During the history of F1, all but the following numbers from 0–136 have been displayed on a car during a F1 GP: 96, 100, 106, 132.

Did You Know That?
Lella Lombardi wore the No 208 on her Brabham-Ford when she first entered F1 on 20 July 1974 at the British GP. She failed to qualify.

❀ THE ARRIVAL OF THE PRANCING HORSE ❀

On 20 May 1950, Ferrari entered Formula One for the first time in only the second official Grand Prix, held in Monaco. Their driver, Alberto Ascari, secured second place in the race behind Juan Manuel Fangio (Alfa Romeo).

❀ GRAHAM HILL ❀

Norman Graham Hill was born on 15 February 1929 in Hampstead, London. Amazingly Graham did not pass his driving test until he was 24 years old and, following a brief career in the military, he began working as a mechanic at the Brands Hatch racing school, where he raced in one of the school's cars in lieu of wages.

Graham then met Colin Chapman of Lotus and worked with him as he built up his racing team. In 1956 Graham built his own Lotus for racing and in 1958 he joined Lotus as a works driver. On 18 May 1958, Graham made his F1 debut in the Monaco Grand Prix, but he broke down after 68 of the race's 100 laps. Nonetheless, Monaco would go on to give Hill much pleasure, as he won five times in the Principality during his career.

In 1960 Hill joined BRM. His best finish was third in the Dutch GP at Zandvoort. He failed to sparkle in 1961, but in 1962 his fortunes started to change. Equipped with a new V8 engine, Hill won his first ever F1 race, the Dutch Grand Prix, and followed it up with wins in the German and Italian GPs of 1962. Going into the final GP of the season, the South African, Hill was three points clear of Jim Clark in the Championship race. When Clark retired, Hill raced to victory and took the first of his two World Championships. In each of the next three years, Hill was World Championship runner-up, to Clark in 1963 and '65 and John Surtees in 1964.

After a problem-filled 1966, Hill returned to Lotus to partner Clark in 1967. Chapman's new Lotus 49-Cosworth was starting to make a big impression, and Clark won the opening GP of 1968, in South Africa. On 7 April 1968 Jim Clark crashed and died in a Formula Two race at Hockenheim. Although Chapman and Hill were devastated by Clark's death, they soldiered on and in the next GP, the Spanish, Hill won. He won two more GPs that year to claim his second drivers' title. At the 1969 US Grand Prix, Hill crashed and broke both his legs. He returned to F1, without success, and when he failed to qualify for the 1975 Monaco Grand Prix, he retired. He had participated in 179 Grands Prix, winning 14, with 36 podium finishes, 13 pole positions and 10 fastest laps. Graham Hill died on 29 November 1975, when his private plane crashed in fog on the outskirts of London, and in 1990, he was inducted into the International Motorsports Hall of Fame.

Did You Know That?
Graham is the only driver to win the "Triple Crown" of motor racing: the F1 World Championship (1962 & 1968), the Indianapolis 500 (1966) and the Le Mans 24 Hours race (1972).

❂ 1950 IN THE BEGINNING ❂

The first ever Grand Prix, the British, took place on 13 May 1950 at Silverstone. Here are the race standings:

Pos	Driver	Team	Laps	Time/Retired	Grid	Pts
1.	Nino Farina	Alfa Romeo	70	2:13'23.6	1	9
2.	Luigi Fagioli	Alfa Romeo	70	+ 2.6	2	6
3.	Reg Parnell	Alfa Romeo	70	+ 52.0	4	4
4.	Yves Giraud Cabantous	TLT[†]	68	+ 2 Laps	6	3
5.	Louis Rosier	TLT	68	+ 2 Laps	9	2
6.	Bob Gerard	ERA	67	+ 3 Laps	13	
7.	Cuth Harrison	ERA	67	+ 3 Laps	15	
8.	Philippe Etancelin	TLT	65	+ 5 Laps	14	
9.	David Hampshire	Maserati	64	+ 6 Laps	16	
10.	Brian Shawe Taylor	Maserati	64	+ 6 Laps	20	
11.	Johnny Claes	TLT	64	+ 6 Laps	21	
Ret.	Juan Manuel Fangio	Alfa Romeo	62	Oil Leak	3	
NC.	Joe Kelly	Alta	57	N/C	19	
Ret.	Prince Bira	Maserati	49	Out of fuel	5	
Ret.	David Murray	Maserati	44	Engine	18	
NC.	Geoff Crossley	Alta	43	N/C	17	
Ret.	Toulo de Graffenried	Maserati	36	Engine	8	
Ret.	Louis Chiron	Maserati	26	Clutch	11	
Ret.	Eugene Martin	TLT	8	Oil pressure	7	
Ret.	Peter Walker	ERA	5	Gearbox	10	
Ret.	Leslie Johnson	ERA	2	Compressor	12	

Fastest Lap: Nino Farina 1'50.600 [†]*Talbot-Lago-Talbot*

❂ DEMOLITION DERBY ❂

The 2006 Australian GP witnessed the safety car being deployed four times during the race.

❂ A PAIR OF WORLD CHAMPIONS ❂

Emerson Fittipaldi quit Lotus in 1974 and joined McLaren-Ford, where Denny Hulme stayed on as his team-mate. The McLaren racing team had acquired substantial financial backing from Texaco and Marlboro, and a third McLaren was entered for the 1974 season in Yardley's colours. The third car was driven by Mike Hailwood. McLaren now had two former F1 World Champions – Hulme (1967) and Fittipaldi (1972).

❀ THE SUPER LICENCE RULE ❀

Prior to the opening GP of 1982, the South African, the drivers protested against a new rule imposed by FISA. This stated that from 1982 all F1 drivers had to hold a "Super Licence". The FISA Super Licence is a qualification allowing the licence holder to take part in F1 races as a driver and is issued by FISA upon request. However, to be eligible for a FISA Super Licence the driver must already possess a Grade A competition licence and meet the requirements of the FISA International Sporting Code. To satisfy these the driver must be either a reigning champion in a lower motor sport racing category (Formula Three, F3000 etc) or must have consistently finished well in these races. Under exceptional circumstances FISA is permitted to award a Super Licence to a driver who does not meet the normal criteria if a subsequent vote results in a unanimous agreement by FISA members. However, despite the drivers' protests the owners and sponsors persuaded them to accept the new rule and race. Alain Prost claimed the chequered flag.

❀ ALONSO CONTINUES WHERE HE LEFT OFF ❀

Fernando Alonso (Renault), the World Drivers' Champion in 2005, opened the 2006 season in Bahrain with a thrilling victory, finishing just in front of Michael Schumacher (Ferrari). Schumacher had started from pole and in much the same way Alain Prost and Ayrton Senna contested F1 GPs in the 1980s "mano a mano". Alonso was up for the fight and in lap 39 he just managed to nip out of the pits ahead of the seven-times World Champion and held the lead to take the chequered flag 1.246 seconds clear. It was Schumacher's first podium finish in seven GPs while Kimi Raikkonen (McLaren-Mercedes) was third despite having to start from 22nd place on the grid.

Did You Know That?
By taking pole position, Michael Schumacher equalled the legendary Ayrton Senna's record of 65 pole positions.

❀ REUTEMANN COMES GOOD ❀

Carlos Reutemann (Brabham-Ford) gained his maiden F1 victory on 30 March 1974 in the South African Grand Prix at Kyalami. It was the marque's first GP win in four long years. Sadly, Peter Revson (Shadow-Ford) crashed and died at Kyalami in 1974 during pre-race testing.

❊ 1982 DRIVERS' WORLD CHAMPIONSHIP ❊

Pos	Driver	Nationality	Team	Pts
1.	Keke Rosberg	Finnish	Williams-Ford	44
2.	Didier Pironi	French	Ferrari	39
3.	John Watson	British	McLaren-Ford	39
4.	Alain Prost	French	Renault	34
5.	Niki Lauda	Austrian	McLaren-Ford	30
6.	Rene Arnoux	French	Renault	28
7.	Patrick Tambay	French	Ferrari	25
8.	Michele Alboreto	Italian	Tyrrell-Ford	25
9.	Elio de Angelis	Italian	Lotus-Ford	23
10.	Riccardo Patrese	Italian	Brabham-Ford & Brabham-BMW	21

❊ 1982 CONSTRUCTORS' CUP ❊

Pos	Constructor	Pts
1.	Ferrari	74
2.	McLaren-Ford	69
3.	Renault	62
4.	Williams-Ford	58
5.	Lotus-Ford	30
6.	Tyrrell-Ford	25
7.	Brabham-BMW	22
8.	Ligier-Matra	20
9.	Brabham-Ford	19
10.	Alfa Romeo	7

❊ FAST TALK (11) ❊

"The reason Michael [Schumacher] did what he did is that he thinks he's better than the rest of us. He thinks he's bigger than the sport, too, but he isn't. And when he retires, and no one really remembers him, that will become clear."
Jacques Villeneuve

❊ REUTEMANN IGNORES PIT INSTRUCTION ❊

In the 1981 Brazilian Grand Prix Carlos Reutemann received a signal from the pits to let Alan Jones overtake him. But the Argentinian driver ignored the instruction and took the chequered flag to win. At the post-race interview Reutemann claimed he did not see the signal.

❂ A UNIQUE TRIO ❂

Three drivers have won the F1 World Drivers' Championship with a nationality different to that of their birth. Jochen Rindt (1970) was born in Mainz, Germany, but brought up in Austria. Mario Andretti was born in Montona, Italy, but had American nationality when he was crowned World Champion in 1978. Keke Rosberg was born in Stockholm, Sweden, but when he won the 1982 World Championship he had Finnish nationality.

Did You Know That?
Jody Scheckter, World Champion in 1979, was born in East London, South Africa.

❂ ALFA'S SWANSONG ❂

After Alfa Romeo had dominated the first ever season of GP racing in 1950, when the top three places in the championship table were all occupied by their drivers, and despite Juan Manuel Fangio winning the 1951 F1 Drivers' World Championship in an Alfa Romeo, the Italian team pulled out of Formula One racing after the final Grand Prix of the 1951 season, the Spanish GP at Pedrables. Juan Manuel Fangio won the 1951 Spanish GP to clinch the world title by six points from Alberto Ascari (Ferrari).

Did You Know That?
The FIA was so concerned that Ferrari would dominate F1 racing in 1952 with their powerful Ferrari 500, they decided that the 1952 F1 season would be raced according to the less powerful F2 rules to give all the teams a chance of success.

❂ THE McLAREN MP4-13 ❂

In 1998, the Adrian Newey-designed McLaren MP4-13 chassis helped Mika Hakkinen to the first of his two Drivers' Championships. Along with team-mate, David Coulthard, the pair won nine of the 16 GPs, took 12 pole positions and recorded nine fastest laps.

❂ TEAM BRABHAM HIT TOP SPOT ❂

Dan Gurney secured Brabham's first ever victory in Formula One when he took the chequered flag at Rouen in the French Grand Prix on 28 June 1964.

❀ WILLIAMS FW18 ❀

The Williams FW18 totally dominated F1 in 1996. The chassis, designed by Patrick Head and Adrian Newey and powered by a Renault V10 engine, was simply awesome, winning 12 of the 16 GPs raced, taking 12 pole positions and securing 11 fastest laps. Damon Hill won eight times in the FW18 and his team-mate, Jacques Villeneuve, four times. Williams won the 1996 Constructors' Cup by a mammoth 105 points from Ferrari (175 points to 70).

❀ SCHUMACHER'S GRIEF IN VICTORY ❀

The day after his mother died, Michael Schumacher (Ferrari) won the 2003 San Marino Grand Prix from pole position on the grid.

❀ NURBURGRING FIRST AND LAST ❀

Erwin Bauer's sole race in Formula One came in the 1953 German GP at the Nurburgring, but it ended disappointingly for him on lap 1.

Did You Know That?
On 3 June 1958, Bauer died at the Nurburgring when he crashed his 2-litre sports Ferrari, unaware that he should have been on his slowing-down lap, having already taken the chequered flag.

❀ F1 WINNERS AT THE BRICKYARD, PART 2 ❀

From 2000 to 2007, the Indianapolis Motor Speedway hosted the United States GP. It used part of the famous 2.5-mile banked oval on which the famous Indianapolis 500 is run. The winners there were:

2000	Michael Schumacher (Ferrari)
2001	Mika Hakkinen (McLaren-Mercedes)
2002	Rubens Barrichello (Ferrari)
2003	Michael Schumacher (Ferrari)
2004	Michael Schumacher (Ferrari)
2005	Michael Schumacher (Ferrari)
2006	Michael Schumacher (Ferrari)
2007	Lewis Hamilton (McLaren-Mercedes)

Did You Know That?
Indianapolis, the capital of the State of Indiana, was founded in 1821 and is nicknamed the "Circle City".

❀ 1983 DRIVERS' WORLD CHAMPIONSHIP ❀

Pos Driver	Nationality	Team	Pts
1. Nelson Piquet	Brazilian	Brabham-BMW	59
2. Alain Prost	French	Renault	57
3. Rene Arnoux	French	Ferrari	49
4. Patrick Tambay	French	Ferrari	40
5. Keke Rosberg	Finnish	Williams-Ford & Williams-Honda	27
6. John Watson	British	McLaren-Ford & McLaren-Tag	22
7. Eddie Cheever	American	Renault	22
8. Andrea de Cesaris	Italian	Alfa Romeo	15
9. Riccardo Patrese	Italian	Brabham-BMW	13
10. Niki Lauda	Austrian	McLaren-Ford & McLaren-Tag	12

❀ 1983 CONSTRUCTORS' CUP ❀

Pos	Constructor	Pts
1.	Ferrari	89
2.	Renault	79
3.	Brabham-BMW	72
4.	Williams-Ford	36
5.	McLaren-Ford	34
6.	Alfa Romeo	18
7.	Tyrrell-Ford	12
8.	Lotus-Renault	11
9.	Toleman-Hart	10
10.	Arrows-Ford	4

❀ 1960 ❀

8-6-4-3-2-1 points awarded to the first six placed drivers. No points were awarded for the fastest lap. Shared drives were no longer permitted.

❀ TURBO POWER REDUCED ❀

For the 1987 F1 season, FISA ordered the constructors to reduce the turbo pressure in their cars to four bars, while all 1,500cm^3 engines were fitted with a pop-off valve. In 1987, FISA allowed the fully aspirated engines to be used again, but with a limit of 3,500cm^3.

❂ CHAOS AT THE 1981 BELGIAN GP ❂

Prior to the start of the 1981 Belgian Grand Prix, Ricardo Patrese was in the second row of the grid, but his engine cut out and he tried furiously to halt the start, waving his arms in the air. His mechanic then ran on to the track to help him, but the green lights were lit. The cars pulled away and the drivers attempted to avoid Patrese's car, but his team-mate, Sigfried Sthor, who started from 13th position on the grid, hit the mechanic, who was now sandwiched between the two Arrows-Fords. Luckily the mechanic did not suffer any serious injuries. The race was stopped and when it was finally restarted, Alan Jones (Williams-Ford) touched wheels with Nelson Piquet (Brabham-Ford), knocking him out of the race before later crashing out himself. The race was won by Carlos Reutemann.

Did You Know That?
During practice at the 1981 Belgian GP, Carlos Reutemann drove over a photographer's foot.

❂ DUAL F1 WORLD CHAMPION ❂

Jack Brabham is the only person in F1 to have been World Champion as a driver (1959, 1960 & 1966) and as a constructor (1966 & 1967).

❂ ROW AT SAN MARINO ❂

Following the post-race disqualification of Nelson Piquet and Keke Rosberg at the 1982 Brazilian Grand Prix, FOCA appealed to FISA in respect of the underweight cars but their appeal was rejected. The FOCA teams then withdrew from the next GP at San Marino, which left only seven teams to compete: ATS, Alfa Romeo, Ferrari, Osella, Renault, Toleman and Tyrrell. The race turned out to be a dogfight between Rene Arnoux (Renault) and the two Ferrari drivers, Didier Pironi and Gilles Villeneuve. At the beginning of the final lap Villeneuve led the race and team orders went out ordering Pironi to stay behind the Canadian. However, Pironi had other ideas and overtook his team-mate at Tosa to snatch victory on the line.

Did You Know That?
Villeneuve felt betrayed and angry at Pironi's lack of discipline and vowed never to speak to his team-mate again. He never did, because Villeneuve died two weeks later in practice before the next GP.

❂ VETTEL COMPLETES HAT-TRICK ❂

Sebastian Vettel won his third consecutive Formula One World Drivers' Championship for Red Bull-Renault in 2012. He went into the final race of the season, the Brazilian Grand Prix, leading Ferrari's Fernando Alonso by 13 points, a not-insurmountable advantage with 25 points for a win and only ten for a fifth-place finish. As it happened, Jenson Button (McLaren-Mercedes) – who was out of the running for the overall prize – won the race, with Alonso in second. This gave him 18 points, but Vettel managed to come in sixth place to earn eight points. When the dust had asettled, Vettel finished with a three-point advantage over the Ferrari man.

Did You Know That?
Vettel became the ninth driver – and second German – in Formula 1 history to claim three or more World Drivers' Championships.

❂ CLARK WINS WORLD TITLE ❂

On 1 August 1965, Jim Clark drove his Lotus-Climax to victory in the German GP at the Nurburgring. It was his fifth successive GP victory and his sixth of the season. There were three races remaining, but Clark had won his second F1 World Drivers' Championship, as he had reached the maximum number of points possible, 60, with only the six best scores from GPs counting.

Did You Know That?
It was Clark's first win at the Nurburgring.

❂ TON-UP BOYS ❂

When Michael Schumacher (Ferrari) won the 2006 German GP at Hockenheim it was his third consecutive GP victory, but only his fourth F1 victory in his home race. It also gave Bridgestone Tyres their 100th GP win. Fernando Alonso's (Renault) 5th-place finish put him on 100 points for the season, which meant Schumacher trailed the World Champion by 11 points with six races to go.

❂ A BRITISH 1-2-3 ❂

British drivers dominated the 1964 Drivers' World Championship, with John Surtees (Ferrari) finishing first, Graham Hill (BRM) second and Jim Clark (Lotus-BRM and Lotus-Climax) third.

❀ 1984 DRIVERS' WORLD CHAMPIONSHIP ❀

Pos	Driver	Nationality	Team	Pts
1.	Niki Lauda	Austrian	McLaren-TAG7	72
2.	Alain Prost	French	McLaren-TAG	71.5
3.	Elio de Angelis	Italian	Lotus-Renault	34
4.	Michele Alboreto	Italian	Ferrari	30.5
5.	Nelson Piquet	Brazilian	Brabham-BMW	29
6.	Rene Arnoux	French	Ferrari	27
7.	Derek Warwick	British	Renault	23
8.	Keke Rosberg	Finnish	Williams-Honda	20.5
9.	Ayrton Senna	Brazilian	Toleman-Hart	13
10.	Nigel Mansell	British	Lotus-Renault	13

❀ 1984 CONSTRUCTORS' CUP ❀

Pos	Constructor	Pts
1.	McLaren-TAG	143.5
2.	Ferrari	57.5
3.	Lotus-Renault	47
4.	Brabham-BMW	38
5.	Renault	34
6.	Williams-Honda	25.5
7.	Toleman-Hart	16
8.	Alfa Romeo	11
9.	Ligier-Renault	3
10.	Arrows-Ford	3

❀ SECOND WITH ONLY THREE WHEELS ❀

Stefan Johansson (McLaren-TAG) finished second to Nelson Piquet (Williams-Honda) in the 1987 German Grand Prix despite only having three wheels on his car as he crossed the finishing line. One of his tyres exploded on the final lap of the race but he managed to crawl home for a podium place.

❀ VETTEL IS YOUNGEST EVER POLE-SITTER ❀

When Sebastian Vettel (Toro Rosso), at 21 years and 73 days old, claimed pole position for the 2008 Italian GP at Monza, he became the youngest driver ever to achieve the feat. Spain's Fernando Alonso was the previous holder of the record at 21 years and 236 days when he took pole position in the 2003 Malaysian Grand Prix.

❀ NIKI LAUDA ❀

Andreas Nikolaus Lauda was born on 22 February 1949 in Vienna, Austria. In 1968 he began his racing career driving a mini in hill climbs, and the following year he took up mini racing, but eventually moved up into single-seaters in Formula Three.

In 1971 "Niki" joined Formula Two and, on 15 August 1971, he made his F1 debut in his home Grand Prix, the Austrian, at the Osterreichring for March-Ford. In 1972, Lauda bought a place in the March-Ford team but failed to score a single championship point.

Niki left March-Ford in 1973 and joined BRM as their third driver behind Jean-Pierre Beltoise and Clay Regazzoni. Lauda's team-mates had both won in Formula One, and when he started to outpace them other teams sat up and took notice. After Lauda finished 17th in the 1973 Drivers' Championship, Enzo Ferrari signed him for the 1974 season. Niki finished second in his debut race for Ferrari, the Argentinian Grand Prix on 13 January 1974. He had his first win for the Scuderia on 28 April 1974 in the Spanish Grand Prix at Jarama and finished the season fourth in the Drivers' Championship. In 1975 Niki won his first World Championship by winning five of the season's 14 GPs. On 1 August 1976, tragedy struck in the German Grand Prix at the Nurburgring. His Ferrari swerved off the track and hit an embankment before rolling back on to the track, where it was hit by Brett Lunger's Surtees-Ford. The Ferrari burst into flames and Lauda, who was trapped in his car, was badly burned. Although he stood up when he was finally hauled from the car by Lunger, Niki later collapsed into a coma and a priest administered the last rites. Despite his injuries, Niki returned just two races later and, going into the final Grand Prix of the season, the Japanese, he still led the Drivers' Championship. However, Niki decided not to race on a rain-soaked circuit in Japan, and James Hunt's (McLaren-Ford) third place gave the British driver the World Championship by a single point over Lauda.

Niki won the F1 crown in 1977 with Ferrari and then left the Scuderia for Brabham. After spending two unsuccessful years with Bernie Ecclestone's team he decided to retire and concentrate on his own charter airline.

In 1982 he returned to Formula One, and in 1984 he won his third World Championship, defeating his McLaren-TAG team-mate, Alain Prost, by half a point. Lauda competed in 170 Grands Prix, winning 25 of them, had 24 fastest laps and 54 podium finishes and secured 24 pole positions. He was inducted into the International Motorsports Hall of Fame in 1993.

❀ PIQUET UNNERVES PROST ❀

After winning the penultimate race of 1983, the European Grand Prix on 25 September 1983 at Brands Hatch, Nelson Piquet (Brabham-BMW) boldly declared: "I am telling you, if we don't have any problems in the final race, nobody can stop us." However, the standings showed Alain Prost (Renault) in the lead on 57 points, Piquet on 55 and Rene Arnoux of Ferrari on 49. In answer to Piquet's statement Prost replied: "We are still in the lead." In the end, the Brazilian's mind games paid dividends as he pipped the Frenchman to the 1983 F1 Drivers' Championship title.

❀ HERRMANN DEBUT ❀

Hans Herrmann made his Formula One debut on home soil in the German Grand Prix on 2 August 1953 and finished ninth in his Veritas. During his career, he participated in 18 GPs, achieved one podium finish and scored a total of 10 championship points. Outside Formula One, Herrmann, along with Britain's Richard Attwood, gave Porsche their first overall victory in the 1970 Le Mans 24 Hours race driving a Porsche 917K.

Did You Know That?
In 1954 Herrmann raced in the Mille Miglia along with his navigator, Herbert Linge, in a Porsche 550 Spyder. Just as the gates of a railroad crossing were being lowered before the arrival of the fast train to Rome, Herrmann decided it was too late to brake. He simply knocked the back of Linge's helmet, forcing him to bend his head forward, as the pair narrowly made it below the gates, as spectators watched in disbelief.

❀ MIRROR IMAGE GIVES SENNA TITLE ❀

Just as Ayrton Senna (McLaren-Honda) had collided with his team-mate, Alain Prost, at the 1989 Japanese Grand Prix, a collision which put Prost out of the race but still handed him the F1 Drivers' Championship when Senna was disqualified despite winning the GP, so the saga continued at the 1990 Japanese Grand Prix. However, this time Senna gained revenge when his McLaren-Honda collided with Prost's Ferrari in the first lap, forcing both drivers to retire from the race. With only the Australian Grand Prix left, Senna was crowned World Champion for the second time in his career.

❀ 1985 DRIVERS' WORLD CHAMPIONSHIP ❀

Pos	Driver	Nationality	Team	Pts
1.	Alain Prost	French	McLaren-TAG	73
2.	Michele Alboreto	Italian	Ferrari	53
3.	Keke Rosberg	Finnish	Williams-Honda	40
4.	Ayrton Senna	Brazilian	Lotus-Renault	38
5.	Elio de Angelis	Italian	Lotus-Renault	33
6.	Nigel Mansell	British	Williams-Honda	31
7.	Stefan Johansson	Swedish	Ferrari	26
8.	Nelson Piquet	Brazilian	Brabham-BMW	21
9.	Jacques Laffite	French	Ligier-Renault	16
10.	Niki Lauda	Austrian	McLaren-TAG	14

❀ 1985 CONSTRUCTORS' CUP ❀

Pos	Constructor	Pts
1.	McLaren-TAG	90
2.	Ferrari	82
3.	Williams-Honda	71
4.	Lotus-Renault	71
5.	Brabham-BMW	26
6.	Ligier-Renault	23
7.	Renault	16
8.	Arrows-BMW	14
9.	Tyrrell-Ford	4
10.	Tyrrell-Renault	3

❀ FAST TALK (12) ❀

"My Italian blood respects Ferrari!"   *Jean Alesi* (Alesi is French)

❀ PIQUET GIVES SENNA THE NOD ❀

During the weekend of the 1987 Hungarian Grand Prix, Lotus-Honda and Nelson Piquet (Williams-Honda) announced a two-year deal starting in season 1988. Piquet had been approached by McLaren but did not accept their offer, claiming that he had lost the 1986 F1 Drivers' Championship as a direct result of Williams' in-house politics and that he was not prepared to risk losing another Championship. Jokingly, Piquet suggested that McLaren should sign Ayrton Senna (Lotus-Honda) – and they did, with Senna winning the world title the following year.

◉ MANSELL WINS IN PIQUET'S CAR ◉

Nigel Mansell won the 1986 British Grand Prix in the car normally driven by his Williams-Honda team-mate, Nelson Piquet. Piquet had secured pole position but in the warm-up lap he opted for the T-car, claiming the balance in his regular car was not quite right. An incident at the start of the GP resulted in a restart being ordered. Mansell, whose engine had broken in the incident, went to the restart in the car Piquet had abandoned. Nigel had no problems with it, winning the 75-lap race ... 5.574 seconds ahead of Piquet.

◉ KING MICHAEL VIII OF FRANCE ◉

On 16 July 2006, Michael Schumacher (Ferrari) won his record eighth French GP at Magny Cours, the first time an F1 driver had ever won the same GP eight times. With Fernando Alonso (Renault) finishing second in the race, he was now just 17 points behind the World Champion in the Drivers' Championship after 11 races. Ironically, in the first three GPs of the 2006 season Alonso scored 28 points to Schuey's 11, a difference of 17 points. It was Schuey's 88th career victory and Ferrari's 187th.

Did You Know That?
Michael Schumacher's victory in the 2006 French GP was the 150th podium finish of his career.

◉ PRANCING HORSE LOSES STEP ◉

In 1957 Ferrari struggled all season and won none of the eight Grands Prix raced. Reigning World Champion Juan Manuel Fangio had moved from the Scuderia to Maserati at the end of the 1956 season. That year Fangio won four GPs for Maserati, Stirling Moss won three in his Vanwall and Sam Hanks won the Indianapolis 500 in an Epperly-Offenhauser.

◉ McLAREN NIPPED FOR SPEED ◉

In the eighth Grand Prix of the 1988 season, the British GP, Gerhard Berger (Ferrari) brought to an end a run of seven consecutive pole positions for McLaren-Honda (Senna 6, Prost 1). However, Senna, starting from P3 on the grid behind Berger and Michele Alboreto (Ferrari), won his fourth Grand Prix of the season and his team's eighth consecutive GP.

❀ FANTASY EUROPEAN STARTING GRID ❀

(excluding France, Germany, Great Britain and Italy)
(up to the end of the 2013 season)

1
Fernando Alonso
(Spa) *(32 GP wins,
217 GPs, World
champion 2005,
2006)*

2
Niki Lauda (Aut) *(25
(GP wins, 177 GPs,
World champion 1975,
1977, 1984)*

3
Mika Hakkinen
(Fin) *(20 GP wins
165 GPs World,
champion 1998
1999)*

4
Kimi Raikkonen
(Fin) *(20 GP wins,
194 GPs, World
champion 2007)*

5
Jochen Rindts
(Aut) *(6 GP wins,
62 GPs, World
champion 1970)*

6
Ronnie Peterson (Swe)
*(10 GP wins, 127
GPs, World champion
best 2nd, 1978)*

7
Gerhard Berger
(Aut) *(10 GP wins,
210 GPs, World
champion best 3rd, ,
1988, 1994)*

8
Jacky Ickx (Bel)
*(8 GP wins, 122 GPs,
World champion best
2nd 1969, 1970)*

9
Keke Rosberg
(Fin) *(5 GP wins,
114 GPs, World
champion 1982)*

10
Clay Regazzoni (Swi)
*(5 GP wins, 132 GPs,
World champion best
2nd 1982)*

❀ 1986 DRIVERS' WORLD CHAMPIONSHIP ❀

Pos	Driver	Nationality	Team	Pts
1.	Alain Prost	French	McLaren-TAG	72
2.	Nigel Mansell	British	Williams-Honda	70
3.	Nelson Piquet	Brazilian	Williams-Honda	69
4.	Ayrton Senna	Brazilian	Lotus-Renault	55
5.	Stefan Johansson	Swedish	Ferrari	23
6.	Keke Rosberg	Finnish	McLaren-TAG	22
7.	Gerhard Berger	Austrian	Benetton-BMW	17
8.	Jacques Laffite	French	Ligier-Renualt	14
9.	Michele Alboreto	Italian	Ferrari	14
10.	Rene Arnoux	French	Ligier-Renault	14

❀ 1986 CONSTRUCTORS' CUP ❀

Pos	Constructor	Pts
1.	Williams-Honda	141
2.	McLaren-TAG	96
3.	Lotus-Renault	58
4.	Ferrari	37
5.	Ligier-Renault	29
6.	Benetton-BMW	19
7.	Tyrrell-Renault	11
8.	Lola-Ford	6
9.	Brabham-BMW	2
10.	Arrows-BMW	1

❀ IMPRESSIVE NUMBERS ❀

Fernando Alonso won the 2006 British GP at Silverstone on 11 June to continue a remarkable run: it was his second consecutive GP victory; fifth win of the season; eighth podium finish (he had been on the podium in every race so far); and 14th consecutive podium place. Michael Schumacher finished second and trailed Alonso by 23 points in the race for the 2006 World Championship crown.

Did You Know That?

British racing fans got a view of the future in the GP2 race over the weekend. The winner of both races was 21-year-old Lewis Hamilton, driving for the French ART Grand Prix team. Already on the books of the McLaren team, Lewis would step up to Formula 1 in 2007 and was World Champion in 2008, having finished second a year before.

❀ THE PAMPAS BULL ❀

Jose Froilan Gonzalez, nicknamed "The Pampas Bull" by his English fans, made his Formula One debut in the 1950 Monaco Grand Prix for the Scuderia Achille Varzi racing team. The Argentinian was forced to retire his Ferrari after lap 1 as his fellow countryman, Juan Manuel Fangio, raced to victory. He raced in 30 Grands Prix between 1950 and 1957, and in those races he won twice (both times in the British GP, 1951 & 1954), took seven second-place and four third-place finishes, had three pole positions and set six fastest lap times. In total he scored 72.14 championship points for the teams he raced for, which included Scuderia Achille Varzi, Scuderia Ferrari, Officine Alfieri Maserati and Vandervell Products.

Did You Know That?
His fellow F1 drivers nicknamed Gonzalez "El Cabezon" (Fat Head).

❀ NEW RULE CHANGES FOR 1989 ❀

FISA, the sport's governing body, decided that for the 1989 Formula One season cars were only permitted to use aspirated engines. Furthermore, as there were now so many teams competing, FISA also decided to introduce a new system of pre-qualifying practice. Those F1 drivers who did not score any points in the last half of the 1988 season now had to pre-qualify for the Grand Prix.

❀ STEWART CALLS IT A DAY BEFORE GP 100 ❀

Jackie Stewart (Tyrrell-Ford) had already clinched the 1973 F1 Drivers' World Championship going into the final race of the season, the US Grand Prix at Watkins Glen. The race was to be the three-times World Champion's hundredth and final GP, as he had earlier taken the decision to hang up his racing helmet. However, Tyrrell pulled out of the race following the death of their driver, Francois Cevert, in practice.

❀ CHAPMAN BREEDS TWO CHAMPIONS ❀

After giving future F1 World Champion, John Surtees, his F1 debut in the 1960 Monaco Grand Prix, Colin Chapman then gave another future World Champion, Jim Clark, his debut in a Lotus-Climax in the very next race, the Dutch Grand Prix at Zandvoort on 6 June 1960. Clark had to retire from the race with transmission failure.

❀ 1987 DRIVERS' WORLD CHAMPIONSHIP ❀

Pos	Driver	Nationality	Team	Pts
1.	Nelson Piquet	Brazilian	Williams-Honda	73
2.	Nigel Mansell	British	Williams-Honda	61
3.	Ayrton Senna	Brazilian	Lotus-Honda	57
4.	Alain Prost	French	McLaren-TAG	46
5.	Gerhard Berger	Austrian	Ferrari	36
6.	Stefan Johansson	Swedish	McLaren-TAG	30
7.	Michele Alboreto	Italian	Ferrari	17
8.	Thierry Boutsen	Belgian	Benetton-Ford	16
9.	Teo Fabi	Italian	Benetton-Ford	12
10.	Eddie Cheever	American	Arrows-Megatron	8

❀ 1987 CONSTRUCTORS' CUP ❀

Pos	Constructor	Pts
1.	Williams-Honda	137
2.	McLaren-TAG	76
3.	Lotus-Honda	64
4.	Ferrari	53
5.	Benetton-Ford	28
6.	Tyrrell-Ford	11
7.	Arrows-Megatron	11
8.	Brabham-BMW	10
9.	Lola-Ford	3
10.	Zakspeed	2

❀ FAST TALK (13) ❀

"Driving in Monte Carlo is like riding a bike in your house."
Nelson Piquet

❀ FANGIO 3 ASCARI 2 ❀

In the 1951 Formula One season, Juan Manuel Fangio won three GPs in his Alfa Romeo 159 compared to Alberto Ascari's two GP victories in his Ferrari. Fangio took the world drivers' crown home to Argentina with a six-point advantage over the Italian driver.

Did You Know That?
Although the Constructors' Cup did not begin until 1958, it was Alfa Romeo's second successive world title for one its drivers.

❂ NAUGHTY NIGEL ❂

At the 1989 Portuguese Grand Prix, Nigel Mansell (Ferrari) was leading the race and decided to pit. However, he overshot his position and had to reverse his car to the Ferrari garage – a prohibited manoeuvre. He re-entered the race in third place behind his team-mate, Gerhard Berger, and Ayrton Senna (McLaren-Honda). The race director informed Ferrari that Mansell was disqualified from the GP and he was shown the black flag for three consecutive laps, but each time he chose to ignore the instruction to leave the track. Then, on lap 48, Mansell tried to overtake Senna at the end of the main straight, and when the Brazilian moved across to block him, they touched wheels and both cars spun off.

Did You Know That?
Mansell was suspended for one race and fined US$55,000.00.

❂ GIUNTI KILLED IN A SPORTS CAR RACE ❂

On 10 January 1971, the Ferrari racing team lost Ignazio Giunti in a horrific accident in a sports car race in Argentina. In the Buenos Aires 1000km race, his first drive of the year, Giunti's Ferrari 312 PB prototype ploughed into the back of a Matra 650 which was stopped and sitting on the track, giving the popular Italian no chance of survival. Giunti had raced in four Grands Prix for Ferrari, making his debut in the Belgian Grand Prix at Spa on 7 June 1970, where he finished a creditable fourth.

❂ ILLEGAL FUEL ❂

Michael Schumacher (Benetton-Renault) won the 1995 Brazilian Grand Prix, from David Coulthard (Williams-Renault). However, after the race – the first of the season – they were both disqualified for using illegal fuel. Although their race positions were later reinstated, both teams were denied their race points in the Constructors' Cup.

❂ TYRRELL BUILDS HIS OWN CAR ❂

The Mexican Grand Prix on 25 October 1970 witnessed the unveiling of a new car built by Ken Tyrrell to replace the March. Jackie Stewart drove the new marque but left the race after lap 33 with suspension trouble. However, the future looked bright for Tyrrell-Ford in the hands of Stewart.

❀ NIGEL MANSELL, OBE ❀

Nigel Ernest James Mansell was born on 8 August 1953 in Upton-on-Severn, England. After a successful period in kart racing and a brief career as an aerospace engineer, Nigel won the British Formula Ford Championship in 1977. In 1979, Nigel and his wife, Rosanna, sold their house to finance his move into Formula 3. Colin Chapman, his F3 manager, gave Nigel with his successful Formula 1 Lotus racing team and in 1980 Nigel made his F1 debut in the Austrian GP driving for Lotus. It was a debut Nigel will always remember and not least of all because he badly burnt his backside as a result of a fuel leak. However, the pain soon disappeared when Colin Chapman gave him a contract to drive in F1 for Lotus during the 1981 season. Following Chapman's death in 1982, Peter Warr took over at Lotus but he and Nigel never got on well. In 1984, he finished in the Top 10 of the Drivers' Championship for the first time in his career.

In 1985, Frank Williams signed Mansell and throughout his Williams career Nigel proudly drove the famous "Red 5" car. On 6 October 1985, Nigel won his first F1 Grand Prix, the European GP at Brands Hatch. His maiden win came after 72 attempts in the cockpit of an F1 car. Nigel then won a second successive F1 GP at the South African Grand Prix in Kyalami. In the 1986 season he won five GP and lost the World Championship when his tyre burst with only 19 laps of the last GP of the season, the Australian, to go. Mansell finished runner-up in the Championship to Alain Prost (McLaren-TAG). Six more wins followed in 1987 including an emotional victory in the British GP at Silverstone and then in 1988 he only managed to finish two of the 14 GPs he appeared in.

In 1989, "Il Leone" ("The Lion") joined Ferrari and won first time out in Brazil. After two unsuccessful years with the Scuderia Mansell joined Williams again in 1991 and finished runner-up to Ayrton Senna in the Drivers' Championship. The following year Mansell won the opening five races and went on to clinch the World Championship with a record number of wins in one season (9) and highest number of pole positions (14). Mansell then fell out with Williams in 1993 and moved to the USA to drive for the Newman/Haas CART Team where he won the CART Championship in his rookie year. Nigel later made a brief return to F1 racing with McLaren in 1985 but quit after just two races. He won the BBC Sports Personality of the Year Award in 1986 and 1992, one of only three people to win it twice. Mansell participated in 187 Grands Prix, winning 31, securing 32 pole positions and recording 30 fastest laps.

✹ THE A–Z OF ENGINE MANUFACTURE ✹

Engine manufacturers from Alfa Romeo to Zakspeed have helped power F1 racing cars throughout the history of the sport.

✹ A STRANGE ENDING TO MONACO GP ✹

Amazingly only one car finished all 76 laps of the 1982 Monaco Grand Prix, Riccardo Patrese in his Brabham-Ford. The last two laps were perhaps the most exciting last two laps of any GP. The two Renault drivers led from the start before both had to leave the race following crashes, Rene Arnoux after 14 laps and Alain Prost after 59. Riccardo Patrese took the lead on the 74th lap before Didier Pironi in his Ferrari overtook him. However, Pironi's car then suffered electrical problems and ran out of fuel on the final lap, allowing the Italian to retake first place and claim victory. Even the third-placed driver, Andrea de Cesaris (Alfa Romeo), failed to cross the finishing line, having also run out of fuel.

Pos	Driver	Team	Laps	Time/Retired	Grid	Pts
1.	Riccardo Patrese	Brabham-Ford	76	1:54'11.259	2	9
2.	Didier Pironi	Ferrari	75	Out of fuel	5	6
3.	Andrea de Cesaris	Alfa Romeo	75	Out of fuel	7	4

✹ F1 DRIVER KIDKNAPPED ✹

After his Formula One career had ended, Hans Herrmann built up a successful automotive supplies company. During the 1990s he was kidnapped and kept in the boot of a car for several hours before he finally managed to free himself and escape.

✹ SCHUMI'S FIVE ENDS ALONSO'S FIVE ✹

Michael Schumacher (Ferrari) won the 2006 United States GP for the second consecutive year – and fifth in seven runnings at Indianapolis Motor Speedway – to prevent Fernando Alonso (Renault) from claiming a fifth straight victory of the season. Schumi's third win of 2006 was his 87th in Formula One and he closed to within 19 points of Alonso in the World Championship with eight races remaining.

Did You Know That?
Felipe Massa was runner-up at Indianapolis to record a second consecutive Ferrari 1–2 in the United States Grand Prix.

❀ 1988 DRIVERS' WORLD CHAMPIONSHIP ❀

Pos	Driver	Nationality	Team	Pts
1.	Ayrton Senna	Brazilian	McLaren-Honda	90
2.	Alain Prost	French	McLaren-Honda	87
3.	Gerhard Berger	Austrian	Ferrari	41
4.	Thierry Boutsen	Belgian	Benetton-Ford	27
5.	Michele Alboreto	Italian	Ferrari	24
6.	Nelson Piquet	Brazilian	Lotus-Honda	22
7.	Ivan Capelli	Italian	March-Judd	17
8.	Derek Warwick	British	Arrows-Megatron	17
9.	Nigel Mansell	British	Williams-Judd	12
10.	Alessandro Nannini	Italian	Benetton-Ford	12

❀ 1988 CONSTRUCTORS' CUP ❀

Pos	Constructor	Pts
1.	McLaren-Honda	199
2.	Ferrari	65
3.	Benetton-Ford	39
4.	Lotus-Honda	23
5.	Arrows-Megatron	23
6.	March-Judd	22
7.	Williams-Judd	20
8.	Tyrrell-Ford	5
9.	Rial-Ford	3
10.	Minardi-Ford	1

❀ ALFA'S RETURN TO THE PODIUM ❀

In the US East Grand Prix, the last race of the 1981 season, the Alfa Romeo team achieved its first podium finish since they returned to GP racing in 1980. It was also the first podium appearance for the Alfa driver, Bruno Giacomelli.

❀ BRABHAM LEAVES REPCO BEHIND ❀

In 1969 Jack Brabham switched from the Australian Repco engine that had propelled his cars to F1 World Championship glory in 1966 (Jack Brabham – Brabham-Repco) and in 1967 (Denny Hulme – Brabham-Repco). His cars now used the highly reliable Ford Cosworth DFV engine. Brabham finished in tenth place in the Drivers' Championship while his second driver, Jacky Ickx, finished in second place.

⬢ THE FIRST EVER F1 WORLD CHAMPION ⬢

Giuseppe (Nino) Farina was the inaugural winner of the F1 Drivers' World Championship in 1950. Along with Juan Manuèl Fangio (winner in Monaco, Belgium & France) he won three of the seven GPs (British, Swiss & Italian) in 1950, with Johnnie Parsons claiming victory in the Indianapolis 500. Farina finished the season on 30 points, with Fangio second on 27 points and Luigi Fagioli third on 24 points.

Did You Know That?
During the 1950 F1 season, points were only awarded to the top five finishers (8, 6, 4, 3 and 2), while one point was awarded for the driver recording the fastest lap. And, at the end of this inaugural F1 season, only the best four of seven scores counted towards the World Championship. Points for shared drives were divided equally between the drivers, regardless of who had driven more laps.

⬢ BRABHAM BT55 HELPS McLAREN ⬢

In 1986, Gordon Murray designed the BT55 for Brabham-BMW. The car was lower and longer than the others, with its engine assembled inclined and it also possessed a special gearbox design by Weissman. However, despite this innovative design, the team never quite got the engine or the suspension quite right. Murray later used the experience he gained designing the BT55 in producing his all-conquering McLaren in 1988.

⬢ HANS DEVICE ⬢

In 2003 FIA stipulated that F1 drivers had to wear the HANS device, a special horseshoe-shaped collar designed to protect the neck in case of an accident. HANS (the Head and Neck Protection System) was developed in the USA to reduce the risk of injury through the movement of the driver's head and neck in an accident as the car decelerates after striking a solid object. F1 drivers can experience g-forces of up to 100g when racing.

⬢ ASCARI TAKES A DIP ⬢

At the 1955 Monaco Grand Prix, Alberto Ascari flipped his Lancia into the harbour on lap 80 of the race. He escaped with minor injuries, but died one week later in a crash at Monza.

❀ 1989 DRIVERS' WORLD CHAMPIONSHIP ❀

Pos	Driver	Nationality	Team	Pts
1.	Alain Prost	French	McLaren-Honda	76
2.	Ayrton Senna	Brazilian	McLaren-Honda	60
3.	Riccardo Patrese	Italian	Williams-Renault	40
4.	Nigel Mansell	British	Ferrari	38
5.	Thierry Boutsen	Belgian	Williams-Renault	37
6.	Alessandro Nannini	Italian	Benetton-Ford	32
7.	Gerhard Berger	Austrian	Ferrari	21
8.	Nelson Piquet	Brazilian	Lotus-Judd	12
9.	Jean Alesi	French	Tyrrell-Ford	8
10.	Derek Warwick	British	Arrows-Ford	7

❀ 1989 CONSTRUCTORS' CUP ❀

Pos	Constructor	Pts
1.	McLaren-Honda	141
2.	Williams-Renault	77
3.	Ferrari	59
4.	Benetton-Ford	39
5.	Tyrrell-Ford	16
6.	Lotus-Judd	15
7.	Arrows-Ford	13
8.	Dallara-Ford	8
9.	Brabham-Judd	8
10.	Onyx-Ford	6

❀ FAST TALK (14) ❀

"He's just a total bloody idiot. Always was, always will be."
Derek Warwick on Rene Arnoux

❀ NINE ON THE TROT ❀

Alberto Ascari (Ferrari) won the last six Grands Prix of the 1952 season and the first three of the 1953 season to record a winning streak of nine in a row.

❀ MISSING ARROWS ❀

The Arrows team failed to appear for the Hungarian Grand Prix on 18 August 2002 and was never seen on a Formula One circuit again.

❀ WILLIAMS-HONDA ALMOST BREAK RECORD ❀

Williams-Honda won the 1987 Constructors' Cup but narrowly missed out on achieving a record points tally in the competition. Nelson Piquet retired after problems with his brakes on lap 58 while Riccardo Patrese, who drove in place of the injured Nigel Mansell, was forced out of the race on lap 76 with an oil leak.

❀ SCHUMI DISQUALIFIED ❀

Although Michael Schumacher (Ferrari) finished as runner-up to Jacques Villeneuve (Williams-Renault) in the 1997 F1 Drivers' Championship, the FIA removed all of his points because of an incident in the final race of the season, the European Grand Prix at Jerez, Spain. Schumi famously pulled across Villeneuve in Jerez, leaving them both in the gravel trap, but the Canadian managed to get back into the race and finish third to clinch the World Championship. Heinz-Harald Frentzen (Williams-Renault) was promoted to second place overall in the final standings, and David Coulthard (McLaren-Mercedes) to third.

❀ GP AND SIX-HOUR WINS IN SAME YEAR ❀

In 1982 Michele Alboreto raced in Formula One for Tyrrell-Ford, winning the US West GP in Las Vegas and finishing eighth in the Drivers' Championship. The same year he also continued his sports car racing with Lancia and won three times: twice with Riccardo Patrese (Silverstone Six Hours & Nurburgring 1000) and once with Piercarlo Ghinzani at Mugello.

Did You Know That?
Riccardo Patrese won the 1982 Monaco GP and finished tenth in the 1982 Drivers' Championship with Brabham-BMW/Brabham-Ford.

❀ RAMPANT BRITS ❀

In 1958 Britain's Mike Hawthorn (Ferrari) won the F1 Drivers' Championship closely followed by four other Brits (Stirling Moss – second, Tony Brooks – third, Roy Salvadori – fourth, and Peter Collins – fifth), British car manufacture Vanwall won the first ever F1 Constructors' Cup, while British drivers won all but one of the season's GPs (Maurice Trintignant won in Monaco in a British Cooper-Climax).

◉ WINNERS OF THE BRITISH GP ◉

Year	Driver	Constructor	Location
1926	*L. Wagner, R. Senechal	Delage	Brooklands
1927	Robert Benoist	Delage	Brooklands
1935	Richard Shuttleworth	Alfa Romeo	Donington
1936	*H. Ruesch, R. Seaman	Alfa Romeo	Donington
1937	Bernd Rosemeyer	Auto Union	Donington
1938	Tazio Nuvolari	Auto Union	Donington
1948	Luigi Villoresi	Maserati	Silverstone
1949	*E de Graffenried	Maserati	Silverstone
1950	Giuseppe Farina	Alfa Romeo	Silverstone
1951	Jose Froilan Gonzalez	Ferrari	Silverstone
1952	Alberto Ascari	Ferrari	Silverstone
1953	Alberto Ascari	Ferrari	Silverstone
1954	Jose Froilan Gonzalez	Ferrari	Silverstone
1955	Stirling Moss	Mercedes	Aintree
1956	Juan-Manuel Fangio	Lancia-Ferrari	Silverstone
1957	*S. Moss, T. Brooks	Vanwall	Aintree
1958	Peter Collins	Ferrari	Silverstone
1959	Jack Brabham	Cooper-Climax	Aintree
1960	Jack Brabham	Cooper-Climax	Silverstone
1961	Wolfgang von Trips	Ferrari	Aintree
1962	Jim Clark	Lotus-Climax	Aintree
1963	Jim Clark	Lotus-Climax	Silverstone
1964	Jim Clark	Lotus-Climax	Brands Hatch
1965	Jim Clark	Lotus-Climax	Silverstone
1966	Jack Brabham	Brabham	Brands Hatch
1967	Jim Clark	Lotus-Cosworth	Silverstone
1968	Jo Siffert	Lotus-Ford	Brands Hatch
1969	Jackie Stewart	Matra-Cosworth	Silverstone
1970	Jochen Rindt	Lotus-Cosworth	Brands Hatch
1971	Jackie Stewart	Tyrrell-Cosworth	Silverstone
1972	Emerson Fittipaldi	Lotus-Cosworth	Brands Hatch
1973	Peter Revson	McLaren-Cosworth	Silverstone
1974	Jody Scheckter	Tyrrell-Cosworth	Brands Hatch
1975	Emerson Fittipaldi	McLaren-Cosworth	Silverstone
1976	Niki Lauda	Ferrari	Brands Hatch
1977	James Hunt	McLaren-Cosworth	Silverstone
1978	Carlos Reutemann	Ferrari	Brands Hatch
1979	Clay Regazzoni	Williams-Cosworth	Silverstone
1980	Alan Jones	Williams-Cosworth	Brands Hatch
1981	John Watson	McLaren-Cosworth	Silverstone

1982	Niki Lauda	McLaren-Cosworth	Brands Hatch
1983	Alain Prost	Renault	Silverstone
1984	Niki Lauda	McLaren-TAG	Brands Hatch
1985	Alain Prost	McLaren-TAG	Silverstone
1986	Nigel Mansell	Williams-Honda	Brands Hatch
1987	Nigel Mansell	Williams-Honda	Silverstone
1988	Ayrton Senna	McLaren-Honda	Silverstone
1989	Alain Prost	McLaren-Honda	Silverstone
1990	Alain Prost	Ferrari	Silverstone
1991	Nigel Mansell	Williams-Renault	Silverstone
1992	Nigel Mansell	Williams-Renault	Silverstone
1993	Alain Prost	Williams-Renault	Silverstone
1994	Damon Hill	Williams-Renault	Silverstone
1995	Johnny Herbert	Benetton-Renault	Silverstone
1996	Jacques Villeneuve	Williams-Renault	Silverstone
1997	Jacques Villeneuve	Williams-Renault	Silverstone
1998	Michael Schumacher	Ferrari	Silverstone
1999	David Coulthard	McLaren-Mercedes	Silverstone
2000	David Coulthard	McLaren-Mercedes	Silverstone
2001	Mika Hakkinen	McLaren-Mercedes	Silverstone
2002	Michael Schumacher	Ferrari	Silverstone
2003	Rubens Barrichello	Ferrari	Silverstone
2004	Michael Schumacher	Ferrari	Silverstone
2005	Juan Pablo Montoya	McLaren-Mercedes	Silverstone
2006	Fernando Alonso	Renault	Silverstone
2007	Kimi Raikkonen	Ferrari	Silverstone
2008	Lewis Hamilton	McLaren-Mercedes	Silverstone
2009	Sebastian Vettel	Red Bull-Renault	Silverstone
2010	Mark Webber	Red Bull-Renault	Silverstone
2011	Fernando Alonso	Ferrari	Silverstone
2012	Mark Webber	Red Bull-Renault	Silverstone
2013	Nico Rosberg	Mercedes	Silverstone

Note: 1926–49 not part of official F1 drivers' Championship, nor 1929–57 Constructors' Cup.
*First names: Wagner, Louis; Senechal, Robert; Ruesch, Hans; Seaman, Richard; De Graffenried, Emmanuel; Moss, Stirling; Brooks, Tony.

✹ F1 LIGHTS UP ✹

Singapore hosted its first ever F1 Grand Prix, at the Marina Bay Street Circuit, on 28 September 2008. It was also F1's first ever night race. Fernando Alonso, driving for Renault, won the race, but it became infamous for the "Crashgate" incident involving Alonso's team-mate Nelson Piquet Jnr..

⚙ 1990 DRIVERS' WORLD CHAMPIONSHIP ⚙

Pos	Driver	Nationality	Team	Pts
1.	Ayrton Senna	Brazilian	McLaren-Honda	78
2.	Alain Prost	French	Ferrari	71
3.	Nelson Piquet	Brazilian	Benetton-Ford	43
4.	Gerhard Berger	Austrian	McLaren-Honda	43
5.	Nigel Mansell	British	Ferrari	37
6.	Thierry Boutsen	Belgian	Williams-Renault	34
7.	Riccardo Patrese	Italian	Williams-Renault	23
8.	Alessandro Nannini	Italian	Benetton-Ford	21
9.	Jean Alesi	French	Tyrrell-Ford	13
10.	Ivan Capelli	Italian	Leyton House-Judd	6

⚙ 1990 CONSTRUCTORS' CUP ⚙

Pos	Constructor	Pts
1.	McLaren-Honda	121
2.	Ferrari	110
3.	Benetton-Ford	71
4.	Williams-Renault	57
5.	Tyrrell-Ford	16
6.	Lola-Lamborghini	11
7.	Leyton House-Judd	7
8.	Lotus-Lamborghini	3
9.	Arrows-Ford	2
10.	Brabham-Judd	2

⚙ AN ALL-ENGLISH AFFAIR ⚙

All 12 F1 Drivers' Champions 1958–69 were English-speaking: Mike Hawthorn (1958), Graham Hill (1962, 1968), Jim Clark (1963, 1965), John Surtees (1964) and Jackie Stewart (1969) were British; Jack Brabham (1959, 1960, 1966) was Australian; Phil Hill (1961) was American; and Denny Hulme (1967) a New Zealander.

⚙ LAUDA RETURNS ⚙

When the 1982 F1 season began in South Africa on 23 January 1982, Niki Lauda, who had retired at the end of the 1979 season, returned to the cockpit of an F1 car and drove like an old master to claim fourth place in the GP for McLaren-Ford. The race was won by Alain Prost in a Renault.

❀ CENTURY FOR MICHELIN ❀

Fernando Alonso's (Renault) win in the Canadian GP in Montreal on 25 June 2006 was Michelin's seventh win of the 2006 F1 season and their 100th Formula One victory. Michelin first entered F1 in 1977 and when it left in 1984 it had notched up 59 victories. The tyre manufacturer then returned to F1 in 2001 and claimed its 41st victory of its second stint in the sport with Alonso's win in Montreal.

Did You Know That?
Carlos Reutemann (Ferrari) won Michelin's first F1 GP in Brazil in 1978. Alain Prost has won the most GPs for Michelin, 16, while Alonso's victory in Japan in 2006 was his 15th for the company.

❀ FLYING RONNIE ❀

Ronnie Peterson (Lotus-Ford) secured his first F1 victory in the French Grand Prix on 1 July 1973. The Swedish ace ended the season with four victories to claim third place in the Drivers' Championship.

❀ FIRST TITLE FOR TURBO-CHARGED CAR ❀

When Nelson Piquet won the 1983 F1 Drivers' World Championship in his Brabham-BMW, it was the first time a driver drove a turbo-charged car to championship glory. Ferrari won their second consecutive Constructors' Cup in 1983, ahead of Renault and Brabham.

❀ MOSS TAKES LOTUS TO DIZZY HEIGHTS ❀

By winning the Monaco Grand Prix on 29 May 1960, Stirling Moss gave Team Lotus their first ever F1 podium finish. Moss also won the final GP of the 1960 season in the USA to secure third place in the Drivers' Championship.

❀ PAPERS COSTS PIQUET HOME GP WIN ❀

In the opening race of the 1987 season, Nelson Piquet (Williams-Honda) was leading his home Grand Prix, the Brazilian, on the seventh lap but then was forced into the pits as the some of the papers strewn around the circuit got into his radiators and he was forced to pit due to overheating. He drove magnificently but could only finish second behind the reigning World Champion, Alain Prost (McLaren-TAG).

❂ ALAIN PROST ❂

Alain Marie Prost was born on 24 February 1955 in Saint-Chamond, Loire, France. Only Michael Schumacher and the legendary Juan Manuel Fangio won more F1 Drivers' World Championships than the man nicknamed "The Professor". Prost won four F1 World Championships during his career, in 1985, 1986, 1989 and 1993.

A teenage Prost was set for a career in professional football until he won the 1973 World Junior Karting Championship, when his career was mapped out for him. Prost slipped his way past Formula Two racing and entered the big stage in 1980 when he participated in the opening Grand Prix of the 1980 season in Argentina on 13 January 1980. Prost (McLaren-Ford) finished in a very creditable sixth place in his maiden GP to claim his first World Championship point. He went on to finish 16th in the drivers' table at the end of the 1980 F1 season. On 5 July 1981, a patriotic Prost won his first ever F1 race and fittingly he won it in a Renault on French soil, in the French Grand Prix at Dijon. By the time he hung up his racing helmet, Prost had won a record six French GPs. During his three years with Renault, Prost won nine Grands Prix but internal conflicts, plus the French media blaming him for finishing runner-up to Nelson Piquet (Brabham-BMW) by two points in the 1983 Drivers' Championship, resulted in him rejoining McLaren in 1984.

Prost spent six successful seasons at McLaren from 1984 to 1989, in which he won 30 Grands Prix, clinched three World Championships and was runner-up twice. His proudest moment came in 1985 when he became the first ever French F1 World Champion. In 1987, he passed Jackie Stewart's record number of F1 wins when he won the 28th Grand Prix of his career. In 1990 Alain joined Ferrari, but disillusionment with his car and the internal politics going on then at the Scuderia led him to speak out once too often and he was fired in 1991. He left F1 and, taking a sabbatical from F1 racing, became a commentator for French television.

Prost returned to Formula One with Williams in 1993 and won seven Grands Prix to claim his fourth drivers' crown. When Prost learned that his arch-rival, Ayrton Senna, was to join him at Williams-Renault in 1994, he tendered his resignation. Prost then became a technical advisor at McLaren before taking over Ligier and renaming it Prost Grand Prix for the 1997 F1 season. Prost was not as successful an owner as he had been a driver, and in 2001 his Prost racing team folded. Prost competed in 200 Grands Prix, winning 51 of them and securing a total of 798.5 championship points. He also managed to secure 41 fastest laps.

❀ 1991 DRIVERS' WORLD CHAMPIONSHIP ❀

Pos	Driver	Nationality	Team	Pts
1.	Ayrton Senna	Brazilian	McLaren-Honda	96
2.	Nigel Mansell	British	Williams-Renault	72
3.	Riccardo Patrese	Italian	Williams-Renault	53
4.	Gerhard Berger	Austrian	McLaren-Honda	43
5.	Alain Prost	French	Ferrari	34
6.	Nelson Piquet	Brazilian	Benetton-Ford	26.5
7.	Jean Alesi	French	Ferrari	21
8.	Stefano Modena	Italian	Tyrrell-Honda	10
9.	Andrea de Cesaris	Italian	Jordan-Ford	9
10.	Roberto Moreno	Brazilian	Benetton-Ford	8

❀ 1991 CONSTRUCTORS' CUP ❀

Pos	Constructor	Pts
1.	McLaren-Honda	139
2.	Williams-Renault	125
3.	Ferrari	46.5
4.	Benetton-Ford	38.5
5.	Jordan-Ford	13
6.	Tyrrell-Honda	12
7.	Minardi-Ferrari	6
8.	Dallara-Judd	5
9.	Brabham-Yamaha	3
10.	Lotus-Judd	3

❀ ARRIVEDERCI AND AU REVOIR ❀

At the end of the 1985 season Alfa Romeo (Italy) and Renault (France) announced their decision not to participate any longer in F1 as GP racing teams, although both stated their desire to continue supplying engines for other teams.

❀ A MASTERFUL DISPLAY ❀

Ayrton Senna (McLaren-Ford) blasted everyone out of sight in the 1993 European Grand Prix held at Donington Park on 11 April 1993. In wet, slippery conditions Senna started from P4 on the grid but inside the first 90 seconds he was leading the race after an awesomely brilliant piece of driving. Senna was so good in the wet that he lapped everyone in the race except Damon Hill (Williams-Renault).

❀ IN MEMORIAM ❀

Since the first F1 GP in 1950, 27 racing drivers have tragically lost
their lives in testing, practice, qualifying or the actual race itself.

No.	Driver	Year/GP	Practice/Qualifying/Race
1.	Onofre Marimon	1954 German	Qualifying
2.	Luigi Musso	1958 French	Race
3.	Peter Collins	1958 German	Race
4.	Stuart Lewis-Evans	1958 Morocco	6 days after GP
5.	Chris Bristow	1960 Belgian	Race
6.	Alan Stacey	1960 Belgian	Race
7.	Wolfgang von Trips	1961 Italian	Race
8.	Carel de Beaufort	1964 German	Qualifying
9.	John Taylor	1966 German	Race
10.	Lorenzo Bandini	1967 Monaco	Race
11.	Jo Schlesser	1968 French	Race
12.	Gerhard Mitter	1969 German	Qualifying
13.	Piers Courage	1970 Dutch	Race
14.	Jochen Rindt	1970 Italian	Qualifying
15.	Roger Williamson	1973 Dutch	Race
16.	Francois Cevert	1973 US	Qualifying
17.	Peter Revson	1974 South African	Free Practice
18.	Helmuth Koinigg	1974 US	Race
19.	Mark Donohue	1975 Austrian	Warm-up session
20.	Tom Pryce	1977 South African	Race
21.	Ronnie Peterson	1978 Italian	7 days after GP
22.	Patrick Depaillier	1980 German	Free Practice
23.	Gilles Villeneuve	1982 Belgian	Qualifying
24.	Riccardo Paletti	1982 Canadian	Race
25.	Elio de Angelis*	1986 France	Testing
26.	Roland Ratzenberger	1994 San Marino	Qualifying
27.	Ayrton Senna	1994 San Marino	Race

Elio de Angelis was testing for Brabham at Le Castellet Circuit

Did You Know That?
Three drivers lost their lives in Hillclimbing races: Ludovico Scarfiotti
(1968), Mark Colton (1995) and Peter Bourne (2003).

❀ AUSTRALIA'S ENGLAND ❀

Paul England from Australia only raced once in Formula One, in the
1957 German Grand Prix in a Formula Two Cooper-Climax.

❀ FAST TALK (15) ❀

"Drivers are just interchangeable light bulbs – you plug them in and they do the job."
Teddy Mayer, McLaren

❀ FERRARI MISSES 13 RACES ❀

Since the first ever official Grand Prix in 1950, Ferrari has only missed 13 GPs. Ferrari did not participate in the 1950 British Grand Prix at Silverstone, the 1961 US Grand Prix at Watkins Glen and the 11 Indy 500 races held between 1950 and 1960, which, then, formed part of the official F1 calendar.

❀ FERRARI'S FIRST GP WIN ❀

Jose Froilan Gonzalez will go down in Ferrari motor racing history as the first driver to win a Formula One race driving the famous Maranello-built red machine. On 14 July 1951, the Argentinian drove Enzo Ferrari's car to victory in the British Grand Prix at Silverstone.

Did You Know That?
In the first GP of the 1951 season, the Swiss, Gonzalez drove for Talbot-Lago-Talbot and retired from the race after an oil pump failure on lap 10. He moved to Ferrari in time for the French GP.

❀ A BEAUTIFUL MACHINE ❀

Colin Chapman's 1962 Lotus 25 is considered by racing enthusiasts to be the most beautiful F1 car ever made. Jim Clark drove the car to F1 World Championship glory for driver and constructor in 1963. It was the first F1 car to use a monocoque chassis and during its racing years, 1962–64, it won 13 GPs, secured 17 pole positions and set 13 fastest laps. It had a Coventry Climax V8 engine with 1,496cc/1,95bhp at 9,800rpm.

❀ HUNGARY FOR SUCCESS ❀

On 24 August 2003, Zsolt Baumgartner became Hungary's first and, to date, only Formula One driver when he participated in his home Grand Prix, substituting for the injured Ralph Firman. However, it was a disappointing maiden race as Baumgartner was forced to retire his Jordan-Ford with engine failure on lap 34.

✪ 1992 DRIVERS' WORLD CHAMPIONSHIP ✪

Pos	Driver	Nationality	Team	Pts
1.	Nigel Mansell	British	Williams-Renault	108
2.	Riccardo Patrese	Italian	Williams-Renault	56
3.	Michael Schumacher	German	Benetton-Ford	53
4.	Ayrton Senna	Brazilian	McLaren-Honda	50
5.	Gerhard Berger	Austrian	McLaren-Honda	49
6.	Martin Brundle	British	Benetton-Ford	38
7.	Jean Alesi	French	Ferrari	18
8.	Mika Hakkinen	Finnish	Lotus-Ford	11
9.	Andrea de Cesaris	Italian	Tyrrell-llmor	8
10.	Michele Alboreto	Italian	Footwork-Mugen-Honda	6

✪ 1992 CONSTRUCTORS' CUP ✪

Pos	Constructor	Pts
1.	Williams-Renault	164
2.	McLaren-Honda	99
3.	Benetton-Ford	91
4.	Ferrari	21
5.	Lotus-Ford	13
6.	Tyrrell-Ilmor	8
7.	Footwork-Mugen-Honda	6
8.	Ligier-Renault	6
9.	March-Ilmor	3
10.	Dallara-Ferrari	2

✪ KNIGHTS OF THE ROAD ✪

Three F1 drivers have received knighthoods from the Queen:

Sir Jack Brabham OBE • Sir Stirling Moss OBE
Sir Jackie Stewart OBE

✪ SCHUMI IGNORES BLACK FLAG ✪

At the 1994 British Grand Prix at Silverstone, Michael Schumacher (Benetton-Ford) broke grid order when he passed pole-sitter Damon Hill (Williams-Renault) on the parade lap. Race officials waved the black flag, but Schumacher ignored it and finished runner-up to Hill in the race. The German's second place was taken away from him and he was handed a two-race ban, although it was subsequently deferred.

❀ FANTASY SOUTH AMERICAN STARTING GRID ❀

(up to the end of the 2013 season)

1
Ayrton Senna (Bra)
(41 GP wins, 161 GPs, World champion 1988, 1990, 1991)

2
Juan Manuel Fangio (Arg) *(25 GP wins, 51 GPs, World champion 1951, 1954, 1955, 1956, 1957)*

3
Nelson Piquet (Bra) *(23 GP wins, 204 GPs, World champion 1981, 1983, 1987)*

4
Emerson Fittipaldi (Bra) *(14 GP wins, 144 GPs, World champion 1972, 1974)*

5
Carlos Reutemann (Arg) *(12 GP wins, 146 GPs, World champion best 2nd 1981)*

6
Felipe Massa (Bra) (Bra) *(11 GP wins, 193 GPs, World champion best 2nd 2008)*

7
Rubens Barrichello (Bra) *(11 GP wins, 326 GPs, World champion best 2nd 2002, 2004)*

8
Juan Pablo Montoya (Col) *(7 GP wins, 95 GPs World champion best 3rd 2002, 2003)*

9
Jose Froilan Gonzalez (Arg) *(2 GP wins, 26 GPs, World champion best 2nd 1954)*

10
Carlos Pace (Bra) *(1 GP win, 72 GPs, World champion best 6th 1975)*

❂ A BRITISH 1-2-3 DOUBLE ❂

In the 1965 season British drivers dominated the World Drivers' Championship for the second year in succession, with Jim Clark (Lotus-BRM, Lotus-Climax and Lotus-Ford) finishing first, Graham Hill (BRM) second and Jackie Stewart (BRM) third.

❂ CHAOS IN SPAIN ❂

At the 1975 Spanish Grand Prix a dispute over safety standards at the Montjuich track almost resulted in a walk-out by the drivers. During the race, half of the drivers crashed and Rolf Stommelen's rear wing of his Hill-Ford broke on lap 25, killing several spectators and forcing him out of the race. The race was stopped after 29 laps and victory was awarded to Jochen Mass (McLaren-Ford).

❂ F1'S FIRST CENTENARIAN ❂

Paul Pietsch was born in Freiburg, Germany on 20 June 1911. In 1932, he began his motor racing career with a privately owned Bugatti and Alfa Romeo. In the 1935 German GP he raced for Auto Union and was 3rd in the Italian GP. Away from the track, Pietsch founded *Das Auto* and his company Motor-Presse-Stuttgart has become Germany's leading motorcycle and automobile magazine publisher. After 1937 he raced in his privately owned Maserati and drove in three Grands Prix, debuting at Monza on 3 September 1950, in last race of the inaugural World Championship season. In 1951 and 1952 he competed in the German Grands Prix, but failed to finish any of his World Championship races. He died, aged 100, on 31 May 2012.

❂ 15 CARS CRASH AT BRITISH GP ❂

No fewer than 15 cars crashed during the rain-soaked British Grand Prix at Silverstone on 19 July 1975. The race was won by Emerson Fittipaldi (McLaren-Ford). Surprisingly, it was the two-times F1 World Champion's last ever GP victory.

❂ CLARK'S MAGNIFICENT SEVEN ❂

Jim Clark (Lotus-Climax), won seven of the 10 Grands Prix raced to win the World Drivers' Championship in the 1963 season. It was a sweet success for Clark following his disappointment in 1962, when he lost the World Championship in the final race.

❀ 1993 DRIVERS' WORLD CHAMPIONSHIP ❀

Pos	Driver	Nationality	Team	Pts
1.	Alain Prost	French	Williams-Renault	99
2.	Ayrton Senna	Brazilian	McLaren-Ford	73
3.	Damon Hill	British	Williams-Renault	69
4.	Michael Schumacher	German	Benetton-Ford	52
5.	Riccardo Patrese	Italian	Benetton-Ford	20
6.	Jean Alesi	French	Ferrari	16
7.	Martin Brundle	British	Ligier-Renault	13
8.	Gerhard Berger	Austrian	Ferrari	12
9.	Johnny Herbert	British	Lotus-Ford	11
10.	Mark Blundell	British	Ligier-Renault	10

❀ 1993 CONSTRUCTORS' CUP ❀

Pos	Constructor	Pts
1.	Williams-Renault	168
2.	McLaren-Ford	84
3.	Benetton-Ford	72
4.	Ferrari	28
5.	Ligier-Renault	23
6.	Lotus-Ford	12
7.	Sauber	12
8.	Minardi-Ford	7
9.	Footwork-Mugen-Honda	4
10.	Larrousse-Lamborghini	3

❀ DUAL DRIVE ❀

Despite being a Maserati driver for the 1956 F1 season, Stirling Moss won the 1956 International Trophy driving for owner Tony Vandervell's Vanwall team.

❀ NIGEL'S SILVERSTONE HAT-TRICK ❀

At the 1991 British Grand Prix, Nigel Mansell (Williams-Renault) took pole position, had the fastest lap in the race and won the GP by +42.293 seconds from Gerhard Berger (McLaren-Honda) much to the delight of his adoring fans at Silverstone. With half of the season gone, Ayrton Senna (McLaren-Honda) led the Drivers' Championship table on 51 points, followed by Mansell on 33, Riccardo Patrese (Williams-Renault) on 22 and Alain Prost (Ferrari) on 21.

⊛ F1 DRIVERS' NICKNAMES ⊛

Fernando Alonso – Matador
Mario Andretti – *Piedone*
Alberto Ascari – *Ciccio* (Chubby)
Rubens Barrichello – Rubinho
Mike Beuttler – Blocker
Jack Brabham – Black Jack
Vitorio Brambilla – The Gorilla
Louis Chiron – *Le Vieux Renard* (The Old Fox)
David Coulthard – DC
Andrea De Cesaris – De Crasheris
Juan Manuel Fangio – *El Chueco* (Bandy Legs) and Maestro
Giancarlo Fisichella – *Fisico* (Fizzy)
Emerson Fittipaldi – *O rato* (The Mouse)
Froilan Gonzalez – The Pampas Bull
Mika Hakkinen – The Flying Finn
Nick Heidfeld – Quick Nick
Graham Hill – Mr Monaco
Denny Hulme – The Bear
James Hunt – Hunt The Shunt
Lella Lombardi – The Tyger
Nigel Mansell – *Il Leone*
Pierluigi Martini – *Puffo* (Smurf)
Carlos Pace – *O moco*
Sergio Perez – The Mexican Wunderkind
Ronnie Petersen – SuperSwede and The Flying Swede
Alain Prost – The Professor
Kimi Raikkonen – Iceman
Carlos Reutemann – *Lole*
Nico Rosberg – Britney
Jody Scheckter – Baby Bear
Michael Schumacher – Schumi and The Red Baron
Ralf Schumacher – Schumi II
Raymond Sommer – *Coeur de Lion* (Lionheart)

⊛ A RARE DOUBLE ⊛

A few weeks after winning the rain-soaked 1966 Belgian Grand Prix at Spa in a Ferrari, John Surtees fell out with the Scuderia outfit and joined Cooper-Maserati. When he won the final race of the 1966 season, the Mexican Grand Prix, he recorded a rare double by winning a GP in the same season for two different works teams.

❀ FAST TALK (16) ❀

"Some drivers are totally willing to accept what their teams tell
them – namely that they're at the bottom of the food chain. You
know, 'You're here to drive, nothing more.'"
Jacques Villeneuve

❀ 1961–1990 ❀

9-6-4-3-2-1 points awarded to the first six placed drivers.

❀ ARNOUX THE UNWANTED WINNER ❀

Rene Arnoux took his home town GP, the French in 1982, but he
was not the driver the Renault team wanted to win. After briefly
leading the race, Arnoux was overtaken by Riccardo Patrese and
Nelson Piquet on lap three, but then Patrese suffered engine
failure before Piquet also had to leave the race for the same reason.
Arnoux then retook the lead but received an order from the pit to
allow his team-mate, Alain Prost, who was lying second, to pass
him. However, Arnoux disobeyed the order and won, much to the
annoyance of the Renault management team and Prost.

❀ INDY FIRST ❀

The 2000 US Grand Prix, staged at the Indianapolis Motor Speedway,
was the first since 1991 (Phoenix), and was the first ever F1 GP staged
within the confines of a facility housing a 2½-mile oval track.

Did You Know That?
The addition of a road course was the first reconfiguration at the
Indianapolis Motor Speedway circuit since it was built in 1909.
However, a road course through the infield did feature in the original
plans for the Indianapolis Motor Speedway drawn up by Carl Fisher,
the founder of the course.

❀ HUNT BRAVES WEATHER TO TAKE CROWN ❀

In the final Grand Prix of the 1976 season, the Japanese GP at Fuji,
torrential rain soaked the track. The reigning World Champion,
Niki Lauda (Ferrari), who was leading the drivers' table at the time
by three points, refused to race, leaving the door open for James
Hunt (McLaren-Ford) to finish third and take the drivers' crown.

❂ MICHAEL SCHUMACHER ❂

Michael Schumacher was born on 3 January 1969 in Hurth-Hermuheim, Germany. Most Drivers' World Championships, most Grand Prix victories, most World Championship points and most pole positions make it hard to argue that Schumi is sport's the greatest ever driver. Possessing a steely determination, extreme bravery, tactical genius and the desire to go even faster; he was the ultimate driving machine

Michael began his racing career driving karts aged just 4½, and in 1987 he won the German Karting Championship. In 1988, he drove in both the Formula Ford and Formula Three series, winning the 1990 German Formula Three Championship. Also in 1990 he competed in the World Sportscar Championships for Mercedes. On 25 August 1991, Michael made his F1 debut driving for Jordan-Ford in the Belgian Grand Prix. He was poached by Benetton and in his first race for them, the 1991 Italian Grand Prix, finished fifth to win his first World Championship points. .

Schumi's first F1 victory came in the 1992 Belgian Grand Prix and he finished third in the Drivers' Championship. A year later, he won in Portugal and was fourth in the Drivers' Championship. Michael won the first of his seven World Championships in 1994, winning eight GPs. In 1995 Schumi's Benetton-Ford was practically unstoppable as he won nine GPs to claim back-to-back world titles. Schumi joined Ferrari in 1996, but their car was no match for the Williams-Renault of Damon Hill. In the 1997 season finale, at Jerez, Michael – leading the World Drivers' Championship race by one point – swerved his Ferrari into Jacques Villeneuve's Williams-Renault. He went out, but Villeneuve raced on to finish third, and to take the title. Schumi's punishment was to have his second-place finish in the Championship removed and he was placed last. In 1998 Mika Hakkinen (McLaren-Mercedes) pipped him to the World title in the final race of the season. A broken leg, at the 1999 British GP, curtailed his season that year.

Michael bounced back in 2000, recording nine wins and taking his third world title, but his first for Ferrari. For five seasons 2000–2004, Schumi and Ferrari blasted the opposition away, until Fernando Alonso snatched the 2005 World Championship. On 10 September 2006, just after winning the Italian Grand Prix – his 90th – Michael announced he would be retiring from racing after the season. There was no fairy-tale finish with an eighth World Drivers' Championship, but he did finish a narrow second to Alonso (Renault).

In 2010, Michael returned to F1, driving for Mercedes and stayed with the team until 2012. He failed to add to his tally of 91 GP wins, and, in fact, achieved only one podium finish, the 2012 European GP.

❖ 1994 DRIVERS' WORLD CHAMPIONSHIP ❖

Pos	Driver	Nationality	Team	Pts
1.	Michael Schumacher	German	Benetton-Ford	92
2.	Damon Hill	British	Williams-Renault	91
3.	Gerhard Berger	Austrian	Ferrari	41
4.	Mika Hakkinen	Finnish	McLaren-Peugeot	26
5.	Jean Alesi	French	Ferrari	24
6.	Rubens Barrichello	Brazilian	Jordan-Hart	19
7.	Martin Brundle	British	McLaren-Peugeot	16
8.	David Coulthard	British	Williams-Renault	14
9.	Nigel Mansell	British	Williams-Renault	13
10.	Jos Verstappen	Dutch	Benetton-Ford	10

❖ 1994 CONSTRUCTORS' CUP ❖

Pos	Constructor	Pts
1.	Williams-Renault	118
2.	Benetton-Ford	103
3.	Ferrari	71
4.	McLaren-Peugeot	42
5.	Jordan-Hart	28
6.	Ligier-Renault	13
7.	Tyrrell-Yamaha	13
8.	Sauber-Mercedes	12
9.	Footwork-Ford	9
10.	Minardi-Ford	5

❖ THE LUXEMBOURG GRAND PRIX ❖

The Luxembourg Grand Prix was staged twice and raced at the Nurburgring, Germany, both times. Jacques Villeneuve (Williams-McLaren) won the inaugural Luxembourg GP in 1997 and Mika Hakkinen (McLaren-Mercedes) won in 1998.

Did You Know That?

The Nurburgring hosted the German GP 23 times from 1951 to 1985 and will alternate with Hockenheim as the venue from 2007.

❖ YARDLEY DUMPS BRM ❖

In 1972, Yardley left Brabham and took up sponsorship of a rejuvenated McLaren racing team.

❀ THE MONZA GORILLA ❀

In 1957 Vittorio Brambilla, nicknamed "The Monza Gorilla", began racing motor-cycles and won the Italian national 175cc title in 1958. He also raced go-karts before becoming a mechanic for his brother, Tino. In 1968 Brambilla returned to racing in Formula Three and won the Italian F3 Championship in 1972, while at the same time also racing in Formula Two with Team March. After winning a few F2 races, and with the financial support of Beta Tools, he bought his way into Formula One in 1974 with the March factory team. Brambilla managed just one F1 victory in his career, the 1975 Austrian GP.

❀ THE BIRTH OF SPONSORSHIP ❀

Overt sponsorship commenced in the world of Formula One in 1968. Colin Chapman's green and yellow Lotuses were now red, white and gold following sponsorship by Gold Leaf cigarettes.

❀ INDY CHAMP LIGHTS UP F1 ❀

On 28 April 1996, Jacques Villeneuve (Williams-Renault) achieved his first victory in Formula One, in the European Grand Prix at the Nurburgring. The young Canadian went on to win three more GPs in his rookie season and ended the year as runner-up in the World Championship to his team-mate, Damon Hill.

Did You Know That?
Jacques Villeneuve won the 1995 Indy Car Championship.

❀ BURNING RUBBER ❀

The following tyre manufacturers have been, or are currently, involved in F1:

Englebert (1950, 1954–58)
Firestone (1950–60, 1966–75)
Pirelli (1950–59, 1981–86, 1989–91, 2011–date)
Continental (1954–55, 1958)
Avon (1958, 1981–82)
Dunlop (1958–66, 1968–70, 1976–77)
Goodyear (1960, 1964–98)
Bridgestone (1976–77, 1997–2010)
Michelin (1977–84, 2001–06)

❀ 1995 DRIVERS' WORLD CHAMPIONSHIP ❀

Pos	Driver	Nationality	Team	Pts
1.	Michael Schumacher	German	Benetton-Renault	102
2.	Damon Hill	British	Williams-Renault	69
3.	David Coulthard	British	Williams-Renault	49
4.	Johnny Herbert	British	Benetton-Renault	45
5.	Jean Alesi	French	Ferrari	42
6.	Gerhard Berger	Austrian	Ferrari	31
7.	Mika Hakkinen	Finnish	McLaren-Mercedes	17
8.	Olivier Panis	French	Ligier-Mugen-Honda	16
9.	Heinz-Harald Frentzen	German	Sauber-Ford	15
10.	Mark Blundell	British	McLaren-Mercedes	13

❀ 1995 CONSTRUCTORS' CUP ❀

Pos	Constructor	Pts
1.	Benetton-Renault	137
2.	Williams-Renault	112
3.	Ferrari	73
4.	McLaren-Mercedes	30
5.	Ligier-Mugen-Honda	24
6.	Jordan-Peugeot	21
7.	Sauber-Ford	18
8.	Footwork-Hart	5
9.	Tyrrell-Yamaha	5
10.	Minardi-Ford	1

❀ SENNA DISQUALIFIED ❀

In the opening Grand Prix of the 1988 season in Brazil, Ayrton Senna (McLaren-Honda) started his amazing series of pole positions, 13 poles in 16 starts, in his hometown GP. However, just before the race began he had a gearbox failure resulting in the start being cancelled. Senna had to drive his T-car and start from the pit, which would lead to his disqualification later.

❀ NEW FACES IN '90 ❀

David Brabham, Claudio Langes, Martin Donnelly, Gianni Morbidelli and Jyrki Jarvilehto Letho all made their Formula One GP debuts in 1990. Meanwhile, Team Life also entered Formula One racing in 1990.

❀ FORMER F1 CIRCUITS ❀

The following 51 circuits were not on the calendar for the 2013 Formula One season. Some have been redeveloped and will never reappear, while others, such as Hockenheim in Germany, are still in regular use.

Circuit	Country*	First GP	Last GP	No.
Buenos Aires	Argentina	1953	1998	20
Adelaide	Australia	1985	1995	11
A1/Osterreichring	Austria	1970	1987	18
Zeltweg	Austria	1964	1964	1
Zolder	Belgium	1973	1984	10
Nivelles-Baulers	Belgium	1972	1974	2
Rio de Janeiro	Brazil	1978	1989	10
Mont Tremblant	Canada	1968	1970	2
Mosport Park	Canada	1967	1977	8
Aintree	England (Britain)	1955	1962	5
Brands Hatch	England (GB/EUR)	1964	1986	12
Donington Park	England (Europe)	1993	1993	1
Le Mans	France	1967	1967	1
Paul Ricard	France	1971	1990	14
Clermont-Ferrand	France	1965	1972	4
Dijon-Prenois	France	1974	1984	6
Magny-Cours	France	1991	2008	18
Reims-Gueux	France	1950	1966	11
Rouen-Les-Essarts	France	1952	1968	5
AVUS	Germany	1959	1959	1
Hockenheim	Germany	1970	2012	33
Imola	Italy (San Marino)	1980	2006	27
Pescara	Italy	1957	1957	1
Fuji	Japan	1976	2008	4
Tanaka	Japan (Pacific)	1994	1995	2
Hermanos Rodriguez	Mexico	1963	1992	15
Agadir	Morocco	1954	1956	3
Ain-Diab	Morocco	1957	1958	2
Zandvoort	Netherlands	1952	1985	29
Boavista	Portugal	1958	1960	2
Monsanto Park	Portugal	1959	1959	1
Estoril	Portugal	1984	1996	13
East London	South Africa	1962	1965	3
Kyalami	South Africa	1967	1993	20
Barcelona (Monjuich)	Spain	1969	1975	4
Barcelona (Pedralbes)	Spain	1951	1954	2

Circuit	Country*	First GP	Last GP	No.
Jarama	Spain	1981	1981	1
Jerez	Spain (Europe)	1994	1997	2
Valencia	Spain (Europe)	2008	2012	2
Anderstorp Raceway	Sweden	1973	1978	6
Bremgarten	Switzerland	1950	1954	5
Istanbul Park	Turkey	2005	2011	7
Caesars Palace	USA	1981	1982	2
Dallas Fair Park	USA	1984	1984	1
Detroit	USA	1983	1988	6
Indianapolis	USA	1950	2007	19
Long Beach	USA	1983	1983	1
Phoenix	USA	1989	1991	3
Riverside	USA	1960	1960	1
Sebring	USA	1959	1959	1
Watkins Glen	USA	1961	1980	20

* Parentheses denote that another national Grand Prix was staged there. Imola (Italy) was the long-time host of the San Marino GP, while Brands Hatch (England) also hosted the European GP.

❁ ACTIVE SUSPENSION WINS IN ITALY ❁

For the 1987 Italian Grand Prix, Nelson Piquet finally managed to convince Williams-Honda to use their active suspension. Piquet rewarded the team with pole position and the chequered flag to become the first driver to win a Formula One race using active suspension.

Did You Know That?
During the last three laps of the 1987 Italian GP, first Nelson Piquet and then Ayrton Senna (Lotus-Honda) broke the track records. However, Piquet managed to cross the winning line in 1:14'47.707, 1.806 seconds ahead of his fellow countryman. Indeed, the racing in the final stages of the GP had been so intense that the race director forgot to wave the flag in time to greet Piquet crossing the line, much to the delight of the crowd.

❁ NOT SO SUPER ❁

Super Aguri was a short-lived team. They began in 2006 but, four races into 2008, with drivers Takuma Sato and Anthony Davidson perpetual also-rans, they withrew from Formula One. Overall, Super Aguri collected just four points in 39 races.

✪ SUPERMAN AT THE MONACO GP ✪

At the 2006 Monaco GP, Red Bull Racing continued with their trend of promoting blockbuster movies when they adopted Warner Bros' new *Superman Returns* movie as the theme for the race. Red Bull Racing turned their famous floating Energy Station into the movie's Daily Planet Headquarters for the GP. Drivers David Coulthard and Christian Klein also carried logos for the movie on their spoilers. Coulthard finished third in the GP to claim the team's maiden podium finish and in true Hollywood style, Coulthard stepped on to the podium to collect his prize wearing the famous crime fighter's red cape.

✪ PORSCHE SECURE FIRST GP WIN ✪

On 8 July 1962, Dan Gurney gave Porsche their first ever victory in Formula One when he won the French Grand Prix at Rouen. Unusually, the first four GPs of the 1962 season were won by four different marques.

✪ SCHUMACHER SWITCHES CAMPS ✪

After the 1991 Belgian Grand Prix, Benetton fired Roberto Moreno, who had finished in fourth place in the race, and replaced him with Michael Schumacher (Jordan-Ford) for the Italian Grand Prix. Moreno moved in the opposite direction and was later awarded US$500,000 by an Italian court for unfair dismissal. Schumacher finished the Italian GP in fifth place for his new team, while Moreno's race was over after two laps when he spun off the track.

✪ RALF ENJOYS SEVEN-UP ✪

When Ralf Schumacher (Williams-BMW) finished in fourth place in the 2003 Monaco GP, it was the seventh consecutive race of the 2003 F1 season that he finished in the points.

✪ PIRONI SHATTERS HIS LEGS ✪

During the Saturday practice at the 1982 German Grand Prix, Didier Pironi of Ferrari had his legs broken in a huge shunt on a very wet Hockenheim track. It was raining heavily, so Pironi did not see Alain Prost's Renault slowing down and he crashed into the back of the French driver and then spun into the barriers.

❀ 1996 DRIVERS' WORLD CHAMPIONSHIP ❀

Pos	Driver	Nationality	Team	Pts
1.	Damon Hill	British	Williams-Renault	97
2.	Jacques Villeneuve	Canadian	Williams-Renault	78
3.	Michael Schumacher	German	Ferrari	59
4.	Jean Alesi	French	Benetton-Renault	47
5.	Mika Hakkinen	Finnish	McLaren-Mercedes	31
6.	Gerhard Berger	Austrian	Benetton-Renault	21
7.	David Coulthard	British	McLaren-Mercedes	18
8.	Rubens Barrichello	Brazilian	Jordan-Peugeot	14
9.	Olivier Panis	French	Ligier-Mugen-Honda	13
10.	Eddie Irvine	British	Ferrari	11

❀ 1996 CONSTRUCTORS' CUP ❀

Pos	Constructor	Pts
1.	Williams-Renault	175
2.	Ferrari	70
3.	Benetton-Renault	68
4.	McLaren-Mercedes	49
5.	Jordan-Peugeot	22
6.	Ligier-Mugen-Honda	15
7.	Sauber-Ford	11
8.	Tyrrell-Yamaha	5
9.	Footwork-Hart	1

❀ FAST TALK (17) ❀

"Racing drivers have balls, unfortunately, none of them are crystal."
David Coulthard

❀ ROYAL FAMILY ATTEND INAUGURAL GP ❀

On 13 May 1950, the Royal Family attended the inaugural Formula One Grand Prix, the British, which was won by Giuseppe (Nino) Farina in his Alfa Romeo at Silverstone. Farina also had the honour of securing Formula One's first ever pole position.

Did You Know That?
A total of 21 cars participated in the first ever official Formula One Grand Prix but, following a disappointing year in 1949, Ferrari was absent.

❂ A MAN OF MANY AWARDS ❂

In 1985, Alain Prost was awarded "Legion d'Honneur" (France); in 1988 the Grand Prix Former Drivers' Club awarded him the "Champion of Champions" award; in 1993 he received an OBE from Queen Elizabeth II (England) and in 1999, he was inducted into the "International Motorsports Hall of Fame".

❂ PIQUET ALMOST HAS ORGASM IN HIS CAR ❂

Nigel Mansell (Williams-Renault) was comfortably leading the 1991 Canadian Grand Prix from Nelson Piquet (Benetton-Ford) going into the last lap of the race and was celebrating victory with the crowd when suddenly electrical problems caused his engine to cut out. When Piquet's pit crew told him that Mansell was out of the race he could hardly believe his luck. After claiming an unlikely win the Brazilian said: "I laughed a lot and almost had an orgasm."

❂ HAWTHORN THE FIRST BRIT ❂

On 5 July 1953, Mike Hawthorn became the first British driver to win a Formula One race. Mike drove to victory in the French Grand Prix at Reims for Ferrari. Juan Manuel Fangio and Jose Froilan Gonzalez trailed behind in their Ferraris.

❂ GETTING CLOSE ❂

In the penultimate race of the 1981 season, the Canadian Grand Prix, Jacques Laffite claimed victory in his Ligier-Matra on a very wet track. But the local boy, Gilles Villeneuve, had an amazing race. After damaging his front wing in a collision he still managed to race on and claim third place on the podium, much to the delight of the crowd. Nelson Piquet came fifth and now had 48 Championship points, with Carlos Reutemann on 49, Laffite on 43, and Alan Jones and Alain Prost both on 37.

❂ BAR ENTERS F1 ❂

On 7 March 1999, British American Racing (BAR) entered its first ever F1 GP. BAR-Supertec, who had bought over Tyrrell in 1998, had a disappointing start to life in F1 when Jacques Villeneuve suffered a broken wing after 13 laps of racing and Ricardo Zonta retired with gearbox failure after lap 48.

❂ 1997 DRIVERS' WORLD CHAMPIONSHIP ❂

Pos	Driver	Nationality	Team	Pts
1.	Jacques Villeneuve	Canadian	Williams-Renault	81
2.	Heinz-Harald Frentzen	German	Williams-Renault	42
3.	David Coulthard	British	McLaren-Mercedes	36
4.	Jean Alesi	French	Benetton-Renault	36
5.	Gerhard Berger	Austrian	Benetton-Renault	27
6.	Mika Hakkinen	Finnish	McLaren-Mercedes	27
7.	Eddie Irvine	British	Ferrari	24
8.	Giancarlo Fisichella	Italian	Jordan-Peugeot	20
9.	Olivier Panis	French	Prost-Mugen-Honda	16
10.	Johnny Herbert	British	Sauber-Petronas	15

❂ 1997 CONSTRUCTORS' CUP ❂

Pos	Constructor	Pts
1.	Williams-Renault	123
2.	Ferrari	102
3.	Benetton-Renault	67
4.	McLaren-Mercedes	63
5.	Jordan-Peugeot	33
6.	Prost-Mugen-Honda	21
7.	Sauber-Petronas	16
8.	Arrows-Yamaha	9
9.	Stewart-Ford	6
10.	Tyrrell-Ford	2

❂ FRANCE'S SECOND ❂

When Francois Cevert (Tyrrell-Ford) won the final Grand Prix of the 1971 season, the US Grand Prix at Watkins Glen, he became only the second French driver to take the chequered flag in Formula One following Maurice Trintignant's two GP wins at Monaco in 1955 and again in 1958. The win helped Cevert to third place in the 1971 Drivers' World Championship behind Jacky Ickx (Ferrari) and the World Champion, Jackie Stewart (Tyrrell-Ford). Two years later, at the 1973 US Grand Prix, Cevert was tragically killed during the Saturday practice session at the age of 29.

Did You Know That?
In 1972 Francois Cevert, along with Howden Ganley, finished second in the Le Mans 24 Hours race driving a Matra-Simca 670.

❂ AYRTON SENNA ❂

Ayrton Senna da Silva was born on 21 March 1960 in Sao Paulo, Brazil. When he was four years old his father, Milton bought Ayrton a kart. Nine years later he entered karting competitions, and in 1977 he won the South American Karting Championship. In 1981 Senna left Brazil and moved to Europe, where he became a British Formula Ford 1600 driver, and around the same time he adopted his mother's maiden name, Senna.

In 1982 Senna won both the British and European Formula Ford 2000 Championships. The following year he won the British Formula Three Championship and in 1984, after periods as a test driver for Brabham, McLaren, Toleman and Williams, he was given his F1 chance by the Toleman-Hart racing team. On 25 March 1984, Senna participated in his first Grand Prix, the Brazilian, but left the race when his turbo broke after just eight laps. In his very next GP, the South African at Kyalami, Senna scored his first F1 Championship point. Fittingly, his first podium place came in the 1984 Monaco Grand Prix, a race he would make his own over the following years, when he finished second.

Senna bought out the year left on his contract with Toleman-Hart, and in 1985 he joined Lotus-Renault. In the opening Grand Prix of the 1985 season, the Brazilian, he secured the first of his 65 career pole positions (only Michael Schumacher has more). Next came the Portuguese Grand Prix, on 21 April 1985 in Estoril, where Senna recorded his first GP win after again taking pole position. He finished in fourth place with Lotus in the F1 Drivers' Championship in both 1985 and 1986, and in 1987 he was third.

In 1988 Senna joined McLaren-Honda as number two to Alain Prost. Between them, they won 15 of the 16 GPs raced in 1988, culminating in Senna winning his first World Championship. The following year the Prost–Senna rivalry continued on and off the track, but it was Prost who captured his third world title after their infamous Suzuka chicane incident in the 1989 Japanese Grand Prix when their cars collided. A year later, on the same circuit, Senna and Prost once again collided, only this time it handed Senna his second drivers' crown. In 1991 Senna won his third World Championship driving for McLaren-Honda. Over the next two years Williams-Renault dominated Formula One and Senna finished fourth in 1992 (McLaren-Honda) and runner-up in 1993 (McLaren-Ford). On 1 May 1994 the world of F1 mourned the death of a true legend when Ayrton Senna crashed and died in the San Marino Grand Prix. He took part in 161 Grands Prix and won 41 of them.

❀ LAST TO FIRST ❀

During the 1970s, Larry Perkins from Australia raced in 15 FI GPs but failed to secure a single championship point. After F1, he returned to Australia and to sports car racing, winning the Bathurst 1,000 on six occasions (1982, 1983, 1984, 1993, 1995 & 1997).

Did You Know That?
During the 1995 Bathurst 1,000 race, Perkins was forced to pit on lap one with a blown tyre. When he was in the pits he was lapped in the race. Amazingly he took the lead with fewer than 10 laps remaining, after Glenn Seton's car was forced to retire with mechanical problems. Perkins went on to win and became only the second person in the history of the race to secure victory from last place.

❀ YEAR OF THE LION ❀

In 1992 one man dominated the world of Formula One, and that man was Britain's Nigel Mansell. On his way to claiming the F1 drivers' crown he won the opening five Grands Prix of the season in his Williams-Renault and followed them up with four further wins to obliterate the opposition. Seldom has a man dominated the F1 World Championship to the extent that Nigel did, finishing the season a massive 52 points ahead of the second-placed driver, his Williams-Honda team-mate Riccardo Patrese.

Did You Know That?
Nigel Mansell claimed the 1992 F1 title with five races remaining.

❀ ONE CAR, SIX WHEELS ❀

In 1976, Ken Tyrrell stunned the F1 world by introducing a six-wheeled car. His Tyrrell P34 had a pair of small front wheels placed one behind the other and supported by two standard-sized wheels at the rear. The thinking behind its design was that the car's reduced frontal area would result in less drag and therefore create better airflow to the rear wing. The extra rubber would also improve road-holding and braking.

❀ PRANCING HORSE RULES F1 ❀

In the 1952 season, Ferrari drivers occupied the top four places in the Drivers' Championship table.

❀ SCOT IS TOP OF US POPS ❀

In 1973 Jackie Stewart received *Sports Illustrated* magazine's 1973 "Sportsman of the Year" award, the only racing driver ever to win the prestigious title.

❀ LUCKY 13 FOR SENNA ❀

On his way to claiming the first of his three Formula One World Drivers' Championships in 1988, Ayrton Senna (McLaren-Honda), took a record-shattering 13 pole positions from the 16 GPs he raced in. The previous record had been nine pole positions, held by Ronnie Peterson, Niki Lauda and Nelson Piquet. The three poles not won by Senna were:

Grand Prix	Date	Pole Position
French	03/07/1988	Alain Prost
British	10/07/1988	Gerhard Berger
Portuguese	25/09/1988	Alain Prost

❀ FORMULA ONE IN THE USA ❀

Between 1950 and 1960, the Indianapolis 500 was considered to be a round of the Formula One World Championship. Although Jim Clark and Graham Hill both won the race, their successes came after it was no longer on the Formula One World Championship calendar. Here are the winners of the Indianapolis 500 when the race was for World Championship points:

1950	Lee Wallard	1956	Pat Flaherty
1951	Johnnie Parsons	1957	Sam Hanks
1952	Troy Ruttman	1958	Jimmy Bryan
1953	Bill Vukovich	1959	Rodger Ward
1954	Bill Vukovich	1960	Jim Rathman
1955	Bob Seikert		

❀ NO CAR FOR SECOND DRIVER ❀

At the start of the 1984 F1 season, FISA decided that second drivers of teams that officially entered only one car were not eligible for points. This new rule affected Jo Gartner (Osella-Alfa Romeo) and Gerhard Berger (ATS-BMW), who finished fifth and sixth at the Italian Grand Prix. Their points were not redistributed.

❂ 1998 DRIVERS' WORLD CHAMPIONSHIP ❂

Pos	Driver	Nationality	Team	Pts
1.	Mika Hakkinen	Finnish	McLaren-Mercedes	100
2.	Michael Schumacher	German	Ferrari	86
3.	David Coulthard	British	McLaren-Mercedes	56
4.	Eddie Irvine	British	Ferrari	47
5.	Jacques Villeneuve	Canadian	Williams-Mecachrome	21
6.	Damon Hill	British	Jordan-Mugen-Honda	20
7.	Heinz-Harald Frentzen	German	Williams-Mecachrome	17
8.	Alexander Wurz	Austrian	Benetton-Playlife	17
9.	Giancarlo Fisichella	Italian	Benetton-Playlife	16
10.	Ralf Schumacher	German	Jordan-Mugen-Honda	14

❂ 1998 CONSTRUCTORS' CUP ❂

Pos	Constructor	Pts
1.	McLaren-Mercedes	156
2.	Ferrari	133
3.	Williams-Mecachrome	38
4.	Jordan-Mugen-Honda	34
5.	Benetton-Playlife	33
6.	Sauber-Petronas	10
7.	Arrows	6
8.	Stewart-Ford	5
9.	Prost-Peugeot	1

❂ TURBOCHARGED ❂

On 16 July 1977, James Hunt (McLaren-Ford) won the British Grand Prix at Silverstone in a race which marked the debut of Jean-Pierre Jabouille's Renault with its V6 turbocharged engine. After 16 laps of racing Jabouille was forced to retire with a broken turbo.

❂ ALL OVER IN FOUR SECONDS ❂

Ayrton Senna (McLaren-Honda) won the 1990 Belgian Grand Prix by +3.550 seconds from World Champion Alain Prost (Ferrari). During the race Senna and Prost were battling it out for the lead when both drivers visited the pits for a change of tyres. However, Senna's mechanics managed to put their driver back in the race four seconds quicker than the Ferrari mechanics, a time difference that proved to be the turning point of the GP.

❀ FANTASY N./C. AMERICAN STARTING GRID ❀

(up to the end of the 2013 season)

1
Mario Andretti
(US) *(12 GP wins,
128 GPs, World
champion 1978)*

2
Jacques Villeneuve
(Can) *(11 GP wins,
165 GPs, World
champion 1997)*

3
Gilles Villeneuve
(Can) *(6 GP wins,
67 GPs, World
champion best 2nd
1979)*

4
Phil Hill (US)
*(4 GP wins, 48 GPs
World champion 1961)*

5
Dan Gurney (US)
*(4 GP wins, 86
GPs, World
champion best 3rd
1961)*

6
Bill Vukovich (US)
*(2 GP wins {both
Indianapolis 500},
world champion best
6th 1954)*

7
Peter Revson (US)
*(2 GP wins, 30
GPs, world
champion best 5th
1972, 1973)*

8
Pedro Rodriguez
(Mex) *(2 GP wins, 55
GPs, World champion
best 6th 1967, 1968)*

9
Bob Sweikert (US)
*(1 GP win, (only
Indianapolis 500),
world champion best
7th 1955)*

10
Jim Rathman (US)
*(1 GP win, {only
Indianapolis 500},
world champion best
8th 1960)*

❁ 1999 DRIVERS' WORLD CHAMPIONSHIP ❁

Pos	Driver	Nationality	Team	Pts
1.	Mika Hakkinen	Finnish	McLaren-Mercedes	76
2.	Eddie Irvine	British	Ferrari	74
3.	Heinz-Harald Frentzen	German	Jordan-Mugen-Honda	54
4.	David Coulthard	British	McLaren-Mercedes	48
5.	Michael Schumacher	German	Ferrari	44
6.	Ralf Schumacher	German	Williams-Supertec	35
7.	Rubens Barrichello	Brazilian	Stewart-Ford	21
8.	Johnny Herbert	British	Stewart-Ford	15
9.	Giancarlo Fisichella	Italian	Benetton-Playlife	13
10.	Mika Salo	Finnish	Ferrari	10

❁ 1999 CONSTRUCTORS' CUP ❁

Pos	Constructor	Pts
1.	Ferrari	128
2.	McLaren-Mercedes	124
3.	Jordan-Mugen-Honda	61
4.	Stewart-Ford	36
5.	Williams-Supertec	35
6.	Benetton-Playlife	16
7.	Prost-Peugeot	9
8.	Sauber-Petronas	5
9.	Arrows	1
10.	Minardi-Ford	1

❁ PELE FORGETS TO WAVE FLAG ❁

Approaching lap 70 of the 71-lap Brazilian GP in 2002, Pele, the legendary Brazilian footballer, took up his position in preparation to wave the chequered flag as the lead cars entered their final lap. However, as Michael Schumacher (Ferrari) crossed the finish line just ahead of his brother Ralf (Williams-BMW) Pele forgot to wave the flag.

❁ MOSS TAKES BROOKS'S CAR TO VICTORY ❁

At the 1957 British Grand Prix at Aintree, the engine of Stirling Moss's Vanwall gave up on him after lap 51 of the 90-lap race. He then took over the Vanwall of his team-mate, Tony Brooks, which was then placed sixth, and raced to a memorable victory.

⚘ TYRRELL THROWN OUT OF F1 ⚘

Team Tyrrell and their drivers were thrown out of the 1984 F1 World Championship and had all points (drivers' and constructors') deducted from them. FISA's decision was based on findings following a fuel sample analysis that occurred just after Martin Brundle's second place in the US East Grand Prix in Detroit. Tyrrell appealed and was only permitted to participate in four more races until FISA made their final decision. Despite support for Tyrrell from John Barnard (McLaren) and Patrick Head (Williams), FISA stood by their decision and Tyrrell packed their bags for home.

⚘ FERRARI'S NEW PRANCING HORSE ⚘

At the 2003 Spanish Grand Prix, Ferrari brought their new car, the F2003GA, and they quickly let the other teams know they were in for a testing time from the Scuderia when Michael Schumacher and Rubens Barrichello sat on the front row of the grid ahead of the local hero, Fernando Alonso (Renault). Schumacher won the race, with Alonso claiming second place in front of Barrichello. It was Michael Schumacher's 66th career GP victory.

⚘ MANSELL SPINS SENNA TO VICTORY ⚘

Going into the penultimate Grand Prix of the 1991 season in Japan, Nigel Mansell (Williams-Renault) had to win the race to stand any chance of catching Ayrton Senna (McLaren-Honda) in the fight to be World Champion. However, on the tenth lap Nigel's aggressive driving resulted in him spinning off the track as he took too big a gamble at the braking point of the main straight. Nigel's despair was Senna's ecstasy as he was now officially declared the 1991 Drivers' World Champion, his third title success. In the final lap of the GP, Senna allowed his team-mate, Gerhard Berger, to overtake him and take the chequered flag for a Honda one-two in their home GP.

⚘ FLYING SCOT MAKES IT TWO FROM THREE ⚘

In 1965 Jim Clark (Lotus-BRM, Lotus-Ford and Lotus-Climax) won his second Drivers' World Championship in three years after driving to victory in six of the season's 10 GPs. Only Graham Hill (BRM), with two GP wins, Richie Ginther (Honda) and the newcomer to F1 racing, Jackie Stewart (BRM), managed to keep the "Flying Scot" off the top place on the podium.

❀ 2000 DRIVERS' WORLD CHAMPIONSHIP ❀

Pos Driver	Nationality	Team	Pts
1. Michael Schumacher	German	Ferrari	108
2. Mika Hakkinen	Finnish	McLaren-Mercedes	89
3. David Coulthard	British	McLaren-Mercedes	73
4. Rubens Barrichello	Brazilian	Ferrari	62
5. Ralf Schumacher	German	Williams-BMW	24
6. Giancarlo Fisichella	Italian	Benetton-Playlife	18
7. Jacques Villeneuve	Canadian	BAR-Honda	17
8. Jenson Button	British	Williams-BMW	12
9. Heinz-Harald Frentzen	German	Jordan-Mugen-Honda	11
10. Jarno Trulli	Italian	Jordan-Mugen-Honda	6

❀ 2000 CONSTRUCTORS' CUP ❀

Pos	Constructor	Pts
1.	Ferrari	170
2.	McLaren-Mercedes	152
3.	Williams-BMW	36
4.	Benetton-Playlife	20
5.	BAR-Honda	20
6.	Jordan-Mugen-Honda	17
7.	Arrows-Supertec	7
8.	Sauber-Petronas	6
9.	Jaguar-Cosworth	4

❀ FAST TALK (18) ❀

"Finishing second means you are the first person to lose."
Gilles Villeneuve

❀ BERGER'S RACE ENDS IN FLAMES ❀

In the second race of the 1989 season, the San Marino Grand Prix, Gerhard Berger lost control of his Ferrari at Tamburello and his car burst into flames when it crashed into the barriers. Thankfully Berger escaped unhurt. When the race was restarted Ayrton Senna (McLaren-Honda) overtook his team-mate, Alain Prost, on the first lap and stayed in front to claim his first victory of the season. Senna's overtaking of Prost was in direct breach of the agreement both drivers made with the team owner, Ron Dennis, that no passing of a team-mate would be done in the first lap of a Grand Prix.

❀ GREEN BERET, ENGINEER AND F1 DRIVER ❀

Robert McGregor Innes Ireland, better known as Innes Ireland, won only one Grand Prix during his career, the Austrian GP in 1961. Ireland was a Scottish military officer, an engineer and a Formula One racing car driver who participated in 53 GPs. In addition to his other talents, Ireland was an accomplished writer whose autobiography was entitled *All Arms and Elbows*. He also was employed as a journalist for the *American Road & Track* magazine and captained trawlers in the North Atlantic. Later in life, Ireland was elected President of the British Racing Drivers' Club (BRDC), a position he held until he died from cancer on 22 October 1993.

Did You Know That?
Innes Ireland was commissioned as a lieutenant in the King's Own Scottish Borderers, serving with the Parachute Regiment in the Suez Canal Zone during 1953 and 1954.

❀ RAIKKONEN SECURES FIRST WIN ❀

Kimi Raikkonen won his first Grand Prix on 23 March 2003, when he drove a superb race in his McLaren-Mercedes at the Malaysian GP, the second of the 2003 season. At the end of the race the young Finnish driver led the Drivers' Championship table with 16 points, from his team-mate, David Coulthard (10).

❀ GHOST ON THE PODIUM ❀

In the opening Grand Prix of the 1983 season, the Brazilian, Keke Rosberg's Williams-Ford caught fire after a pit stop for refuelling. The car became engulfed in flames, and Rosberg jumped out of it as the marshals put the fire out. Rosberg then jumped back in his car and was given a push-start by the marshals. He drove magnificently to finish in second place behind the home crowd's favourite and reigning World Champion, Nelson Piquet in his all-conquering Brabham-BMW. When the race finished, FISA disqualified Rosberg for receiving a push-start, and so only Piquet and Niki Lauda (McLaren-Ford) appeared on the podium.

1983 Brazilian Grand Prix

Pos	Driver	Team	Laps	Time/Retired	Grid	Pts
1.	Nelson Piquet	Brabham-BMW	63	1:48'27.731	4	9
3.	Niki Lauda	McLaren-Ford	63	+ 51.883	9	4

❁ 2001 DRIVERS' WORLD CHAMPIONSHIP ❁

Pos	Driver	Nationality	Team	Pts
1.	Michael Schumacher	German	Ferrari	123
2.	David Coulthard	British	McLaren-Mercedes	65
3.	Rubens Barrichello	Brazilian	Ferrari	56
4.	Ralf Schumacher	German	Williams-BMW	49
5.	Mika Hakkinen	Finnish	McLaren-Mercedes	37
6.	Juan Pablo Montoya	Colombian	Williams-BMW	31
7.	Jacques Villeneuve	Canadian	BAR-Honda	12
8.	Nick Heidfeld	German	Sauber-Petronas	12
9.	Jarno Trulli	Italian	Jordan-Honda	12
10.	Kimi Raikkonen	Finnish	Sauber-Petronas	9

❁ 2001 CONSTRUCTORS' CUP ❁

Pos	Constructor	Pts
1.	Ferrari	179
2.	McLaren-Mercedes	102
3.	Williams-BMW	80
4.	Sauber-Petronas	21
5.	Jordan-Honda	19
6.	BAR-Honda	17
7.	Benetton-Renault	10
8.	Jaguar-Cosworth	9
9.	Prost-Acer	4
10.	Arrows-Asiatech	1

❁ F1 CARS RACE ON THE NATIONAL CIRCUIT ❁

Up until 1987, the British Grand Prix alternated between Silverstone, Aintree (1955–62, the home of horse racing's Grand National) and Brands Hatch (1964–86). In 1987 Silverstone became the main circuit for the British GP and has hosted the race every year since.

❁ NEW BULL ON THE CIRCUIT ❁

Toro Rosso succeeded Minardi at the end of the 2005 season. In their 21-year history Minardi never claimed a pole position in a Formula 1 Grand Prix, let alone won a race. Minardi's best ever qualifying position was Pierluigi Martini's second at Phoenix in the 1990 USA Grand Prix. Toro Rosso is owned by Dietrich Mateschitz, founder of the Red Bull drinks company, and the F1 team of the same name,

❀ SIR JACKIE STEWART, OBE ❀

John Young "Jackie" Stewart was born on 11 June 1939 in Milton, West Dumbartonshire, Scotland. In his early days Jackie was an excellent clay-pigeon shooter and was a member of the 1959 British team. However, in 1961 he followed his brother Jimmy's lead and entered circuit racing in a Marcos sports car. In 1963 he won two races in a Jaguar and was then entered by Ecurie Ecosse in a Tojeiro and then in a Cooper-Monaco, winning a race at Goodwood.

Ken Tyrrell signed him in 1964 for Formula Three and, after winning his first F3 race at Snetterton, he turned down a chance to move up into F1. However, in 1965 Jackie made his F1 debut and finished sixth in a BRM at the South African Grand Prix. Seven GPs later he won his first F1 race, driving for BRM in the Italian GP at Monza and finished the season third in the Drivers' World Championship. Jackie started the 1966 season in scintillating form, winning the opening race at Monaco. But his BRM was no match for Jack Brabham in his Brabham-Repco and it wasn't until 1968, at the Dutch Grand Prix, that Jackie won again. When he won at Zandvoort he was reunited with Ken Tyrrell at Matra-Ford. Jackie was runner-up to Graham Hill (Lotus-Ford) in the 1969 Drivers' Championship.

Jackie and Matra-Ford came good in 1969, as he won six of the 11 GPs raced and claimed the 1969 World Drivers' Championship. He could not retain his title in 1970, as his Matra-Ford was replaced by a March-Ford which was no match for Jochen Rindt's Lotus-Ford, and Stewart finished a disappointing sixth in the Championship. A year later Jackie moved to Tyrrell and in 1971 won six of the 11 GPs driving a Tyrrell-Ford to claim his second F1 drivers' crown. His Tyrrell-Ford was competitive in 1972, winning four times, but he was runner-up to Emerson Fittipaldi (Lotus-Ford) in the Drivers' Championship.

Jackie won his third World Championship in 1973, again for Tyrrell-Ford. He won five GPs, and his win at the Nurburgring in Germany on 5 August 1973 was his 27th GP victory, the most by any driver at the time. Indeed, it would be 14 years before his record was broken (by Alain Prost). When his team-mate, Francois Cevert, was killed in practice for the final GP of the 1973 season, the US Grand Prix at Watkins Glen, Stewart called it a day after 99 Grands Prix.

In 1990 he was inducted into the International Motorsports Hall of Fame. and, from 1997 to 2000, Jackie was head of Stewart Racing. The team recorded one victory, Johnny Herbert driving to glory at the 1999 European Grand Prix, before he sold it to Jaguar

In 2001 Jackie received a knighthood. He remains a passionate and eloquent campaigner for safety for cars and circuits in Formula 1.

❀ 2002 DRIVERS' WORLD CHAMPIONSHIP ❀

Pos	Driver	Nationality	Team	Pts
1.	Michael Schumacher	German	Ferrari	144
2.	Rubens Barrichello	Brazilian	Ferrari	77
3.	Juan Pablo Montoya	Colombian	Williams-BMW	50
4.	Ralf Schumacher	German	Williams-BMW	42
5.	David Coulthard	British	McLaren-Mercedes	41
6.	Kimi Raikkonen	Finnish	McLaren-Mercedes	24
7.	Jenson Button	British	Renault	14
8.	Jarno Trulli	Italian	Renault	9
9.	Eddie Irvine	British	Jaguar-Cosworth	8
10.	Nick Heidfeld	German	Sauber-Petronas	7

❀ 2002 CONSTRUCTORS' CUP ❀

Pos	Constructor	Pts
1.	Ferrari	221
2.	Williams-BMW	92
3.	McLaren-Mercedes	65
4.	Renault	23
5.	Sauber-Petronas	11
6.	Jordan-Honda	9
7.	Jaguar-Cosworth	8
8.	BAR-Honda	7
9.	Minardi-Asiatech	2
10.	Toyota	2

❀ MR PERSEVERANCE ❀

Andrea de Cesaris entered 208 Grands Prix during his career and never once stood on the top step of the podium.

❀ 1991–2002 ❀

10-6-4-3-2-1 points awarded to the first six placed drivers.

❀ AN EVER SO SLIM VICTORY ❀

On 5 September 1971, Peter Gethin won the Italian Grand Prix at Monza in his BRM. His winning time of 1:18'12.60 was just 0.01 second ahead of Ronnie Peterson in his March-Ford. Remarkably, he had only led four of the 55 laps raced.

❂ FAST TALK (19) ❂

"Winning is like a drug ... I can't settle for second or third in any circumstances whatsoever."
Ayrton Senna

❂ F1 CARS RACE AROUND LONDON ❂

The City of London has considered hosting the 2007 British Grand Prix on the streets of the capital. In July 2004, eight F1 cars drove on a special course laid out between Regent Street and Piccadilly Circus in a display. Nothing came of the plan and it was quietly dropped.

❂ BRABHAM WRAPS UP TITLE EARLY ❂

When Jack Brabham (Brabham-Repco) won his fourth consecutive Grand Prix, the German GP on 7 August 1966, he clinched the Formula One Drivers' Championship despite the fact that three more GPs still had to be raced (Italy, US and Mexico).

❂ MULTIPLE RACING ❂

In 1981, Michele Alboreto won Minardi's only F2 victory at Misano and then made his F1 debut at the 1981 San Marino Grand Prix for Tyrrell-Ford. On lap 31 he was involved in a collision with Beppe Gabbiani (Osella-Ford). The same year, he also partnered Riccardo Patrese to victory in the Watkins Six Hour endurance race for Lancia and helped the Italian car manufacturer to win the manufacturers' title.

❂ FABI MATCHES PIQUET TWICE ❂

In the 1984 Brazilian Grand Prix, Nelson Piquet's race was over after lap 32 with a broken engine, as was that of his Brabham-BMW team-mate Teo Fabi with turbo failure on the same lap. Three GPs later, in San Marino, Piquet's race was over after lap 48 with a broken turbo, as was Fabi's on the very same lap, also with turbo failure.

❂ SURTEES' FIRST GP WIN ❂

John Surtees claimed his first ever F1 victory at the Nurburgring in the German Grand Prix on 4 August 1963. It was the first for Ferrari since Phil Hill won the 1961 Italian GP at Monza.

❁ BOUTSEN WINS FIRST OF THREE ❁

Thierry Boutsen (Williams-Honda) won the first of his three Grands Prix at the rain-soaked 1989 Canadian GP. He also won the 1989 Australian GP and the 1990 Hungarian GP.

Did You Know That?
When Thierry Boutsen retired from racing in 1999, he formed his own aviation company, Boutsen Aviation, in Monaco.

❁ DRINK AND DRIVE ❁

On 20 March 2005 at the 2005 Malaysian GP, Toyota's Jarno Trulli took the team's first ever F1 podium position finishing second to Fernando Alonso (Renault), just one of five such finishes the team enjoyed that season.

Did You Know That?
Jarno Trulli owns his own wine vineyard in Italy.

❁ A FALL FROM GRACE ❁

After winning four consecutive F1 Drivers' Championships (1954–57), Juan Manuel Fangio (Ferrari) finished in 14th place in the drivers' table of 1958. Although he started the first Grand Prix of the season in Argentina in pole position, and recorded the fastest lap, he finished the race in fourth place and only took part in one further GP in 1958, the French, again finishing fourth.

❁ LOTUS STRUGGLE AT SPA ❁

For the first time in the history of the Lotus racing team, both Lotus cars failed to qualify for a Formula One race when both Nelson Piquet and Satoru Nakajima had engine problems prior to the 1989 Belgian Grand Prix at Spa.

❁ SPA'S BLACKEST DAY ❁

At the Belgian Grand Prix on 19 June 1960, Stirling Moss (Lotus-Climax) crashed and broke both his legs at Spa. On lap 19 of the same race, Chris Bristow crashed his Cooper-Climax, and then, on lap 24, Alan Stacey also crashed in his Lotus-Climax. Both young Britons lost their lives at Spa.

❀ 2003 DRIVERS' WORLD CHAMPIONSHIP ❀

Pos	Driver	Nationality	Team	Pts
1.	Michael Schumacher	German	Ferrari	93
2.	Kimi Raikkonen	Finnish	McLaren-Mercedes	91
3.	Juan Pablo Montoya	Colombian	Williams-BMW	82
4.	Rubens Barrichello	Brazilian	Ferrari	65
5.	Ralf Schumacher	German	Williams-BMW	58
6.	Fernando Alonso	Spanish	Renault	55
7.	David Coulthard	British	McLaren-Mercedes	51
8.	Jarno Trulli	Italian	Renault	33
9.	Jenson Button	British	BAR-Honda	17
10.	Mark Webber	Australian	Jaguar-Cosworth	17

❀ 2003 CONSTRUCTORS' CUP ❀

Pos	Constructor	Pts
1.	Ferrari	158
2.	Williams-BMW	144
3.	McLaren-Mercedes	142
4.	Renault	88
5.	BAR-Honda	26
6.	Sauber-Petronas	19
7.	Jaguar-Cosworth	18
8.	Toyota	16
9.	Jordan-Ford	13

❀ BBC SPORTS TEAM OF THE YEAR AWARD ❀

The BBC Sports Personality of the Year Team Award is presented annually to the sporting team or partnership considered to have made the most substantial contribution to sport in that year. In its inaugural year, 1960, it was won by "Cooper Racing".

❀ BRITAIN'S FIRST F1 WORLD CHAMPION ❀

In 1958, Mike Hawthorn (Ferrari) became Britain's first ever F1 Drivers' World Champion when he beat his fellow countryman, Stirling Moss (Cooper & Vanwall), by a single point in the title race.

Did You Know That?
It was the fourth consecutive year in which Moss finished runner-up in the F1 Championship race.

❀ TRAFFIC CONGESTION ❀

The 1990 F1 season saw a record number of cars, 35, entered but as the rules did not permit more than 30 cars to compete in the official practices, FISA established a pre-qualifying section with nine cars, made up from those teams that fell outside the top thirteen places in the last half of the previous season. Meanwhile, for the GP itself only the 26 fastest cars were permitted to enter the GP and take up a place on the grid.

❀ SCHUMI WINS FIRST BAHRAIN GP ❀

On 4 April 2004, Bahrain hosted its inaugural Formula One race, which was won by Michael Schumacher (Ferrari). The Grand Prix was raced on the Bahrain International Circuit.

❀ 8 FROM 10 ❀

In the 1967 season Denny Hulme (Brabham-Climax and Brabham-Repco) scored points in eight of the 10 GPs he raced in. He won the World Championship by five points from the 1966 champion, his team-mate Jack Brabham (Brabham-Climax and Brabham-Repco).

❀ DONNELLY SERIOUSLY INJURED ❀

In 1990, Martin Donnelly (Lotus-Lamborghini) was involved in an accident during qualifying for the Portuguese Grand Prix at Jerez. He crashed his Lotus at 230kmh. The impact was so hard that Donnelly was thrown from his car in an accident very similar to the one that claimed the life of Gilles Villeneuve during practice for the Belgian Grand Prix at Zolder in 1982.

❀ McLAREN'S KIWI RESTORES PRIDE ❀

When New Zealand's Denny Hulme, the 1967 F1 World Champion, took the chequered flag in the 1972 South African Grand Prix, he gave the McLaren racing team their first F1 win since the Mexican GP in 1969.

❀ SCHUMI MOVES CAMPS ❀

In 1996 Michael Schumacher, the World Champion of 1994 and 1995, left Benetton and joined Ferrari.

❀ 2004 DRIVERS' WORLD CHAMPIONSHIP ❀

Pos	Driver	Nationality	Team	Pts
1.	Michael Schumacher	German	Ferrari	148
2.	Rubens Barrichello	Brazilian	Ferrari	114
3.	Jenson Button	British	BAR-Honda	85
4.	Fernando Alonso	Spanish	Renault	59
5.	Juan Pablo Montoya	Colombian	Williams-BMW	58
6.	Jarno Trulli	Italian	Renault	46
7.	Kimi Raikkonen	Finnish	McLaren-Mercedes	45
8.	Takuma Sato	Japanese	BAR-Honda	34
9.	Ralf Schumacher	German	Williams-BMW	24
10.	David Coulthard	British	McLaren-Mercedes	24

❀ 2004 CONSTRUCTORS' CUP ❀

Pos	Constructor	Pts
1.	Ferrari	262
2.	BAR-Honda	119
3.	Renault	105
4.	Williams-BMW	88
5.	McLaren-Mercedes	69
6.	Sauber-Petronas	34
7.	Jaguar-Cosworth	10
8.	Toyota	9
9.	Jordan-Ford	5
10.	Minardi-Cosworth	1

❀ FROM HILL TO HILL ❀

When Graham Hill (BRM) won the 1962 Drivers' World Championship, following the success of Phil Hill (Ferrari) in 1961, it was the first time in the history of GP racing that two drivers sharing the same surname won consecutive world titles.

❀ LIFE IN THE FAST LANE ❀

Nigel Mansell (Williams-Renault) was leading the 1991 Portuguese Grand Prix when he pitted on lap 51 for new tyres. When he drove away, one of his wheels was noticeably loose. The team mechanics rushed down the speed lane of the pit and secured the wheel, which ultimately led to Mansell's disqualification from the race. Nigel's team-mate, Riccardo Patrese, raced to victory.

⚙ ON THE BUTTON ⚙

In 2000 Williams signed 20-year-old Jenson Button straight from Formula Three and changed their Supertec engines to BMW, who were making a long-awaited return to F1. Button ended the season in eighth place in the Drivers' Championship.

⚙ 11 OUT OF 12 ⚙

The Ford Cosworth DFV engine completely dominated F1 racing during the 1968 season, winning 11 of the 12 races. The only victory by a non-Ford Cosworth engine car was the French Grand Prix, which was won by Jacky Ickx in a Ferrari. Graham Hill (Lotus-Ford) was crowned World Champion.

⚙ SPEEDY DEBUT ⚙

Scott Speed made his F1 debut in the opening GP of the 2006 season in Bahrain. He finished in 13th place in his Scuderia Toro Rosso-Cosworth. Speed had originally finished in 8th place at the end of the race but was handed a 25-second penalty, pushing him to 13th place, for paying insufficient attention to yellow flags. That meant he dropped behind David Coulthard (Red Bull Racing-Ferrari) and lost him and the STR-Cosworth team their first World Championship point. The race stewards also fined the American $5,000 for using abusive language during the subsequent hearing towards a fellow driver, believed to be Coulthard.

Did You Know That?
Scott Speed became the first American since Michael Andretti (Italy, 1993) to drive in an F1 GP.

⚙ ALFA ROMEO DENIED A CLEAN SWEEP ⚙

Johnnie Parsons won the Indianapolis 500 in a Kurtis Kraft-Offenhauser on 30 May 1950. The race was the third of the 1950 F1 season, but the European-based teams, such as Alfa Romeo, ERA, Ferrari, Maserati and Talbot-Lago-Talbot, did not travel to the Indianapolis Motor Speedway circuit.

Did You Know That?
The 1950 Indy 500 was the only Grand Prix of the inaugural 1950 F1 season in which Alfa Romeo failed to take the chequered flag.

❀ FANTASY WORLD SELECT STARTING GRID ❀

(up to the end of the 2007 season)

1
Jack Brabham
(Aus) *(14 GP wins, 126 GPs, World champion 1959, 1960, 1966)*

2
Alan Jones (Aus)
(12 GP wins, 116 GPs, World champion 1980)

3
Jody Scheckter
(SAf) *(10 GP wins, 112 GPs, World champion 1979)*

4
Mark Webber (Aus)
(9 GP win, 217 GPs, World champion best 3rd 2010, 2011)

5
Denny Hulme
(NZ) *(8 GP wins, 112 GPs, World champion 1967)*

6
John Watson (NI)
(5 GP wins, 152 GPs, World champion best 2nd 1982)

7
Bruce McLaren
(NZ) *(4 GP wins, 101 GPs, World champion best 2nd 1960)*

8
Eddie Irvine (NI)
(4 GP wins, 147 GPs, World champion best 2nd 1999)

9
Mike Hawthorn
(Eng) *(3 GP wins, 45 GPs World champion 1958)*

10
Pastor Maldonado
(Ven) *(1 GP win, 58, GPs, World champion best 15th 2012)*

❀ FROZEN FUEL BANNED ❀

At the start of the 1985 F1 season, FISA banned the use of frozen fuel and refuelling during the races, continuing with the maximum limit of 220 litres in the fuel tanks. This rule forced the teams to concentrate on the use of electronic innovations to maximise fuel usage, and it proved decisive in the championship as many teams were not capable of properly managing their fuel consumption without losing speed.

Did You Know That?
Some constructors used a bottom on the panel of the fuel tank that allowed the driver to control turbo-pressure. The BMW, Honda and Renault engines dominated the practices, but when it came to race day, the constructors had to reduce turbo-pressure, allowing Ferrari and Porsche engines to compete equally.

❀ VILLENEUVE CRASHES AND DIES ❀

The 1982 Belgian Grand Prix at Zolder will be always remembered for the death of the Canadian driver, Gilles Villeneuve, who crashed and tragically died in practice on 8 May 1982. On his final qualifying lap the front left wheel of his Ferrari hit the rear of Jochen Mass's car, which was then on a slow "in-lap". Villeneuve's car was catapulted into the air and nose-dived, crashing to the ground as it somersaulted along the side of the track. Just before the car crashed to the ground for the final time, Villeneuve, still strapped to his seat, was thrown out into the catch fencing at the other side of the track. However, he was not breathing when the medical team arrived, and died a short time later in hospital. Ferrari retired from the race, which was won by John Watson in a McLaren-Ford.

Did You Know That?
Gilles' son, Jacques, also had a successful racing career, winning the 1995 Indianapolis 500 and the 1995 CART championships. Jacques then followed in his father's footsteps and joined the Formula One circuit in 1996, claiming pole position in his maiden GP and winning the F1 Drivers' World Championship in 1997.

❀ SPANISH TROT ❀

Michael Schumacher (Benetton-Renault) won the 1995 Spanish Grand Prix from pole position, having led for all 65 laps of the race.

❂ SPELLING ERROR ❂

Johnnie Parsons won one Grand Prix during his career, the Indianapolis 500 in 1950, and died on 8 September 1984. Parsons participated in nine GPs (the Indianapolis 500 was included in the Formula One World Championship from 1950 to 1960), making his debut on 30 May 1950. In addition to his solitary GP win, Parsons also enjoyed a total of 12 championship points. Parsons is the only Indianapolis 500 winner to have his name misspelt on the famous "Borg-Warner Trophy" when the appointed race silversmiths carved "Johnny" instead of "Johnnie". However, the error was corrected posthumously when the trophy was restored in 1991.

❂ SENNA FIGHTS BACK IN SPAIN ❂

Ayrton Senna (McLaren-Honda) won the 1989 Spanish GP from pole position ahead of Gerhard Berger (Ferrari) and Alain Prost (McLaren-Honda). At that stage, Prost led the Drivers' World Championship table on 81 points from Senna on 60 points. However, as only the best 11 results counted, Prost could only claim a maximum of 78 points, which left the door open for his team-mate Senna. The title was decided in Prost's favour at the next race, the Japanese GP, when Senna finished first – but was disqualified after colliding with the Frenchman.

❂ SUPER MARIO RETURNS ❂

Following the shock retirement of Carlos Reutemann after the 1982 Brazilian GP, Williams had just two weeks in which to find a replacement in time for the US West Grand Prix on 4 April 1982. After a frantic search Williams turned to the 1978 F1 World Champion, the American Mario Andretti, who raced for the team in the US West and San Marino GPs. He was then replaced by Northern Ireland's Derek Daly.

Did You Know That?
Mario Andretti is mentioned in the Beastie Boys' song "Shadrach" in the line "You love Mario Andretti cause he always drives his car well."

❂ PIQUET CLOCKS UP 200 GPS ❂

For Nelson Piquet (Benetton-Ford) the 1991 Italian Grand Prix was his 200th GP. The Brazilian three-times former World Champion finished sixth in the race.

❀ 2005 DRIVERS' WORLD CHAMPIONSHIP ❀

Pos	Driver	Nationality	Team	Pts
1.	Fernando Alonso	Spanish	Renault	133
2.	Kimi Raikkonen	Finnish	McLaren-Mercedes	112
3.	Michael Schumacher	German	Ferrari	62
4.	Juan Pablo Montoya	Colombian	McLaren-Mercedes	60
5.	Giancarlo Fisichella	Italian	Renault	58
6.	Ralf Schumacher	German	Toyota	45
7.	Jarno Trulli	Italian	Toyota	43
8.	Rubens Barrichello	Brazilian	Ferrari	38
9.	Jenson Button	British	BAR-Honda	37
10.	Mark Webber	Australian	Williams-BMW	36

❀ 2005 CONSTRUCTORS' CUP ❀

Pos	Constructor	Pts
1.	Renault	191
2.	McLaren-Mercedes	182
3.	Ferrari	100
4.	Toyota	88
5.	Williams-BMW	66
6.	BAR-Honda	38
7.	RBR-Cosworth	34
8.	Sauber-Petronas	20
9.	Jordan-Toyota	12
10.	Minardi-Cosworth	7

❀ FAST TALK (20) ❀

"It would be a personal victory for me to convince Ayrton that there are more things in life rather than just racing."
Alain Prost

❀ FANGIO RULES ❀

Juan Manuel Fangio won the Formula One Drivers' Championship in four consecutive years from 1954 to 1957. His 1957 crown was his fifth and last World Championship title.

Did You Know That?
During his 1953–57 championship years, Fangio won 16 of the GPs held (six races in 1954, four in 1955, two in 1956 and four in 1957).

❀ 2006 WORLD DRIVERS' CHAMPIONSHIP ❀

Pos	Driver	Nationality	Team	Pts
1.	Fernando Alonso	Spanish	Renault	134
2.	Michael Schumacher	German	Ferrari	121
3.	Felipe Massa	Brazilian	Ferrari	80
4.	Giancarlo Fisichella	Italian	Renault	72
5.	Kimi Raikkonen	Finnish	McLaren-Mercedes	65
6.	Jenson Button	British	Honda	56
7.	Rubens Barrichello	Brazilian	Honda	30
7.	Juan Pablo Montoya	Colombian	McLaren-Mercedes	26
9.	Nick Heidfeld	German	Sauber-BMW	23
10.	Ralf Schumacher	German	Toyota	20

❀ 2006 CONSTRUCTORS' CUP ❀

Pos	Constructor	Pts
1.	Renault	206
2.	Ferrari	201
3.	McLaren Mercedes	110
4.	Honda	86
5.	Sauber-BMW	36
6.	Toyota	35
7.	Red Bull-Ferrari	16
8.	Williams-Cosworth	11
9.	Toro Roso-Cosworth	1

❀ A DARK YEAR ❀

The 1968 F1 season witnessed a number of driver deaths including: Mike Spence, testing a Lotus-Turbina at Indianapolis; Ludovico Scarfiotti in a hill climb race; Jo Schlesser at the French Grand Prix in Rouen; and former World Champion Jim Clark in an F2 race at Hockenheim. The last driver fatality during an F1 race was Ayrton Senna (at Imola, 1994).

❀ SPEEDY FERNANDO ❀

Fernando Alonso (Renault) scored the first fastest lap of his F1 career at the Canadian Grand Prix on 15 June 2003 when he set a time of 1'16.040. He finished in fourth place behind the winner, Michael Schumacher (Ferrari). Ralf Schumacher (Williams-BMW) finished in second place, making it the eighth consecutive race of the 2003 F1 season in which he finished in the points.

◉ F1'S 200 CLUB ◉

Only 13 drivers have entered more than 200 Formula One Grands Prix. Riccardo Patrese was the first to reach 200., at the 1990 British Grand Prix, having broken Jacques Laffite's 176-race record in 1989. Twelve men have followed Patrese into the 200 Club, with two passing 300. If he competes in 2014, Felipe Massa will reach 200 in his seventh GP.

Driver	200th Grand Prix	Total GPs*
Rubens Barrichello	2005 San Marino	326
Michael Schumacher	2004 Monaco GP	308
Riccardo Patrese	1990 British GP	257
Jarno Trulli	2009 Australian GP	256
Jenson Button	2011 Hungarian GP	249
David Coulthard	2006 Monaco GP	247
Giancarlo Fisichella	2008 Monte Carlo GP	231
Fernando Alonso	2013 Chinese GP	218
Mark Webber	2013 Bahrain GP	217
Andrea de Cesaris	1994 Canadian GP	214
Gerhard Berger	1997 San Marino GP	210
Nelson Piquet	1991 Italian GP	207
Jean Alesi	2001 USA GP	202

Did You Know That?
Jenson Button is the only driver to have won his 200th Grand Prix.

◉ FIRST GP WIN FOR WILLIAMS-HONDA ◉

Keke Rosberg (Williams-Honda) won the US West Grand Prix on 8 July 1984, to claim Williams-Honda's first victory using the Japanese car manufacturer's new turbo engine. Rene Arnoux (Ferrari) had an unbelievable drive, coming from last place in the race to second place on the podium just ahead of Elio de Angelis in his Lotus-Renault. Piercarlo Ghinzani (Osella-Alfa Romeo) won the first ever championship points for the team and himself with his fifth place behind Jacques Laffite (Williams-Honda). On a very bumpy and dirty race track, 12 drivers brushed or hit the wall.

Did You Know That?
Nigel Mansell's gearbox, in his Lotus-Renault, packed in on him and in very humid conditions he pushed his car over the finishing line to claim sixth place and one championship point. He then collapsed on the track with heat exhaustion.

❂ FOUR-WHEEL LEGEND IS TWO-WHEEL FAN ❂

Alain Prost, awarded an OBE in 1993, is a road cycling enthusiast, who has helped design bicycle frames for the French frame-builder Cyfac.

❂ NOT SO TURKISH DELIGHT ❂

On 19 September 2006, the World Motor Sport Council handed the National Sporting Authority of Turkey and the organizers of the Turkish Grand Prix the largest fine in the history of the sport – €5 million (£2.66 million) – and nearly dropped the race from the 2007 F1 calendar. The winner of the 2006 Turkish GP, Felipe Massa, received his trophy from Turkish-Cypriot leader Mehmet Ali Talat. However, the United Nations do not recognize the Turkish-controlled area of Cyprus as a separate country, so the FIA took action on the grounds that the organizers had violated its political neutrality policy.

❂ FAST TALK (21) ❂

"Michael Schumacher is the most unsporting driver with the largest number of sanctions (against him) in the history of Formula One. That doesn't mean he hasn't been the best driver, and fighting against him has been an honour and a pleasure."
Fernando Alonso

❂ I'M OFF ❂

Fernando Alonso emulated Michael Schumacher and Juan Manuel Fangio by changing teams after winning back-to-back World Drivers' Championships. Alonso signed to drive for McLaren in 2007 after winning two titles with Renault, Schumi went from Benetton to Ferrari in 1995 and Fangio won the 1956 title for Ferrari after winning titles in 1954 and 1955 for Maserati/Mercedes and Mercedes, respectively.

❂ BABY-FACED DRIVER ❂

On 25 August 2006, Sebastian Vettel of Germany broke a number of F1 records prior to the 2006 Turkish GP. At 19 years and 53 days, Vettel became the youngest person ever to drive an F1 car during a Grand Prix weekend. By the end of the first day's practice, Vettel had set the fastest time of the day in his Sauber-BMW. New Zealander Mike Thackwell had been the youngest driver when he drove a Tyrrell in practice for the 1980 Canadian GP at 19 years and 180 days.

✦ IMPRESSIVE DEBUT ✦

Lewis Hamilton's third place in the 2007 Australian GP made him the first debutant to finish on the podium since Jacques Villeneuve was second to his Williams team-mate Damon Hill in Australia in 1996.

✦ RULE BRITANNIA (1) ✦

Great Britain has enjoyed more success in the F1 World Drivers' Championship than all other countries. Ten drivers have won 14 titles: Mike Hawthorn (1958), Jim Clark (1963 and 1965), Graham Hill (1962 and 1968), John Surtees (1964), Jackie Stewart (1969, 1971 and 1973), James Hunt (1976), Nigel Mansell (1992), Damon Hill (1996), Lewis Hamilton (2008) and Jenson Button (2009).

✦ HAPPY 50TH BIRTHDAY FERRARI ✦

On 29 June 1997, Ferrari celebrated 50 years of manufacturing street legal motor cars. The company had been founded in 1929 as Scuderia Ferrari by Enzo Ferrari but, until 1947, only racing cars were built.

✦ COULTHARD'S EATING DISORDER ✦

In his autobiography, published in 2007, British driver David Coulthard revealed that he suffered from bulimia when he was battling to break into Formula One as a teenager. "I stopped eating fattening food and, before I knew what had happened, I was bulimic. In my mind the only way to keep my weight down was making myself vomit."

✦ "I HAD THAT SCHUMACHER IN MY CAB" ✦

A German taxi driver was left shaken but not stirred after he found himself a passenger in his own car with the seven-times F1 World Champion Michael Schumacher at the wheel. Michael and his family were in Coburg, Bavaria, to collect a dog they had just bought. However, when Schumi realised they were running late to catch their flight back to Switzerland he asked the taxi driver for the keys and drove the car to the local aerodrome himself. "I found myself a passenger, which was strange enough, but having 'Schumi' behind the wheel was incredible. He drove at full throttle around the corners and overtook in some unbelievable places," said Tuncer Yilmaz. Schumacher's generous €100 tip probably eased Yilmaz's concerns.

❂ FERNANDO ALONSO ❂

Fernando Alonso Díaz was born on 29 July 1981 in Oviedo, Spain. His racing career began in karting, and he won four consecutive junior category Spanish Championships between 1993 and 1996, and the Junior World Cup in 1996. In 1997 he won the Spanish and Italian Inter-A titles and the following year he retained his Spanish Inter-A title as well as finishing runner-up in the European Karting Championships. Aged 17-years old Adrian Campos, a former F1 driver for Minardi, gave Fernando his first test in a race car in October 1998. After three days of testing, the young Spaniard's times equalled the lap times of Campos' previous test driver Marc Gene of Switzerland. Campos signed Alonso to race for him in the 1999 Spanish Euro Open MoviStar Series. His first victory came in only his second race and Fernando went on to win the Championship by a single point.

In 1999 Alonso tested for the Minardi Formula One team and was the fastest driver at the test. But Formula 3000 beckoned for Fernando when he signed for Team Astromega in 2000. He found life in Formula 3000 tough and failed to score a point in his opening six races. However, a second place and a win in his last two races enabled him to end the season fourth overall. The following year he made his F1 debut with Minardi in the 2001 Australian Grand Prix to become the third-youngest driver ever to start an F1 race. Alonso signed for Benetton as their test driver in 2002, shortly before the team was taken over by Renault. When boss Flavio Briatore dropped Jenson Button in 2003, he promoted Alonso into the team's second seat alongside Jarno Trulli. Briatore's faith in Alonso paid off when, at the Malaysian Grand Prix, he became the youngest driver to achieve a F1 pole position. A few weeks later, in Hungary, he became the youngest driver to win a Formula One race. Fernando finished the season sixth in the Drivers' Championship, and improved to fourth in 2004, scoring 59 points and taking four podiums.

With a third-place finish at the 2005 Brazilian GP, Fernando claimed his first F1 World Drivers' Championship to become the youngest F1 World Champion, aged 24 years and 59 days. His win at the Chinese GP clinched Renault's first Constructor's Championship. He and Renault retained their championships in 2006, before the pair split, with Alonso signing for McLaren. It was not a successful move. Alonso struggled to match tyro Lewis Hamilton and there was a very public falling out. Eventually the pair finished a point behind eventual Champion Kimi Raikkonen, but Fernando decided to return to Renault for 2008.

In 2010, Alonso left Renault and joined Ferrari where he enjoyed many Grand Prix victories, but was regularly bested by Sebastian Vettel (Red Bull Racing) in the race for the Driver's Championship.

❂ GREEN LIGHT FOR NIGHT RACE ❂

On 25 October 2007, the FIA announced that the 2008 Formula One season will feature a night race for the first time in its history. The streets of Singapore were chosen as the venue for the historic race and it was scheduled for 28 September 2008. Singapore will thus be the fourth venue in eastern Asia, joining Malaysia, China and Japan. Until 1999, however, only Japan had hosted Formula One races. In addition, the circuit at Singapore will be only the third one on the streets in the current championship. The other two are at Monaco and the European GP at Valencia, which also debuted in 2008.

❂ THE SPYGATE ROW ❂

On 4 July 2007, McLaren was at the centre of a spying row involving one of their senior employees, Mike Coughlan, and Ferrari's Performance Director Nigel Stepney. Ferrari claimed that McLaren had obtained confidential team documents and when a 780-page Ferari technical dossier was found at his home, Coughlan was suspended. Nine days later the FIA charged McLaren with breaking the sport's rules.

The hearing took place in Paris on 26 July 2007 and McLaren were found not guilty. The World Motorsport Council (WMSC) ruled there had been insufficient evidence that the rules breach had made any impact on the 2007 World Championship race. However, they made it clear that McLaren were still facing the possibility of a Championship ban if any future information proved they gained an unfair advantage from the documents. Ferrari was furious with the decision, and released a statement that suggested the decision not only legitimized dishonest behaviour in Formula One but also set a very serious precedent.

The story rumbled on and a further WMSC hearing was convened in Paris on 13 September. This time McLaren was stripped of all their points in the 2007 Formula One Constructors' Championship. Ron Dennis's team was also handed a whopping record $100m (£49.2m) fine, which included any prize money or television money the British team would have earned from participating in the Constructors' Cup. However, much to the relief of Dennis and McLaren's two drivers, Fernando Alonso and Lewis Hamilton, they were not stripped of their Drivers' Championship points. The WMSC also stated that McLaren would have to prove that their cars did not contain any Ferrari "intellectual property" before they would be allowed to compete in the 2008 F1 season.

❀ FANTASY FERRARI STARTING GRID ❀

(GP wins and World champion years are those only as Ferrari drivers)

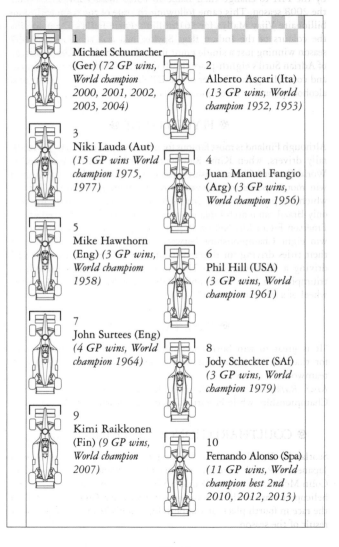

1
Michael Schumacher
(Ger) *(72 GP wins,
World champion
2000, 2001, 2002,
2003, 2004)*

2
Alberto Ascari (Ita)
*(13 GP wins, World
champion 1952, 1953)*

3
Niki Lauda (Aut)
*(15 GP wins World
champion 1975,
1977)*

4
Juan Manuel Fangio
(Arg) *(3 GP wins,
World champion 1956)*

5
Mike Hawthorn
(Eng) *(3 GP wins,
World champiom
1958)*

6
Phil Hill (USA)
*(3 GP wins, World
champion 1961)*

7
John Surtees (Eng)
*(4 GP wins, World
champion 1964)*

8
Jody Scheckter (SAf)
*(3 GP wins, World
champion 1979)*

9
Kimi Raikkonen
(Fin) *(9 GP wins,
World champion
2007)*

10
Fernando Alonso (Spa)
*(11 GP wins, World
champion best 2nd
2010, 2012, 2013)*

❁ A FORCE TO BE RECKONED WITH ❁

In October 2007 Formula One team Spyker was given permission by the FIA to change their name to Force India Formula One for the 2008 season. This came following the sale of the team to Indian billionaire Vijay Mallya for £61 million. Force India's logo contains the colours of the Indian flag. Spyker had a disappointing 2007 season winning just a single point in the Constructors' Cup, courtesy of Adrian Sutil's eighth-place finish in Japan. Mallya is the chairman and controlling shareholder of the UB Group, which has airline and alcohol operations throughout India.

❁ FLYING FINNS ❁

Although Finland is most famous for producing World Championship rally drivers, when Kimi Raikkonen won the 2007 Formula One World Drivers' Championship he became the third Finnish diver to win motor sport's most coveted crown. Apart from Great Britain, which has produced eight drivers to win 12 World Championships, only Brazil can match Finland's total of three different title-winners. Emerson Fittipaldi, Nelson Piquet and Ayrton Senna did, however, win eight Championships between them. Each of the Finns won their titles driving for different teams: Keke Rosberg won in 1982 driving a Williams, Mika Hakkinen was with McLaren when he triumphed in both 1988 and 1989, while Raikkonen was at the wheel of a Ferarrari in 2007.

❁ FAST TALK (22) ❁

"It is great to win both championships. I thank the whole team for that, for all their hard work, and Felipe, too. It was perfect teamwork."
Kimi Raikkonen after winning the 2007 F1 World Drivers' Championship, while Ferrari claimed the Constructors' Cup

❁ COULTHARD HONOURS COLIN McRAE ❁

Scotland's David Coulthard changed his helmet for the 2007 Japanese GP and wore the colours of his friend and fellow Scot, Colin McRae, the former World Rally Champion, who had died in a helicopter crash with his son a few weeks earlier. Coulthard finished the race in fourth place. It was both his and his Team Red Bull's best result of the season.

⚙ 2007 DRIVERS' WORLD CHAMPIONSHIP ⚙

Pos	Driver	Nationality	Team	Pts
1.	Kimi Raikkonen	Finnish	Ferrari	110
2.	Lewis Hamilton	British	McLaren-Mercedes	109
3.	Fernando Alonso	Spanish	McLaren-Mercedes	109
4.	Felipe Massa	Brazilian	Ferrari	94
5.	Nick Heidfeld	German	BMW	61
6.	Robert Kubica	Polish	BMW	39
7.	Heikki Kovalainen	Finnish	Renault	30
8.	Giancarlo Fisichella	Italian	Renault	21
9.	Nico Rosberg	German	Williams-Toyota	20
10	David Coulthard	British	Red Bull-Renault	14

⚙ 2007 CONSTRUCTORS' CUP ⚙

Pos	Constructor	Pts
1.	Ferrari	204
2.	BMW	101
3.	Renault	51
4.	Williams-Toyota	33
5.	Red Bull-Renault	24
6.	Toyota	13
7.	STR-Ferrari	8
8.	Honda	6
9.	Super Aguri-Honda	4
10.	Spyker-Ferrari	1
—	McLaren-Mercedes	0*

McLaren was stripped of all 2007 Constructors' Championship points after the Belgian Grand Prix when it was discovered that the team was found to be in breach of the International Sporting Code through possession of confidential Ferrari data.

⚙ SUPER AGURI BREAKS DUCK ⚙

At the 2007 Spanish GP, the Japanese Super Aguri team, founded by ex-F1 driver Aguri Suzuki in 2006, claimed its first ever F1 World Championship point when Takuma Sato finished eighth. Two races later, in Montreal, Sato collected another three points with a sixth-place finish, but they were the only points collected by the team

Did You Know That?
Aguri Suzuki started and ended his F1 career driving in the Japanese Grands Prix of 1988 and 1995, respectively.

⬡ LEWIS HAMILTON BREAKS ROOKIE RECORDS ⬡

McLaren's young British driver Lewis Hamilton broke all sorts of records in his rookie season of 2007. He was the first rookie to go on the podium in his first ever race since Jacques Villeneuve did so for Williams in 1996. Hamilton then became the first driver to be on the podium at the end of his first three races, with second places in both Malaysia and Bahrain. And he went on to stretch his run of top-three finishes to an unprecedented first nine races of his career.

Hamilton also became the youngest driver ever to lead the World Drivers' Championship, taking away the record of his team's founder, Bruce McLaren, who drove in Formula One from 1959 until his death in 1970. It took until race six, in Montreal, for Hamilton to win a race, but he went on to win three more – also matching McLaren's career mark. His points total of 109 was identical to that of the defending double World Champion and team-mate Fernando Alonso, but one less than the man who became champion, Kimi Raikkonen of Ferrari. So Hamilton emulated Villeneuve by finishing second in his debut season in Formula One, but the big difference is that Villeneuve had first gained experience in US open wheel racing.

Did You Know That?
One of Lewis Hamilton's classmates at John Henry Newman School in Stevenage was England international midfield footballer Ashley Young and the pair briefly played in the same school football team.

⬡ CONCORDE AGREEMENT ENDS ⬡

The Concorde Agreement between the existing F1 Constructors and F1 Supremo, Bernie Ecclestone came to an end with the conclusion of the 2007 Formula One season. The Concorde Agreement, which is an expressly secret document, sets out the terms and conditions by which the teams compete in F1 races and take their share of the television revenues and prize money. Concorde Agreements date back more than a quarter of a century, to 1981, when the first one was signed. Documents were later agreed in 1987, 1992, 1997 and 1998.

⬡ F1 MEETS THE BUDDH ⬡

The 2011 season saw the first ever Indian Formula One Grand Prix. The race was held at the Buddh International Circuit, close to the capital Delhi in the state of Uttar Pradesh. The inaugural winner was World Champion elect Sebastian Vettel, for Red Bull-Renault.

❂ BILLIONAIRES' PLAYGROUND ❂

The Monaco Grand Prix, round the tight streets of tiny principality on the Mediterranean coast, is the most famous and glamorous race of the Formula One season. Many of the great Formula One drivers have made their homes the Principality, inlcuding Scotsman David Coulthard. There is a story that Brazilian legend Ayrton Senna actually walked home to his apartment during the 1988 race after crashing out when leading. Despite Monaco's tiny population – it is just over 30,000 – three drivers are listed as being Monagasque: Louis Chiron, Andre Testut and Olivier Beretta (although Testut was born in Lyon).

Did You Know That?
The Monaco GP has enjoyed the patronage of three generations of the Principality's royal family: Louis II, Rainer III and Albert II have all taken a passionate interest in the race.

❂ A STREET CALLED HAMILTON ❂

Shortly after the end of the 2007 Formula One season, Stevenage Borough Council announced that they would honour local-boy-made-good, Lewis Hamilton, who was educated in the town, by naming a street after him in a new town centre development.

❂ KIMI KEEPS IT LIGHT ❂

Ferrari's flying Finn Kimi Raikkonen fulfilled a lifetime's ambition in 2007 by winning the Formula One World Drivers' Championship. But he had fun on the way. As his rivals were arriving in Australia in preparation for the first GP of the season, Kimi was back home in Finland taking part in a snowmobile race. In an effort to prevent the media from learning about his entry in the race he entered the event under a false name – James Hunt. Then, a week before the Hungarian GP, he raced in a motorboat event in Finland. Keen to avoid the *paparazzi*, Kimi and his two friends wore gorilla outfits on the boat. The *paparazzi* weren't fooled, and snapped away at the gorilla costumes on board the boat.

❂ 100TH WINNER IN F1 ❂

When Finland's Heikki Kovalainen won the 2008 Hungarian Grand Prix for McLaren-Mercedes he became the 100th different driver to win a Formula One Grand Prix.

⊛ SILVERSTONE ⊛

Silverstone, the venue of the British Grand Prix and, in 1950, the first ever race in the Formula One Drivers' Championship, is believed to be an early English word for a wooded area. It opened in 1943 as an airfield and with the help of the RAC was turned into racetrack in 1948. Viewed from above, the old runways of RAF Bomber Command Silverstone can still be seen. The various sections of the track have their own history and this is how they got their names:

Maggotts Curve	Was close to Maggotts Moor
Becketts Corner/Chapel Curve	Ruins of the Chapel of Thomas à Becket are nearby
Hangar Straight	Two WW2 aircraft hangars once stood alongside the straight
Stowe Corner	The famous independent school is just south of the track
Club Corner	In honour of the RAC, the Royal Automobile Club in Pall Mall, London
Abbey Curve	Near the site of Luffield Abbey
Woodcote	Another reference to the RAC, this one the country club at Woodcote, near Epsom, Surrey

⊛ A PARTING OF THE WAYS ⊛

On 2 November 2007 it was announced that Fernando Alonso had left McLaren by mutual consent. The double World Champion secured an early release from his contract after an acrimonious 2007. Matters came to a head at Hungary, when Alonso denied team-mate Lewis Hamilton the chance to claim pole position in qualifying. Alonso individually and McLaren as a team were both punished and the two drivers barely spoke to each other in the final months of the season. Alonso returned to drive for Renault in 2008.

⊛ RULE BRITANNIA (2) ⊛

In addition to the ten British drivers who have been crowned Formula One World Drivers' Champion, four others have finished runners-up in the Championship but never won the title. They are: Tony Brooks, Sir Stirling Moss (runner-up on four consecutive occasions), Eddie Irvine and David Coulthard.

❀ 2008 DRIVERS' WORLD CHAMPIONSHIP ❀

Pos	Driver	Nationality	Team	Pts
1.	Lewis Hamilton	British	McLaren-Mercedes	98
2.	Felipe Massa	Brazilian	Ferrari	97
3.	Kimi Räikkönen	Finnish	Ferrari	75
4.	Robert Kubica	Polish	BMW Sauber	75
5.	Fernando Alonso	Spanish	Renault	61
6.	Nick Heidfeld	German	BMW Sauber	60
7.	Hekki Kovalainen	Finnish	McLaren-Mercedes	53
8.	Sebastian Vettel	German	Red Bull-Renault	35
9.	Jarno Trulli	Italian	Toyota	31
10.	Timo Glock	German	Toyota	25

❀ 2008 CONSTRUCTORS' CUP ❀

Pos	Constructor	Pts
1	Ferrari	172
2	McLaren-Mercedes	151
3	BMW Sauber	135
4	Renault	80
5	Toyota	56
6	Toro Rosso-Ferrari	39
7	Red Bull-Renault	29
8	Williams-Toyota	26
9	Honda	14

❀ FAST TALK (23) ❀

"My job isn't for people to love and hug me … it's not a love-in."
Ron Dennis, McLaren boss

❀ HAWKINS AND ASCARI HARBOUR-BOUND ❀

The narrow streets of Monaco have seen some terrible crashes and, sadly, a number of fatalities. Amazingly two drivers have not only left the track, but also dry land and lived to tell the tale. Alberto Ascari crashed into the water in 1955 and nearly drowned. Ten years later, Ausralian driver Paul Hawkins, in a private Lotus entered by Dickie Stoop, lost control at the chicane, went over the wall and ended up in the water. Hawkins was able to swim to safety. In another eerie coincidence with Ascari, Hawkins, too, died in a racing accident, at Oulton Park, England, in May 1967.

❀ FANTASY McLAREN STARTING GRID ❀

(Wins and World champion years are those only as McLaren drivers)

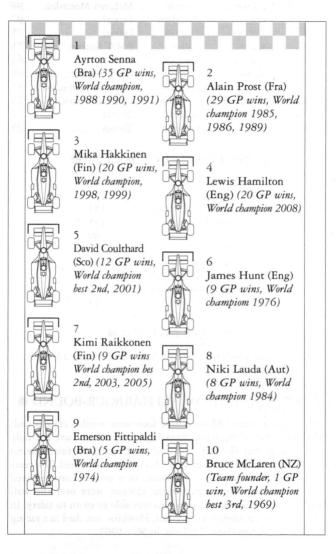

1
Ayrton Senna
(Bra) *(35 GP wins,*
World champion,
1988 1990, 1991)

2
Alain Prost (Fra)
(29 GP wins, World
champion 1985,
1986, 1989)

3
Mika Hakkinen
(Fin) *(20 GP wins,*
World champion,
1998, 1999)

4
Lewis Hamilton
(Eng) *(20 GP wins,*
World champion 2008)

5
David Coulthard
(Sco) *(12 GP wins,*
World champion
best 2nd, 2001)

6
James Hunt (Eng)
(9 GP wins, World
champiom 1976)

7
Kimi Raikkonen
(Fin) *(9 GP wins*
World champion bes
2nd, 2003, 2005)

8
Niki Lauda (Aut)
(8 GP wins, World
champion 1984)

9
Emerson Fittipaldi
(Bra) *(5 GP wins,*
World champion
1974)

10
Bruce McLaren (NZ)
(Team founder, 1 GP
win, World champion
best 3rd, 1969)

❋ CAN THESE CARS FLY? ❋

Images of a charging red bull could be seen on four cars in the 2008
F1 season because the name Red Bull appeared in both English and
Italian translations. Dietrich Mateschitz, co-founder of Red Bull
GmbH, Chairman of Red Bull Racing and joint Chairman of Scuderia
Toro Rosso, headed both teams. Although they shared a website, the
teams had nothing in common: staff, engines, chassis or home base.

❋ MONACO GRAND PRIX WINNERS 1929–2013 ❋

Year	Driver	Team
1929	William Grover-Williams	Bugatti
1930	Rene Dreyfus	Bugatti
1931	Louis Chrion	Bugatti
1932	Tazio Nuvolari	Alfa Romeo
1933	Achille Varzi	Bugatti
1934	Guy Moll	Alfa Romeo
1935	Luigi Fagioli	Mercedes-Benz
1936	Rudolf Carraciola	Mercedes-Benz
1937	Manfred von Brauchitsch	Mercedes-Benz
1948	Giuseppe Farina	Maserati
1950*	Juan Manuel Fangio	Alfa Romeo
1952	Vittorio Marzotto	Ferrari
1955	Maurice Trintignant	Ferrari
1956	Stirling Moss	Maserati
1957	Juan Manuel Fangio	Maserati
1958	Maurice Trintignant	Cooper-Climax
1959	Jack Brabham	Cooper-Climax
1960	Stirling Moss	Lotus-Climax
1961	Stirling Moss	Lotus-Climax
1962	Bruce McLaren	Cooper-Climax
1963	Graham Hill	BRM
1964	Graham Hill	BRM
1965	Graham Hill	BRM
1966	Jackie Stewart	BRM
1967	Denny Hulme	Brabham-Repco
1968	Graham Hill	Lotus-Ford
1969	Graham Hill	Lotus-Ford
1970	Jochen Rindt	Lotus-Ford
1971	Jackie Stewart	Tyrrell-Ford
1972	Jean-Pierre Beltoise	BRM
1973	Jackie Stewart	Tyrrell-Ford

Year	Driver	Team
1974	Ronnie Petersen	Lotus-Ford
1975	Niki Lauda	Ferrari
1976	Niki Lauda	Ferrari
1977	Jody Scheckter	Wolf-Ford
1978	Patrick Depailler	Tyrrell-Ford
1979	Jody Scheckter	Ferrari
1980	Carlos Reutemann	Williams-Ford
1981	Gilles Villeneuvev	Ferrari
1982	Riccardo Patrese	Brabham-Ford
1983	Keke Rosberg	Williams-Ford
1984	Alain Prost	McLaren-TAG
1985	Alain Prost	McLaren-TAG
1986	Alain Prost	McLaren-TAG
1987	Ayrton Senna	Lotus-Honda
1988	Alain Prost	McLaren-Honda
1989	Ayrton Senna	McLaren-Honda
1990	Ayrton Senna	McLaren-Honda
1991	Ayrton Senna	McLaren-Honda
1992	Ayrton Senna	McLaren-Honda
1993	Ayrton Senna	McLaren-Ford
1994	Michael Schumacher	Benetton-Ford
1995	Michael Schumacher	Benetton-Renault
1996	Olivier Panis	Ligier-Mugen Honda
1997	Michael Schumacher	Ferrari
1998	Mika Hakkinen	McLaren-Mercedes
1999	Michael Schumacher	Ferrari
2000	David Coutlhard	McLaren-Mercedes
2001	Michael Schumacher	Ferrari
2002	David Coutlhard	McLaren-Mercedes
2003	Juan Pablo Montoya	Williams-BMW
2004	Jarno Trulli	Renault
2005	Kimi Raikkonen	McLaren-Mercedes
2006	Fernando Alonso	Renault
2007	Fernando Alonso	McLaren-Mercedes
2008	Lewis Hamilton	McLaren-Mercedes
2009	Jenson Button	Brawn-Mercedes
2010	Mark Webber	Red Bull-Renault
2011	Sebastian Vettel	Red Bull-Renault
2012	Mark Webber	Red Bull-Renault
2013	Nico Rosberg	Mercedes

* *World Drivers Championship from 1950. No race held in 1938–47, 1949, 1951, 1953–54.*

⬢ GP AT NURBURGRING BUT NO GERMAN GP ⬢

In 2006, the FIA revealed that the European Grand Prix was to be removed from the calendar. It was also announced that the German Grand Prix would alternate between the Hockenheimring and the Nurburgring, but this arrangement would start only from 2008, with the Nurburgring hosting the race in 2007. This created a problem because the title of German Grand Prix was owned by the operators at Hockenheim and they weren'r prepared to release it to the Nurburgring in 2007. The upshot was that the 2007 race at the Nurburgring was actually called the *Grosser Preis von Europa* (European Grand Prix – won by McLaren's Fernando Alonso). With the 2008 arrival of the street race in Valencia, Spain, gaining the European GP designation, the 2008 GP at Hockenheim was called the German Grand Prix.

Did You Know That?
The first race to be called the "European Grand Prix" was the 1923 Italian Grand Prix at Monza won by Italy's Carlo Salmano in a Fiat.

⬢ RACING COLOURS ⬢

Until sponsorship became commonplace in Formula One in the 1960s, cars raced in what was considered their national colours. Some of these reflected the colours of their flags or national colours of reprsentative teams, others were more arbitrary. The six main competing nations were France, Germany, Great Britain, Italy, Japan and the United States, though there were regular entrants from Argentina, Australia, Brazil, South Africa, Spain and Sweden. These were the colours of the 12 nations:

Argentina:............Blue, with yellow bonnet and black chassis
Australia:..............Green and gold with blue
Brazil:...................Pale yellow with green chassis and wheels
France:..................Blue
Germany:..............White*
Great Britain:....Green (a dark shade, known as British Racing Green)
Italy:......................Red
Japan:...................Ivory white with a red disk on the bonnet
South Africa:.....Gold and green
Spain:...................Red with yellow bonnet, red chassis and springs
Sweden:...............Blue with yellow on top and three blue bands
United States:...White with blue sripes

* German teams often raced in base metal, believing that without paint the cars would be lighter.

❈ THINGS AREN'T QUITE WHAT THEY SEEM ❈

A quick glance at the calendar for the 2008 Formula One Grand Prix season would have suggested almost perfect continuity. After all, six of the seven venues hosting races in 1950, the inaugural year of the World Drivers' Championship, were among of the 18 venues for the 2008 title race: Britain, Monaco, USA, Belgium, France and Italy.

Monza in Italy, however, was the only racetrack to have staged the same race in all 59 championships. The French GP was staged every year (except 1955) until 2008, but it was at Reims, Rouen, Clermont-Ferrand, Le Mans, Paul Ricard, Dijon and Magny-Cours. In America, the Indianapolis 500 – which dates back to 1911 – was a part of the Formula One Championship from 1950 to 1960, but using a section of the 2.5-mile banked circuit, it hosted the US GP from 2000 to 2007. Monaco was used every year, apart from 1951, 1953 and 1954, always on the famous street circuit. The British GP was staged every year, but Aintree and Brands Hatch both hosted races. Belgium's Grand Prix has been off the calendar six times in the 59 years and from 1972 to 1982, it was at either Nivelles or Zolder.

The one GP from 1950 which was no longer part of the calendar was the Swiss Grand Prix, at Bremgarten, near Bern. It ran for only five years before the Swiss Government, reacting to the 80 fatalities at the Le Mans 24 Hour in 1955, banned the sport in the country. There was a Swiss Grand Prix in 1975 and 1982, but the races were in nearby Dijon, France. In that former race, there was even a "home" victory for Swiss driver Clay Regazzoni.

❈ HOW PRANCING HORSE FLEW ONTO A CAR ❈

The Prancing Horse emblem of Ferrari has a history all its own. It was originally emblazoned on the SPAD fighter plane flown by Italy's most famous World War 1 pilot, Francesco Baracca. After Baracca's death in a plane crash, his parents took the prancing horse logo in his memory. Friends of young racing driver Enzo Ferrari, they were so taken his skill and talent that they asked him to continue Baracca's tradition of sportsmanship, gallantry and boldness.

❈ FAST TALK (24) ❈

"A miss is as good as a mile."
Eddie Irvine, responding to an angry Ayrton Senna after Irvine had nearly made contact with the race leader during his F1 debut in the 1993 Japanese Grand Prix

❂ LEWIS HAMILTON DONE FOR SPEEDING ❂

On 18 December 2007, British Formula One sensation Lewis Hamilton was fined, and had his driving licence suspended in France for one month, 48 hours after being caught speeding on a French motorway. He was clocked travelling at 196km/h (122mph) in a Mercedes near to Laon in northern France. The motorway speed limit in France is 130 km/h (81 mph).

❂ THE ICEMAN MELTS AWAY OPPONENTS ❂

Ferrari's Kimi Raikkonen won his first Formula One World Drivers' Championship after winning the season-ending Brazilian Grand Prix. Few gave the Finn nicknamed "The Iceman" much hope of winning the title as he trailed Lewis Hamilton by seven points and Hamilton's McLaren team-mate and defending double World Champion Fernando Alonso by three. Hamilton, seeking to become the first ever rookie to win Formula One's World Championship, could finish only seventh, while Alonso was third, behind the second Ferrari of hometown favourite Felipe Massa. Second place would have been good enough for Alonso to retain his title but Raikkonen – who won two more GPs than both Hamilton and Alonso – clinched the Championship with 110 points, one more than Hamilton and Alonso, with Massa a further 15 points adrift. Second place in the Championship eventually went to Hamilton, on a second count-back rule, having scored one more second-place race finish than Alonso.

❂ FAST TALK (25) ❂

"It's pretty impossible to put into words. I thought do I have it? Do I have it? And when they told me I was ecstatic."
Lewis Hamilton, after becoming the 2008 Drivers' World Champion

❂ EURO LEGENDS ❂

The European Grand Prix's history, stretches back to the 1920s, even though, for more than 50 years. it was not actually a race. One Grand Prix almost every year from 1923 to 1977 was designated as the European GP – predating the World Championship by 27 years. It had its own race 1983–85 and again 1993–2012, except for 1998. England's Brands Hatch (1983, 1985) and Donington (1993), Germany's Nurburgring (1984, 1995–96, 1999–2007) and Spain's Jerez (1994, 1997) and Valencia (2008–12) hosted the European GP.

❀ 2009 DRIVERS' WORLD CHAMPIONSHIP ❀

Pos	Driver	Nationality	Team	Pts
1.	Jenson Button	British	Brawn GP-Mercedes	95
2.	Sebastian Vettel	German	Red Bull-Renault	84
3.	Rubens Barrichello	Brazilian	Brawn GP-Mercedes	77
4.	Mark Webber	Australian	Red Bull-Renault	69.5
5.	Lewis Hamilton	British	McLaren-Mercedes	49
6.	Kimi Räikkönen	Finnish	Ferrari	48
7.	Nico Rosberg	German	Williams-Toyota	34.5
8.	Jarno Trulli	Italian	Toyota	32.5
9.	Fernando Alonso	Spanish	Renault	26
10.	Timo Glock	German	Toyota	24

❀ 2009 CONSTRUCTORS' CUP ❀

Pos	Constructor	Pts
1.	Brawn GP-Mercedes	172
2.	Red Bull-Renault	153.5
3.	McLaren-Mercedes	71
4.	Ferrari	70
5.	Toyota	59.5
6.	BMW Sauber	36
7.	Williams-Toyota	34.5
8.	Renault	26
9.	Force India-Mercedes	13
10.	Toro Rosso-Ferrari	8

Did You Know That?
The 2009 season was the first time since 2005 that all participating teams had scored World Championship points.

❀ NO HOME ADVANTAGE ❀

Ten different Frenchmen have won the French Grand Prix, but only three did so after 1950, the first year of the Drivers World Championship. Germany's Michael Schumacher won the race eight times, the most success a driver has enjoyed at any Grand Prix worldwide. Second on the list is actually a home driver, Alain Prost, whose six wins came at three circuits, Paul Ricard (four times), Dijon and Magny-Cours (once each). Jean-Pierre Jabouille – at Dijon in 1979 – and Rene Arnoux – Paul Ricard. 1982 – were the other post-1950 home winners. Louis Chiron, from Monaco, won five French GPs between 1931 and 1949.

❂ 2010 DRIVERS' WORLD CHAMPIONSHIP ❂

Pos	Driver	Nationality	Team	Pts
1.	Sebastian Vettel	German	Red Bull-Renault	256
2.	Fernando Alonso	Spanish	Ferrari	252
3.	Mark Webber	Australian	Red Bull-Renault	242
4.	Lewis Hamilton	British	McLaren-Mercedes	240
5.	Jenson Button	British	McLaren-Mercedes	214
6.	Felipe Massa	Brazilian	Ferrari	144
7.	Nico Rosberg	German	Mercedes GP	142
8.	Robert Kubica	Polish	Renault	136
9.	Michael Schumacher	German	Mercedes	72
10.	Rubens Barrichello	Brazilian	Williams-Cosworth	47

❂ 2010 CONSTRUCTORS' CUP ❂

Pos	Constructor	Pts
1.	Red Bull-Renault	498
2.	McLaren-Mercedes	454
3.	Ferrari	396
4.	Mercedes	214
5.	Renault	163
6.	Williams-Cosworth	69
7.	Force India-Mercedes	68
8.	BMW Sauber-Ferrari	44
9.	Toro Rosso-Ferrari	13
10.	Lotus-Cosworth	0

❂ SWITCHING HOMES ❂

Following the FIA decision to drop the European Grand Prix from the calendar in 2013, it was agreed that the Spanish Grand Prix would alternate between the Circuit de Catalunya, just outside of Barcelona – the long-time home of the race – and the Valencia street circuit, where the European event had been staged 2008–12. And home fans had much to celebrate in that final running of the European GP as Fernando Alonso won the race driving for Ferrari.

❂ SHARING IT AROUND ❂

The first seven races of the 2012 F1 season had seven different winners: Jenson Button, Fernando Alonso, Nico Rosberg, Sebastian Vettel, Pastor Maldonado Mark Webber and Lewis Hamilton.

❁ BRAWN AND BRAINS IN PERFECT SYNCH ❁

The Brawn GP-Mercedes F1 team was formed as a result of a management buy-out from the former Honda team in late 2008. Brawn GP won six of the first seven races of the 2009 season with Jenson Button triumphing each time. Button and Brawn won their respective championships in 2009, after which Mercedes bought the team and Button went to McLaren. Ross Brawn, the eponymous team principal, took the same role at Mercedes in 2010, but retired, aged 59, in December 2013.

❁ NO CHANGES, UNIQUELY ❁

The 2008 Formula One Drivers' World Championship was the first one in which all 11 teams used the same two drivers throughout the season, though Super Aguri did pull out after four races..

❁ A GOOD PLACE TO START WINNING ❁

Five drivers have broken their Formula One ducks in the Canadian Grand Prix. A Canadian, Gilles Villeneuve, was the first in 1978, and he has been succeeded by Thierry Boutsen in 1989, Jean Alesi, 1995 (his only win, and on his 31st birthday), Lewis Hamilton, 2007, and Robert Kubica, 2008. Hamilton is the only one of the quintet to go on to win the Canadian GP again, in 2010 and 2012.

❁ LONG WAIT ❁

When Mark Webber claimed his first pole position, at the 2009 German Grand Prix, at the Nurburgring, it was the firsr time an Australian had been at the front of an F1 World Championship grid since World Champion to be Alan Jones, at Hockenheim, Germany, in 1980. Webber went on to take his first chequered flag too.

❁ NEW KIDS ON THE BLOCK ❁

In season 2011, DRS (Drag Reduction System) rear wings were introduced as an aid to overtaking. It could only be used if the driver behind was within one second of the man he was trying to overtake, and would automatically switch off on the application of the brakes. The advantage gained by using the system differed from circuit to circuit, with the Abu Dhabi GP seeing 89 percent of the moves with DRS on, but at the twisty Monaco Grand Prix only 13 percent of the overtaking manoeuvres came with DRS being used.

❋ AS CLOSE AS IT GETS ❋

Entering the final race of the 2008 Drivers' World Championship, Lewis Hamilton held a seven-point lead over Felipe Massa, who was on home soil at Interlago, Brazil. The Ferrari driver had to win and hope that Hamilton finished no better than sixth, or finish second with the McLaren-Mercedes out of the points. Massa did his bit, driving a masterful race, but the drama happened behind him as heavy rain fell in the dying stages. Hamilton pitted for intermediate tyres and slipped from fourth to sixth, just behind Sebastian Vettel and a long way behind Timo Glock, who decided not to change his rubber. Despite his best efforts, Hamilton could not finad a way past the German in his Toro-Rosso Ferrari as they sped around the final lap. Massa took the chequered flag and, for about 35 seconds, was World Champion. However, without any traction, Glock's Toyota was slipping and sliding all over the track. At the final corner, Vettel held his line, keeping Hamilton behind him, but Glock couldn't defend his place and the young Brit sped past him into fifth place. The three points Hamilton won were enough to finish on 98, one more than the devastated Massa. Ferrari's only consolation came with Kimi Raikkonen's third place which secured the Constructor's Cup.

❋ SEBASTIAN VETTEL, POP STAR ❋

In the summer of 2012, Sebastian Vettel displayed his driving skills away the track when he appeared in a music video for Melanie Fiona's song "Watch Me Work." In the music video he takes her for a drive in a red Infiniti G37 convertible and performs as a DJ.

❋ RUSSIA ENTERS FORMULA ONE ❋

The 2014 Formula One calendar includes a stop at Sochi, Russia, for the first time. In 2013, Sauber announced the signing of 17-year-old Russian Formula Renault 3.5 series driver Sergey Sirotkin. Sauber hoped to have him racing for them in 2014. which would have made him the youngest ever Formula One driver, surpassing Spaniard Jaime Alguersuari, who was 19 when he made his debut in 2009.

❋ FAST TALK (26) ❋

"Jenson won it and deserved it but he won it in the first six or seven races. The second half of the season was mine."
Rubens Barrichello, on his Brawn GP team-mate, in 2009.

● POSSESSION IS NO PARTS OF THE LAW ●

The 2010 Formula One season had a unique trait in that no man actually won a Grand Prix when they were leading World Drivers' Championship. The lead changed hands on many occasions, with Fernando Alonso (Ferrari), Mark Webber (Red Bull-Renault) and Lewis Hamilton (McLaren-Mercedes) and eventual champion Sebastian Vettel (Red Bull-Renault) all occupying top spot. When Vettel became World Champion he emulated James Hunt, in 1977, as the overall champion in the same season he had first been at the top of the table.

● WHAT'S IN A NAME? ●

A dispute over naming rights between Team Lotus and Group Lotus (Lotus Renault GP) flared up before the 2011 Formula One season. It was eventually settled by the courts, in favour of Team Lotus, the result of which was that both Team Lotus and Lotus Renault GP were on the starting grid – to say nothing of Red Bull and Toro Rosso, who were at least owned by the same man, Dieter Materschitz.

Did You Know That?
The name games continued in 2012 as Team Lotus became Caterham F1 Team, Lotus Renault GP was Lotus F1 Team and Marussia Virgin changed to Marussia F1 Team.

● VETTEL CLAIMS MORE RECORDS ●

Sebastian Vettel rewrote the Formula One record books at the end of the 2013 season. Records Vettel set or equalled in the season include:

◈ Points total.............397 (his own previous mark was 392 in 2011) ◈
◈ Winning margin......155 (Jenson Button was 122 behind in 2011) ◈
◈ Consecutive wins.....9 (beating Michael Schumacher's 7 in 2004) ◈
◈ Wins in a season......13 (matching Michael Schumacher in 2004) ◈

● IT'S NOT ALL ABOUT MICHAEL ●

Michael Schumacher holds the Formula One record for most wins, 91, and runners-up finishes, 43, but when it comes to third place, two men lead the way and both have Ferrari links. Rubens Barrichello, Michael's long-time team-mate, and Kimi Raikkonen, his successor as Ferrari's No. 1, have been on the bottom step of the podium 28 times, two more than Fernando Alonso and seven more than Michael.

❁ 2011 DRIVERS' WORLD CHAMPIONSHIP ❁

Pos	Driver	Nationality	Team	Pts
1.	Sebastian Vettel	German	Red Bull-Renault	392
2.	Jenson Button	British	McLaren-Mercedes	270
3.	Fernando Alonso	Spanish	Ferrari	258
4.	Mark Webber	Australian	Red Bull-Renault	257
5.	Lewis Hamilton	British	McLaren-Mercedes	227
6.	Felipe Massa	Brazilian	Ferrari	118
7.	Nico Rosberg	German	Mercedes GP	89
8.	Michael Schumacher	German	Mercedes GP	76
9.	Adrian Sutil	German	Force India-Mercedes	42
10.	Vitaly Petrov	Russian	Renault	37

❁ 2011 CONSTRUCTORS' CUP ❁

Pos	Constructor	Pts
1.	Red Bull-Renault	650
2.	McLaren-Mercedes	497
3.	Ferrari	375
4.	Mercedes GP	165
5.	Renault	73
6.	Force India-Mercedes	69
7.	Sauber-Ferrari	44
8.	Toro Rosso-Ferrari	41
9.	Williams-Cosworth	5
10.	Lotus-Renault	0

❁ ONE WORLD CHAMPION REPLACES ANOTHER ❁

Michael Schumacher's three year contract with Mercedes GP came to an end at the end of the 2012 Formula One season and the seven times former World Drivers' Champion declined to renew his contract. The German team signed up the 2008 World Champion, Lewis Hamilton from McLaren, to replace from for the 2013 season

❁ MASSA THE ETERNAL BRIDESMAID ❁

Felipe Massa never won the World Drivers' Championship, but his team-mates won 11 between them. At Sauber in 2005, it was 1997 World Champion Jacques Villeneuve. Then, at Ferrari, he was No. 2 to World Champions Michael Schumacher, (1994–95, 2000–2004) Kimi Raikkonen (2007) and Fernando Alonso (2005–06).

⚙ INDIA'S FIRST FORMULA ONE DRIVER ⚙

Kumar Ran Narain Karthikeyan – he used the forename Narain – was the India's first Formula One driver. He made his Formula One debut at the 2005 Australian Grand Prix for Jordan, collecting five points from 20 rances. After spending 2006–07 as Williams' test driver, Narain moved to stock car racing before returning to Formula One with back-markers HRT (Hispana Racing Team) during the 2011 season. He spent all of 2012 with the uncompetitive HRT team, and in 29 races for them didn't manage a single top-ten finish. HRT did not take part in the 2013 Constructors' Cup and Karthikeyan was left without a drive, competing instead in the Auto GP World Series (formerly the Euroseries 3000)..

⚙ ALMOST HALF A LIFETIME ⚙

The youngest average age of the three drivers to stand on the podium after a Formula One Grand Prix is 23 years and 350 days, at the Italian Grand Prix at Monza on 14 September 2008. The winner was Sebastian Vettel (Scuderia Toro Rosso, born 2 July 1987), He was followed home by Heikki Kovalainen (McLaren-Mercedes, born 19 October 1981) and Robert Kubicka (BMW-Sauber, born 7 December 1984). Vettel was also the youngest driver ever to win a Formula One Grand Prix. By comparison, the oldest ever trio to finish 1–2–3 came in the first year of the Drivers' World Championship. Nino Farina (born 30 October 1906), Luigi Fagioli (born 9 June 1898) and Louis Rosier (born 5 November 1905) occupied the first three places at the Swiss Grand Prix at Bremgarten on 4 June 1950 and their average was 46 years and 235 days.

⚙ LIKE FATHER, LIKE SON ⚙

On 15 April 2012, Nico Rosberg (Mercedes), won the Chinese Grand Prix, and became the third second-generation driver to match his father and a Grand Prix. The two families who had done it previously were Damon (son of Graham) Hill and Jacques (son of Gilles Villeneuve). Both Keke Rosberg, Nico's dad, and Graham Hill were Drivers' World Champions (Damon followed in his father's footsteps), whereas Jacques was Champion but his father was not.

Did You Know That?
Nico became the first son of a former Monaco Grand Prix winner when he won around the strees of the principality in 2013.

❀ A RAPID ASCENT ❀

Excluding the first few years of the Drivers' World Championship in the 1950s, the earliest a man has become World Champion is in his second season of F1. The first man to achieve it was Jacques Villeneuve, who made his debut for Williams in 1996 and was World Champion a year later. He did, however, have a number of years of open-wheel experience, racing in North America's CART Championship, which he won – along with that year's Indianapolis 500 – in 1995. Lewis Hamilton (McLaren), was new to Formula 1 in 2007 (aged 22 years and 70 days when making his debut) and World Champion in 2008.

❀ BREAKING ALL THE RECORDS ❀

Sebastian Vettel has long been considered one of the greatest drivers in Formula One history but, remarkably, he entered the 2013 season almost four months short of his 26th birthday. He holds the records for the youngest F1 race-winner, youngest Drivers' World Champion, youngest two-time World Champion, youngest three-time World Champion and, of course, the youngest four-time winner too.

❀ AFTER THE MADNESS ❀

After the frantic start to the 2012 Formula One season, when seven different drivers triumphed in the first seven races, normality was restord. In fact, those seven drivers shared 12 of the remaining 13 races – Sebastian Vettel taking the lion's share with four more, Lewis Hamilton, three, and Fernando Alonso and Jenson Button, two each. The only other driver to win a race in 2012 was Kimi Raikkonen, who claimed the Abu Dhabi GP for. Lotus.

❀ STEPPING UP ❀

The best training ground for Formula One drivers is now accepted to be the GP2 series. The up-and-coming drivers learn their trade on the same circuits as the Formula One men – there were 11 races in 2013, and all were part of the F1 Grand Prix weekends. Instituted in 2005, six of the seven champions before 2012 had graduated to Formula One, whilst the other, 2008 winner Giorgio Pantano, had driven for Jordan in Formula One during the 2004 season. Only one, however, had gone on to win the Formula One Drivers' World Championship and that was the 2006 champion, Lewis Hamilton, who went on to complete this so far unique double in 2008.

❁ 2012 DRIVERS' WORLD CHAMPIONSHIP ❁

Pos	Driver	Nationality	Team	Pts
1.	Sebastian Vettel	German	Red Bull-Renault	281
2.	Fernando Alonso	Spanish	Ferrari	278
3.	Kimi Räikkönen	Finnish	Lotus-Renault	207
4.	Lewis Hamilton	British	McLaren-Mercedes	190
5.	Jenson Button	British	McLaren-Mercedes	188
6.	Mark Webber	Australian	Red Bull-Renault	179
7.	Felipe Massa	Brazilian	Ferrari	122
8.	Romain Grosjean	French	Lotus-Renault	96
9.	Nico Rosberg	German	Mercedes GP	93
10.	Sergio Perez	Mexican	Sauber-Ferrari	66

❁ 2012 CONSTRUCTORS' CUP ❁

Pos	Constructor	Pts
1.	Red Bull-Renault	460
2.	Ferrari	400
3.	McLaren-Mercedes	378
4.	Lotus-Renault	303
5.	Mercedes	142
6.	Sauber-Ferrari	126
7.	Force India-Mercedes	109
8.	Williams-Renault	76
9.	Toro Rosso-Ferrari	26
10.	Caterham-Renault	0

❁ PODIUM VETERAN ❁

When Michael Schumacher stood on the podium for the first time, at the Mexican Grand Prix on 22 March 1992, Jean-Eric Vergne had not celebrated his second birthday. When Schumi made it to the podium after the European Grand Prix at Valencia on 24 June 2012, Vergne was in the field (he retired after 26 laps). However, Schumacher's span of 20 years, three months and two days (7,369 days) remains the longest time between first and last podium finishes.

❁ FAST TALK (27) ❁

"Not bad for a No. 2 driver."
Mark Webber, definitely not top dog at Red Bull Racing, but the winner of the 2010 British Grand Prix at Silverstone

❀ SEBASTIAN VETTEL ❀

Sebastian Vettel was born in Heppenheim, then West Germany, on 3 July 1987. Like so many future champions, he began racing competitively in karts when he was just eight years old. His talents were quickly spotted and, in 1998, 11-year-old Sebastian joined the Red Bull Junior team. His first important victory came in the Junior Monaco Kart Cup, in 2001. Two years later, he moved to open-wheel cars and was almost unstoppable in the 2004 German Formula BMW Championship, claiming victory 18 times in 20 races.

The next step up was to Formula 3 Euro Series racing, where he finished fifth for the ASL Mucke Motorsport team and won rookie of the season honours. His reward included a testing session with the Sauber F1 team, and he was taken on as a test driver in 2007, although he also competed in the Formula 3.5 series. On 15 June 2007, following an injury to Robert Kubica, Sebastian made his Formula One debut and it was a spectacular success. He qualified seventh for the United States Grand Prix and finished eighth, becoming, at 19 years and 357 days, the youngest driver to earn a World Championship point. Sauber released Sebastian from his contract as Toro Rosso offered him a regular seat for the final seven races of the 2007 season and at Shanghai, China, he took a brilliant fourth-place finish. In 2008, he became the youngest-ever Formula One World Championship race-winner, at Monza, Italy,

For the 2009 season, Sebastian moved to Red Bull Racing, a team moving towards the top of the Formula One ladder and Vettel was the perfect driver for them. He finished runner-up in the World Championship, 11 points behind Brawn's Jenson Button, but three retirements in mid-season proved costly. Sebastian would not be denied in 2010. He won five races, including the three of the last four, to pip Fernando Alonso to the World Championship by four points.

Seabstian set a new record, 392 points, in winning the 2011 title. Supported by Red Bull No.2 driver Mark Webber, he claimed pole position 15 times in 19 races and won 11 races. A third World Championship came in 2012, followed, a year later by more record-breaking. His points total was 397, he matched Michael Schumacher's 2004 mark of 13 victories, and he set a new standard with nine consecutive wins to end the season, and 11 in the last 12 races. Aged 29, people now talk about Sebastian as being possibly F1's best-ever driver.

Did You Know That?
Sebastian's early heroes were the "Three Michaels" – Schumacher, Jordan and Jackson. His wanted to be a singer, but soon realised he didn't have the voice for it.

❀ MOURNING FOR MARIA ❀

Formula 1 suffered a sad loss on 11 October 2013, when Maria De Villota was found dead in Valencia. The 33-year-old daughter of former F1 driver Emilo De Villota had been a test driver for Marussia in July 2012, but a terrible accident in testing at Duxford Aerodrome, Cambridgeshire, resulted in the loss of an eye. Her death was due to natural causes resulting from her injuries.

❀ FAST TALK (28) ❀

"To finish first in a motor race, first you must finish."
Maybe the single most important piece of advice in Formula One

❀ NEW LOOK COMING FOR SILVERSTONE ❀

On 11 September 2013, Silverstone's owners signed a £32 million deal with MEPC to build warehouses and hotels alongside the circuit.

❀ A LONG, LONG WAIT ❀

Nico Rosberg's victory in the 2012 Chinese Grand Prix for Mercedes GP was the team's first Grand Prix victory as a works squad since 1955 when Juan Manuel Fangio won the Italian GP. Of course, Mercedes did not run a works team after 1955, until they bought the Brawn Racing team following its 2009 Constructors' Cup triumph.

❀ THREE TIMES FOUR ❀

The 2013 Forumla One grid contained ten different nationalities, but Great Britain, France and Germany all provided four. Germany's World Champion Sebastian Vettel was joined by compatriots Nico Rosberg, Adrian Sutil and Nico Hulkenburg; the four Frenchmen were Romain Grosjean, Jean-Eric Vergne, Charles Pic and Jules Bianchi; the British flag was flown by Lewis Hamilton, Jenson Button, Paul di Resta and Max Chilton.

❀ POWER CUTS ❀

The 2013 season was the final year in which Formula One teams could use the 2.4-litre V8 engine configuration which was introduced in 2006. From the 2014 season, the engines would be 1.6-litre turbocharged V6s.

❂ 2013 DRIVERS' WORLD CHAMPIONSHIP ❂

Pos	Driver	Nationality	Team	Pts
1.	Sebastian Vettel	German	Red Bull	397
2.	Fernando Alonso	Spanish	Ferrari	242
5.	Mark Webber	Australian	Red Bull	199
4.	Lewis Hamilton	British	Mercedes	189
3.	Kimi Raikkonen	Finnish	Lotus	183
6.	Nico Rosberg	German	Mercedes	171
7.	Romain Grosjean	French	Lotus	132
8.	Felipe Massa	Brazilian	Ferrari	112
9.	Jenson Button	British	McLaren	73
10.	Nico Hulkenberg	German	Sauber	51

❂ 2013 CONSTRUCTORS' CUP ❂

Pos	Constructor	Pts
1.	Red Bull	596
2.	Mercedes	360
3.	Ferrari	354
4.	Lotus	315
5.	McLaren	122
6.	Force India	77
7.	Sauber	57
8.	Toro Rosso	33
9.	Williams	5
10.	Marussia	0

❂ MICHAEL SAYS "NEIN" ❂

When Kimi Raikkonen had back surgery at the end of the 2013 season, Lotus needed a driver for the last three races. After Michael Schumacher rejected their approach, Heikki Koivalainen stepped in.

❂ MERRY-GO-ROUND STARTS EARLY ❂

The 2014 Formula One season was going to look different following the departure of two veterans in 2013. Red Bull Racing quickly replaced their No. 2, Mark Webber, with another Australian, Daniel Ricciardo, from sister team Torro Roso. Ferrari, meanwhile, turned back the clock to replace Felipe Massa with their last World Champion (in 2007), Kimi Raikkonen, who had been with Lotus. It set up a busy off-season, as many teams either hired rival drivers or brought in fresh faces.

❀ MANY HAPPY RETURNS ❀

The United States Grand Prix was off the Formula One calendar between 2008 and 2012. The race had been staged on and off throughout the history of the Drivers' World Championship, and had been at a special circuit at the Indianapolis Motor Speedway from 2000. A brand new circuit was built to host the 2012 US GP, at the Circuit of the Americas, close to Austin, the capital of Texas. Some things don't change, however, and the winner of the last race at Indianapolis was also the first at the Circuit of the Americas: Lewis Hamilton, driving for McLaren.

❀ KEEP OUT OF THE WAY ❀

A TV cameraman was hit by a tyre which came off Mark Webber's car in the pits at the 2013 German Grand Prix. He was airlifted to hospital, after which the FIA rules that film crews and other media were no longer allowed to patrol inside the pitlane during racess.

❀ VETTEL'S WORLD TITLE FOUR-TIMER ❀

After a very tightly contested first half of the 2013 season, Sebastian Vettel and Red Bull ran away with the Drivers' and Constructors' World Championships, both with record totals. Vettel won all of the last nine races to match Michael Schumacher's 2004 total of 13 Grand Prix wins in a season. The German maestro finished a record on a best-ever 397 points, 155 ahead of his nearest challenge, Fernando Alonso of Ferrari, with Red Bull team-mate almost 200 behind in third place. Red Bull's points total of 596 was also a record. Mercedes drivers Louis Hamilton and Nico Rosberg finished fourth and sixth in the Drivers' table, but their team total of 360 was the second-best overall.

Did You Know That?
Only three men had won the Drivers' World Championship four times before Vettel, (Michael Schumacher with seven – including five in a row – Juan Manuel Fangio, who won five, and Alain Prost).

❀ FAST TALK (29) ❀

"I can't wait to be driving a Ferrari car again and to reacquaint myself with so many people with whom I had such close links, as well as working with Fernando, whom I consider a great driver."
Kimi Raikkonen, announcing his return to Ferrari for the 2014 season.

❀ INDEX ❀

Abecassis, George 48
Abu Dhabi Grand Prix 173, 175
Adams, Phillipe 65
Africa 38
AGS 52
Alboreto, Michele 21, 35, 55, 84, 90,
    93, 96, 98, 102, 105, 114, 142
Alesi, Jean 54, 68, 93, 104, 108, 111,
    114, 117, 121, 123, 127, 129,
    153, 173
Alfa Romeo 22, 80, 84, 85, 87, 90,
    102, 111
Alguersari, Jaime 174
Alliot, Phillipe 39
Allison, Cliff 38
Alonso, Fernando 8, 19, 42, 46, 49,
    52, 56, 73, 83, 89, 90, 95, 96, 101,
    107, 118, 120, 144, 146, 151, 151,
    152, 153, 154, 156, 157, 158. 163,
    164, 168, 170, 171, 172, 175, 176,
    178, 179, 180, 182, 183
Amon, Chris 42, 43, 45, 51, 56, 78
Anderson, Bob 19
Andretti, Mario 38, 49, 53, 69, 71,
    73, 75, 85, 118, 134, 150
Andretti, Michael 17, 18
Angelis, Elio de 35, 79, 80, 84, 90,
    93, 112
Argentinian Grand Prix 25, 42
Arnoux, Rene 54, 77, 79, 80, 84, 87,
    90, 96, 104, 118, 153, 171
Arrows 104, 133, 135
Arrows-Asiatech 139
Arrows-BMW 93, 96
Arrows-Ford 75, 77, 79, 80, 87, 90,
    104, 108
Arrows-Megatron 98, 102
Arrows-Supertec 137
Arrows-Yamaha 57, 129
Arundell, Peter 36, 107
Ascari, Alberto 8, 10, 11, 12, 15, 25,
    27, 29, 35, 49, 55, 61, 98, 103,
    104, 118, 158, 164
Ascari, Antonio 61
Ashley, Ian 62
Australian Grand Prix 41, 67, 82
Austrian Grand Prix 48
Avon Tyres 122

Baghetti, Giancarlo 31, 35, 68
Bahrain Grand Prix 145
Baldi, Mauro 39
Bandini, Lorenzo 34, 35, 36, 39, 41,
    68, 112
BAR 32, 128
BAR-Honda 139, 141, 144, 146, 151
Baracca, Francesco 169
Barnard, John 42
Barrichello, Rubens 48, 58, 63, 73,
    86, 115, 118, 121, 127, 135, 137,
    139, 141, 144, 146, 151, 152, 153,
    171, 172, 174, 175
Bauer, Erwin 86
Baumgartner, Zsolt 113
Beaufort, Carel de 112
Behra, Jean 18, 21, 47
Belgian Grand Prix 88, 169
Beltoise, Jean-Pierre 45, 46, 51,
    59, 68
Benetton-BMW 96
Benetton-Ford 98, 102, 104,
    108, 111, 114, 117, 120, 121,
    152, 154
Benetton-Playlife 133, 135, 137
Benetton-Renault 66, 123, 127,
    129, 139
Beretta, Olivier 162
Berger, Gerhard 55, 94, 95, 96, 98,
    102, 104, 108, 111, 114, 117, 121,
    123, 127, 129, 137, 152, 153
Beuttler, Mike 118
Bianchi, Jules 181
Bira, Prince 8
Blundell, Mark 117, 123
Bonetto, Felice 11, 15
Bonnier, Joakim 26, 37, 68, 95
Boutsen, Thierry 95, 98, 102, 104,
    108, 143, 173
Brabham-Alfa Romeo 69, 71, 75, 77
Brabham-BMW 84, 87, 90, 93, 96,
    98, 103, 109
Brabham-BRM 36
Brabham BT19 65
Brabham-Climax 32, 34, 36, 39, 41
Brabham, David 123
Brabham-Ford 46, 51, 53, 56, 59, 63,
    64, 79, 80, 84, 102

Brabham, Jack 20, 26, 27, 29, 32, 34, 36, 37, 39, 41, 43, 46, 49, 51, 88, 114, 118, 142, 148
Brabham-Judd 104, 108
Brabham-Repco 41, 43, 45, 66, 102
Brabham-Yamaha 111
Brambilla, Vittorio 68, 118, 122
Brawn, Ross 173
Brawn GP 66, 171, 173, 174
Brazilian Grand Prix 44, 58, 120, 135, 154, 174
Briatore, Flavio 52
Bridgestone Tyres 33, 89, 122
Brise, Tony 37
Bristow, Chris 112, 143
British Grand Prix 9, 22, 44, 82, 106–7, 116, 120, 127, 139, 142
British Racing Drivers' Club (BRDC) 9
BRM 24, 26, 29, 34, 36, 37, 39, 41, 43, 45, 46, 51, 53, 56, 59, 63, 66
BRM-Climax 31
BRM-Honda 137
Brooks, Tony 23, 24, 26, 31, 38, 76, 105, 135, 163
BRP-BRM 34, 36
Brundle, Martin 114, 117, 121
Bryan, Jimmy 16
Button, Jenson 9, 14, 19, 49, 89, 137, 141, 144, 146, 147, 151, 153, 155, 167, 171, 172, 174, 175, 176, 178, 179, 180, 181, 182, 183

Canadian Grand Prix 27, 109, 143, 154, 173
Capelli, Ivan 102, 108
Castellotti, Eugenio 18, 21, 27
Catalunya Circuit 52
Caterham Team 175, 179
Cesaris, Andrea de 15, 87, 101, 111, 114, 118, 141, 153
Cevert, Francois 16, 53, 54, 56, 59, 68, 112, 129
Chapman, Colin 11, 97, 113
Cheever, Eddie 87, 98
Chilton, Max 181
Chiron, Louis 8, 69, 118, 162, 171
Circuit Paul Richard 52
Clark, Jim 13, 14, 18, 29, 30, 31, 32, 34, 36, 39, 41, 42, 43, 49,

58, 72, 73, 89, 97, 107, 116, 136, 152, 155
Collins, Peter 21, 23, 24, 112
Concorde Agreement 161
Connaught-Alta 33
Constructors' Cup
all-time 66
1958–59: 24, 26, 66
1960–69: 29, 31, 32, 34, 36, 39, 41, 43, 45, 46, 51, 66, 116
1970–79: 51, 53, 56, 59, 63, 64, 66, 69, 71, 75, 77
1980–89: 66, 79, 80, 84, 87, 90, 93, 96, 98, 102, 104, 105
1990–99: 24, 66, 108, 111, 114, 117, 121, 123, 127, 129, 133, 135
2000–09: 66, 137, 139, 141, 144, 146, 151, 152, 160, 171, 174, 176, 179
2010–13: 172, 176, 179, 180, 182, 183
Continental tyres 122
Cooper 51
Cooper-BRM 45
Cooper-Castellotti 29
Cooper-Climax 24, 26, 29, 31, 32, 34, 36, 39, 43, 66
Cooper-Maserati 29, 41, 43
Cooper T51 37
Coughlan, Mike 157
Coulthard, David 14, 15, 19, 73, 99, 118, 121, 123, 127, 129, 133, 135, 137, 139, 141, 144, 146, 153, 155, 159, 162, 163, 165
Courage, Piers 46, 76, 112
Cross, Art 15

Dallara-Ferrari 114
Dallara-Ford 104
Dallara-Judd 111
Davidson, Anthony 125
Dennis, Ron 164
Depailler, Patrick 54, 63, 64, 69, 71, 75, 77, 112
Di Resta, Paul 181
Dijon-Prenois 52
Donington Park 9
Donnelly, Martin 123, 145
Donohue, Mark 112
Drag Reduction System (DRS) 173
Drivers' World Championship
all-time 49

1950–59: 8, 11, 12, 15, 16, 18, 21, 23, 24, 26, 108
1960–69: 29, 31, 32, 34, 36, 39, 41, 43, 45, 46
1970–79: 51, 53, 56, 59, 63, 64, 69, 71, 75, 77
1980–89: 79, 80, 84, 87, 90, 93, 96, 98, 102, 104
1990–99: 108, 111, 114, 117, 121, 124, 127, 129, 133, 135
2000–09: 137, 139, 114, 141, 144, 146, 151, 152. 160, 170, 171, 173
2010–13: 89, 103, 172, 175, 176, 178, 179, 181, 182, 183
points system 12
DRS (Drag Reduction System) 173
Dunlop tyres 122

Eagle-Climax 41
Eagle-Weslake 43
Ecclestone, Bernie 9, 33, 161
England, Paul 112
Englebert tyres 122
Ensign-Ford 71
European Grand Prix 172
Evans, Stuart-Lewis 33

Fabi, Teo 48, 98, 142
Fagioli, Luigi 11, 22, 68, 177
Fairman, Jack 21
Fangio, Juan Manuel 8, 11, 15, 16, 18, 21, 23, 28, 29, 40, 49, 55, 94, 98, 103, 115, 118, 143, 151, 158, 181, 183
Farina, Giuseppe (Nino) 8, 11, 12, 15, 16, 18, 22, 29, 35, 49, 50, 98, 103, 177
Federation Internationale du Sport Automobile (FISA) 33, 43, 76, 83, 85, 87, 97, 132, 157
Ferrari 11, 13, 23, 24, 26, 29, 31, 32, 34, 36, 39, 41, 42, 43, 44, 45, 46, 51, 53, 56, 59, 63, 64, 66, 69, 71, 75, 77, 79, 80, 84, 87, 90, 93, 94, 96, 98, 102, 104, 108, 111, 113, 114, 117, 120, 121, 123, 127, 129, 131, 133, 135, 136, 137, 139, 141, 144, 146, 151, 152, 154, 155, 157, 158, 159, 169, 171, 172, 174, 176, 179. 182, 183

Ferrari, Enzo 11, 13, 44, 55, 155, 169
Firestone tyres 122
Fischer, Rudi 12
Fisichella, Giancarlo 15, 19, 35, 73, 118, 129, 133, 135, 137, 151, 153
Fittipaldi, Emerson 18, 27, 49, 51, 53, 56, 59, 60, 63, 64, 73, 75, 82, 115, 118, 159, 165
Fittipaldi-Ford 71, 75, 79
Flaherty, Pat 21
Force India 159, 171, 172, 176, 179, 182
Footwork-Ford 121
Footwork-Hart 123, 127
Footwork-Mugen-Honda 114, 117
Formula One Constructors' Association (FOCA) 33
Foyt, A.J. 73
Frentzen, Heinz-Harald 74, 123, 129, 133, 135, 137
Frere, Paul 21

Gachot, Bertrand 62
Ganley, Howard 129
Gendebien, Olivier 29
German Grand Prix 47, 121, 168, 173, 183
Gethin, Peter 53, 68, 141
Ghinzani, Piercarlo 153
Giacomelli, Bruno 102
Ginther, Richie 29, 31, 32, 34, 36, 39, 68
Giunti, Ignazio 99
Glock, Timo, 74, 171, 174
Godia, Paco 21
Gonzalez, Jose Froilan 11, 12, 15, 16, 97, 113, 115, 118
Goodyear tyres 122
GP2 series 178
Graffenried, Toulo de 15
Grand Prix
  Abu Dhabi 173, 175
  Argentina 25, 42
  Australia 41, 67, 82
  Austria 48
  Bahrain 145
  Belgium 88, 169
  Brazil 44, 58, 120, 135, 154, 170, 174
  Britain 9, 22, 44, 82, 96, 106-7, 116, 120, 127, 139, 142, 169

Canada 27, 109, 143, 154, 173
circuits 72, 124–5, 169
Europe 34, 100, 168, 170, 172
France 20, 22, 40, 94, 110, 169, 171
Germany 47, 121, 168, 173, 183
Hungary 8, 9, 39, 56, 143, 162
India 161
Italy 23, 29, 44, 52, 71, 72, 81, 116, 125, 126, 169, 177
Japan 119
Luxembourg 121
Malaysia 90, 138, 143
Monaco 21, 38, 62, 101, 126, 164, 169, 173, 177
Russia 174
San Marino 68, 88
Singapore 52, 107
Spain 68, 116, 172
Switzerland 8, 169, 177
Turkey 154
United States 13, 18, 32, 38, 58, 86, 101, 119, 169, 180, 183
US East 21
US West 105
Gregory, Masten 23, 26
Grosjean, Romain 179, 181, 182
Gurney, Dan 26, 31, 32, 34, 36, 39, 43, 85, 126, 134

Hailwood, Mike 56
Hakkinen, Mika 12, 17, 49, 86, 95, 114, 118, 121, 123, 127, 129, 133, 135, 137, 139, 159, 165
Hamilton, Lewis 9, 14, 44, 46, 49, 86, 96, 107, 155, 156, 157, 161, 162, 164, 165, 167, 170, 181, 172, 173, 174, 175, 176, 178, 179, 181, 182, 183
Hanks, Sam 21, 23
HANS 103
Hawkins, Paul 164
Hawthorn, Mike 12, 15, 16, 23, 24, 38, 49, 62, 67, 70, 76, 105, 128, 144, 148, 155, 158
Head, Patrick 24
Heidfeld, Nick 74, 118, 139, 141
Herbert, Johnny 9, 38, 78, 117, 123, 129, 135
Herrmann, Hans 16, 93, 101
Hesketh-Ford 63, 64

Heyer, Hans 47
Hill, Damon 14, 19, 49, 57, 65, 117, 121, 123, 127, 133, 155, 177
Hill, Graham 13, 14, 18, 25, 27, 31, 32, 34, 36, 37, 38, 39, 41, 43, 45, 46, 49, 58, 73, 78, 81, 89, 118, 146, 155, 177
Hill, Phil 13, 24, 26, 29, 31, 32, 49, 134, 146, 158
Hockenheim 52, 168
Holland, Bill 8
Honda 22, 36, 39, 41, 43, 45, 49
Hulkenberg, Nico 74, 181, 182
Hulme, Denny 41, 43, 45, 46, 49, 51, 56, 59, 63, 82, 118, 145, 148
Hungarian Grand Prix 8, 9, 39, 56, 143, 162
Hunt, James 14, 22, 49, 59, 63, 64, 69, 71, 118, 119, 133, 155, 165, 175

Ickx, Jacky 33, 45, 46, 51, 53, 56, 59, 63, 95
Indianapolis 500 – 18, 27, 62, 68, 73, 132, 147, 169
Indianapolis Motor Speedway 86, 119, 169
Ireland, Innes 23, 29, 31, 34, 53, 68, 138
Irvine, Eddie 12, 17, 127, 129, 133, 135, 141, 148, 163, 169
Ishibashi, Shojiro 33
Iso Marlborough-Ford 59, 63
Italian Grand Prix 23, 29, 44, 52, 71, 72, 81, 116, 125, 126, 169, 177

Jabouille, Jean-Pierre 48, 54, 79, 171
Jaguar-Cosworth 137, 139, 141, 144, 146
Johansson, Stefan 90, 93, 96, 98
Johnson, Leslie 22
Jones, Alan 49, 71, 77, 79, 80, 84, 148, 173
Jordan, Eddie 15, 62
Jordan-Ford 111, 120, 144, 146
Jordan-Hart 121
Jordan-Honda 139, 141
Jordan-Mugen-Honda 133, 135, 137
Jordan-Peugeot 123, 127, 129
Jordan-Toyota 151

Karthikeyan, Narain 177
Kinnunen, Leo 118
Kling, Karl 16
Koinigg, Helmuth 112
Koivalainen, Heikki 68, 162, 177, 182
Kubica, Robert 8, 68, 172, 173, 177

Laffite, Jacques 54, 69, 71, 75, 77, 79, 80, 93, 96, 128, 153
Lancia 27
Langes, Claudio 123
Larrousse Lamborghini 117
Lauda, Niki 15, 28, 37, 49, 51, 56, 63, 64, 69, 71, 75, 84, 87, 90, 91, 93, 95, 108, 119, 158, 165
Le Mans 24 Hours 31, 42, 73, 129
Lehto, Jyrki Jarvilehto 28, 123
Levegh, Pierre 42
Lewis-Evans, Stuart 24, 77, 112
Leyton-House Judd 108
Ligier 52
Ligier-Ford 69, 77, 79
Ligier-Matra 71, 75, 80, 84
Ligier-Mugen-Honda 123, 127
Ligier-Renault 93, 96, 114, 117, 121
Lola-Climax 32, 36, 41
Lola-Ford 96, 98
Lola-Lamborghini 108
Lola Larrousse 52
Lombardi, Lella 80, 118
Lotus 23, 27, 49, 51, 82, 109, 113, 143, 175, 182
Lotus-BRM 32, 34, 36, 39, 41, 43
Lotus-Climax 24, 26, 29, 31, 32, 34, 36, 66
Lotus-Cosworth 172
Lotus-Ford 43, 45, 46, 51, 53, 56, 59, 63, 64, 66, 69, 71, 75, 77, 79, 80, 84, 114, 117
Lotus-Honda 98, 102
Lotus-Judd 104, 111
Lotus-Lamborghini 108
Lotus-Renault 87, 90, 93, 96, 175, 176, 179, 182
Lunger, Brett 91
Luxembourg Grand Prix 121

McLaren 24, 145, 156, 157, 162, 165
McLaren-BRM 43, 45
McLaren, Bruce 18, 26, 29, 31, 32,

34, 36, 39, 45, 46, 56, 148, 165
McLaren-Ford 41, 45, 46, 51, 53, 56, 59, 63, 64, 66, 69, 71, 75, 77, 79, 80, 82, 84, 87, 117
McLaren-Honda 66, 94, 102, 104, 108, 111, 114
McLaren-Mercedes 66, 123, 127, 129, 133, 135, 137, 139, 141, 144, 146, 151, 162, 171, 172, 176, 182, 183
McLaren-Peugeot 121
McLaren-TAG 37, 66, 90, 93, 96, 98
Maddock, Owen 37
Maggs, Tony 32, 34
Magnussen, Jan 45
Magny-Cours 52
Maldonado, Pastor 68, 158, 172, 183
Mallya, Vijay 159
Mansell, Greg 75
Mansell, Leo 75
Mansell, Nigel 14, 17, 19, 24, 25, 44, 48, 49, 59, 65, 73, 78, 90, 93, 94, 96, 98, 99, 100, 102, 104, 108, 111, 114, 117, 118, 121, 128, 131, 136, 146, 153, 155
Manzon, Robert 12
March-Ford 51, 53, 56, 59, 63, 64, 69
March-Ilmor 114
March-Judd 102
Marimon, Onofre Agustin 79, 112
Martini, Pierluigi 118, 139
Marussia 175
Maserati 24
Mass, Jochen 64, 68, 69, 71, 74
Massa, Felipe 101, 170, 182, 176, 179, 182
Mateschitz, Dietrich 139, 166, 175
Matra 45, 51, 53, 56
Matra-Ford 45, 46, 66
Matta, Cristiano Da 45
Mayer, Teddy 113
Mercedes 26, 28, 40, 55, 73, 120, 154, 172, 173, 175, 176, 177, 179, 181, 182, 183
Michelin Tyres 33, 42, 58, 109, 122
Mieres, Roberto 18
Minardi-Asiatech 141
Minardi-Cosworth 146, 151
Minardi-Ferrari 111
Minardi-Ford 102, 117, 121, 123, 135, 139

Mitter, Gerhard 112
Modena, Stefano 111
Monaco 52, 162, 164
Monaco Grand Prix 21, 38, 62, 101,
    126, 164, 166–7, 169, 173, 177
Montoya, Juan Pablo 73, 115, 139,
    141, 144, 146, 151
Montreal 52
Monza 44, 52, 169
Morbidelli, Gianni 67, 123
Moreno, Roberto 42, 111, 126
Moss, Stirling 14, 18, 21, 23, 24, 26,
    28, 29, 31, 53, 67, 76, 77, 105,
    109, 114, 118, 135, 143, 144, 163
Murray, Gordon 103
Musso, Luigi 16, 18, 23, 24, 68,
    112, 148

Nannini, Alessandro 35, 68, 102,
    104, 108
Nazaruk, Mike 11
Newey, Adrian 24, 85, 86
Night race 157
Nilsson, Gunnar 11, 68, 69, 71, 95
Nissen, Kris 47
Nurburgring 168

Oldest:
  driver 69
  podium 177
Onyx-Ford 104
Osterreichring 52

Pace, Carlos 64, 68, 115, 118
Paletti, Riccardo 112
Panis, Olivier 68, 123, 127, 129
Pantano, Giorgio 178
Parkes, Mike 41
Parnell, Reg 11, 22
Parnelli-Ford 64
Parsons, Johnnie 8, 47, 147, 150
Patrese, Riccardo 24, 35, 79, 84, 87,
    88, 101, 104, 105, 108, 111, 114,
    117, 153
Penske-Ford 69
Perez, Sergio 118, 179, 182, 183
Perkins, Larry 131
Peterson, Ronnie 44, 53, 56, 59, 63,
    75, 95, 109, 112, 118
Petrov, Vitaly 176

Pian, Alfredo 12
Pic, Charles 181
Pietsch, Paul 116
Piquet, Nelsinho 63
Piquet, Nelson 13, 25, 28, 46, 48, 49,
    73, 79, 80, 87, 90, 92, 93, 94, 96,
    98, 102, 104, 108, 109, 111, 115,
    125, 128, 142, 150, 152, 153, 159
Piquet Jr, Nelson 52, 63
Pirelli tyres 22, 122
Pironi, Didier 54, 77, 79, 84, 88,
    101, 126
pit babes 34
Porsche 29, 31, 32, 34, 126
Prost-Acer 139
Prost, Alain 25, 37, 49, 51, 54, 55,
    62, 64, 65, 66, 78, 80, 84, 87, 90,
    92, 93, 96, 98, 102, 104, 108, 109,
    110, 111, 117, 118, 128, 133, 151,
    154, 165, 171, 183
Prost-Mugen-Honda 129
Prost-Peugeot 133, 135
Pryce, Tom 64, 112

Racing colours 168
Raikkonen, Kimi 15, 19, 37, 49, 73,
    95, 118, 138, 139, 141, 144, 146,
    151, 158, 159, 162, 164, 165, 170,
    171, 176, 178, 179, 182, 183
Rathmann, Jim 23, 29, 134
Ratzenberger, Roland 28, 112
RBR-Cosworth 151
Rebaque, Hector 80
Red Bull Racing 66, 161, 166, 171,
    172, 175, 176, 179, 180, 182, 183
Regazzoni, Clay 41, 51, 53, 56, 63,
    64, 69, 77, 95
Renault 48, 66, 77, 79, 80, 84, 87, 90,
    93, 111, 141, 144, 146, 151, 152,
    154, 156, 163, 171, 172, 176, 179
Reutemann, Carlos 59, 63, 64, 71, 73,
    75, 77, 79, 80, 83, 84, 88, 109,
    115, 118
Revson, Peter 56, 59, 112, 134
Rial-Ford 102
Ricciardo, Daniel 182
Rindt, Jochen 25, 31, 33, 41, 46, 49,
    51, 85, 95, 112
Rodriguez, Pedro 43, 45, 51, 53,
    76, 134

Rodriguez, Ricardo 76
Rosberg, Keke 16, 21, 44, 49, 62, 79, 84, 85, 87, 90, 93, 95, 96, 138, 153, 159, 177
Rosberg, Nico 16, 19, 74, 107, 118, 167, 171, 172, 176, 177, 179, 181, 182, 183
Rosier, Louis 8, 177
Russian Grand Prix 174
Ruttman, Troy 12, 148

Salo, Mika 135
Salvadori, Roy 24, 105
San Marino Grand Prix 88
Sato, Takuma 125, 146
Sauber 117
Sauber-Ferrari 176, 179, 180
Sauber-Ford 123, 127
Sauber-Mercedes 121
Sauber-Petronas 129, 133, 135, 137, 139, 141, 144, 146, 151, 171
Scarfiotti, Ludovico 41, 68, 152
Scheckter, Jody 11, 18, 49, 63, 64, 69, 71, 75, 77, 85, 118, 148, 158
Schell, Harry 23, 24
Schessler, Jo 22, 112, 152
Schumacher, Michael 8, 12, 19, 23, 34, 37, 44, 46, 48, 49, 52, 57, 58, 62, 63, 65, 68, 73, 74, 77, 83, 84, 86, 89, 94, 99, 101, 105, 114, 117, 118, 120, 121, 123, 126, 127, 133, 135, 137, 139, 141, 144, 145, 146, 149, 151, 152, 153, 154, 155, 157, 171, 172, 176, 179, 182, 183
Schumacher, Ralf 73, 74, 118, 126, 133, 135, 137, 139, 141, 144, 146, 151
Seagrave, Harry 9
Senechal, Robert 9
Senna, Ayrton 17, 21, 27, 28, 44, 46, 49, 55, 61, 65, 66, 67, 68, 78, 83, 90, 92, 93, 96, 98, 99, 102, 104, 108, 111, 112, 114, 115, 117, 123, 125, 130, 133, 136, 142, 150, 152, 159, 162, 165, 169
Shadow-Ford 59, 63, 64, 69, 71, 77
Siffert, Jo 36, 45, 46, 53, 95
Silverstone 9, 19, 52, 82, 163, 169, 181
Singapore Grand Prix 52

Sirotkin, Sergey 174
Sommer, Raymond 118
Spa-Francochamps 52, 169
Spanish Grand Prix 68, 116, 172
Speed, Scott 147
Spence, Mike 39, 43, 153
sponsorship 22, 61, 122
Spyker Racing 159
Stacey, Alan 112, 143
starting grids, fantasy
    British 14
    European 95
    Ferrari 158
    French 54
    German 74
    Italian 35
    McLaren 165
    N./C. American 134
    South American 115
    World 148
Stepney, Nigel 157
Stewart-Ford 129, 133, 135
Stewart, Jackie 14, 19, 38, 39, 41, 43, 45, 46, 49, 51, 53, 56, 59, 67, 73, 79, 97, 99, 114, 140, 155
Sthor, Sigfried 88
Sullivan, Danny 62
Super Aguri 125, 160, 173
Surtees-Ford 51, 53, 56, 59, 69
Surtees, John 22, 32, 34, 36, 39, 41, 43, 45, 49, 57, 58, 89, 97, 118, 142, 155, 158
Sutil, Adrian 159, 176, 181
Suzuka, 52
Suzuki, Aguri 160
Sweikert, Bob 18, 134
Swiss Grand Prix 8, 169, 177
Symonds, Pat 52

Tambay, Patrick 54, 84, 87
Taruffi, Lee 11
Taruffi, Piero 12, 18, 68
Taylor, John 112
Taylor, Trevor 32
Testut, Andre 162
Tobacco advertising 61
Toleman-Hart 87, 90
Toro Rosso 52, 166, 171, 172, 175, 176, 179, 180, 182
Toyota 141, 144, 146, 151, 171

Trintignant, Maurice 16, 18, 24, 26, 54, 129
Trips, Wolfgang von 13, 29, 31, 44, 74, 112
Trulli, Jarno 35, 68, 137, 139, 141, 143, 144, 146, 151, 153, 171
Turkish Grand Prix 154
Tyrrell 136
Tyrrell-Ford 53, 56, 59, 63, 64, 66, 69, 71, 75, 77, 79, 80, 84, 87, 93, 98, 102, 104, 108, 129
Tyrrell-Honda 111
Tyrrell-Ilmor 114
Tyrrell, Ken 18, 99, 131
Tyrrell-Renault 93, 96
Tyrrell-Yamaha 121, 123, 127

United States Grand Prix 13, 18, 32, 38, 58, 86, 101, 119, 180, 183
US East Grand Prix 21
US West Grand Prix 105

Valencia 168
Vanwall 24, 38, 66, 67, 105, 117
Vergne, Jean-Eric 179, 181
Verstappen, Jos 121
Vettel, Sebastian 19, 49, 52, 74, 89, 90, 107, 155, 161, 167, 171, 172, 174, 175, 176, 177, 178, 179, 180, 181, 182, 183
Villeneuve, Gilles 15, 18, 75, 88, 112, 128, 134, 149, 175, 179
Villeneuve, Jacques 23, 49, 57, 73, 77, 80, 84, 105, 118, 120, 122, 127, 129, 133, 134, 137, 139, 149, 155, 161, 176, 177, 179
Villota, Maria de 181
Villoresi, Luigi 11, 12, 15
Vukovich, Bill 15, 16, 134

Wagner, Louis 9
Walker, David 27
Walker, Murray 19, 57
Wallard, Lee 11
Ward, Rodger 26
Warwick, Derek 71, 90, 102, 104
Watkins, Syd 53
Watson, John 21, 62, 69, 75, 77, 80, 84, 87, 148
Webber, Mark 19, 107, 144, 148, 151,
153, 167, 171, 172, 173, 175, 176, 179, 180, 182, 183
Whitehead, Louis 8
Williams 16, 21, 24, 32, 41, 65
Williams-BMW 137, 139, 141, 144, 146, 151
Williams-Cosworth 172, 176
Williams-Ford 64, 66, 75, 77, 79, 80, 84, 87
Williams FW18 86
Williams-Honda 66, 90, 93, 96, 98, 105, 125
Williams-Judd 102
Williams-Mecachrome 133
Williams-Renault 66, 104, 108, 111, 114, 117, 121, 123, 127, 129, 179, 182
Williams-Supertec 135
Williams-Toyota 171
Williamson, Roger 112
Wisell, Reine 27
Wolf-Ford 71, 75
World Motorsport Council (WMSC) 157
Wurz, Alexander 133

Youngest:
  driver 114, 161, 174
  multiple World Champion 178, 180
  podium 177
  point-winner 180
  pole-setter 90, 156
  race-winner 52, 56, 156, 177, 178, 180
  test-driver 16, 154
  World Champion 46, 60, 156, 178

Zakspeed 98
Zandvoort 52

⊛ ABOUT THE AUTHOR ⊛

John White is a lifelong sports fanatic who has devoted all
his spare time to compiling an impressively comprehensive
computer database of sporting facts and figures. A Belfast
man, he has followed Formula One since his compatriot
John Watson nearly became Northern Ireland's first World
Champion (he finished joint second in 1982). He is the author
of all the books in Carlton Books' *Sports Miscellany* series.